COMPLETE MUSHROOM BOOK
the quiet hunt

Antonio Carluccio

Special photography by **Alastair Hendy**

Quadrille

I should like to mention, and dedicate this book to, my dog Jan, who lived with me for thirteen years, giving me the best companionship one could desire, especially when out mushroom picking.

First published in 2003 by
Quadrille Publishing Limited
Alhambra House
27–31 Charing Cross Road
London WC2H oLS

This paperback edition first published in 2005

British Library Cataloguing-in-Publication Data A catalogue record for this book is available from the British Library.

ISBN 1 84400 163 6

Printed in Hong Kong

CONTENTS

INTRODUCTION
THE QUIET HUNT

I wrote my first book on the subject of mushrooms almost twenty years ago. At that time, I had about forty years' experience, having begun my mycological education at the early age of seven, for in Italy, you start to hunt from a very young age, either with parents or friends. It was in Castelnuovo Belbo, in the province of Alessandria in Piedmont, where my family was living, that I was initiated into the joys of the 'quiet hunt', the collecting of wild mushrooms and truffles.

It wasn't until I was about ten, and by then living in Borgofranco d'Ivrea, that I started to learn properly about mycology. Still under the super-vision of either my father or friends of the family, it always gave me great satisfaction to arrive back home with mushrooms I had collected after a day out hunting in the woods. The pleasure of eating them was just as immense for all of my family!

After having investigated all the hills and mountains near Borgofranco, I then decided to move abroad to Vienna to further my studies. Austria has very fertile ground as well, ideal for the growth of wild fungi, and the people have a good general knowledge of mushrooms. I continued the pursuit of my passion, and my 'booty' was always very useful when feeding my friends. Students don't have much money, and wild mushrooms are free! After Austria I then moved

to Hamburg in Germany, where I stayed for the next twelve years, becoming a dealer in Italian wine.

I then moved to England in 1975, to continue my wine business, and have remained here ever since. I couldn't believe the attitude to fungi there was here in England – a country so near to the fungi-lovers of the rest of Europe. Here wild mushrooms have usually been regarded as something suspicious that only witches would collect and eat. But for me, the English soil was rich and full of wonderful examples of fungi just waiting to be picked. And often waiting until they faded and rotted, for no-one had any interest. The British government apparently did consider publishing a booklet at the end of the war, detailing edible mushrooms that could be picked in the British Isles, a result of there not being much food available due to rationing. Despite this, it seemed only to have been mycologists or Continentals who went mushroom-hunting in Britain at that time. And this idea that wild fungi are inedible has spread to most English-speaking countries since – America, Canada, Australia, New Zealand, and so on. Nowhere do they have the same enthusiasm as we do in Continental Europe.

But one cannot say that the British did not know anything about mushrooms, because when I arrived some books had already been published on the subject. The late Jane Grigson, a wonderful and erudite woman whom I had the good fortune to know, had written *The Mushroom Feast*, a very good cookery book. Roger Phillips, a botanist and photographer, had written and photographed an excellent scientific book about mushrooms (and other books on other aspects of nature).

Despite this, it is only in the last twenty years that mushrooms have started to become truly part of the British culinary scene, with both wild and cultivated sold in specialist markets and delicatessens. European countries, on the contrary, have had thousands of years of experience with these 'jewels of nature'. The Ancient Romans, for instance, were passionate about fungi, and would eat them regularly at banquets. The present-day Italians are just as enthusiastic, as are the Swedes, Poles, Yugoslavs, the Germans and French. In Russia there is actually a special train that departs every Saturday morning from Moscow, full of fungi-hunters bound for the country, who return in the evening with their baskets laden.

In all these countries you are able to buy fungi direct from markets. These have been collected by farmers, and are perfectly safe to eat as the authorities have checked them. But even in these places where people are quite knowledgeable, there are still deaths caused by over-enthusiastic pickers not checking the fungi properly before eating. I cannot stress enough how careful you need to be when picking mushrooms, and I shall repeat this warning many times throughout this book.

The most wonderful aspect of collecting and eating fungi is that people from all social strata can become 'hooked'. Drew McPherson, a Scottish friend of mine, started selling wild mushrooms collected in Scotland. Twenty years later, he has a multi-million-pound business, due to the demand for mushrooms increasing so rapidly, for there is no respectable restaurant that doesn't use wild mushrooms from time to time. The demand is now so high that Drew has to import mushrooms from all over the world, wherever they are in season.

Even supermarkets are selling cultivated mushrooms, which can compete favourably with wild varieties.

I'll never forget when I started to run my restaurant in 1981, that I had personally to collect all the mushrooms to be used in the kitchen! I used to go picking in the break between lunch and dinner service, and prepare the mushrooms before cooking them in the evening. I then put an advert in a Polish newspaper printed for expatriates living in Britain, asking for mushroom pickers. A queue of Poles with baskets laden with mushrooms turned up at the restaurant almost immediately. I trusted their expertise, and they earned good money, so this made for a fruitful partnership. For many years, too, I employed an Italian called Gennaro, who used to bring me baskets of mushrooms. I then gave him a permanent job at the restaurant, where he was responsible for collecting, cleaning and storing all the mushrooms. I'm glad to say he now has his own successful restaurant. It's always good to see people who have worked with you moving on and doing their 'own thing'.

It is due to the enormous surge of general interest, in both wild and cultivated mushrooms, that I decided it was time to update my twenty-year-old *A Passion for Mushrooms*. The present book's subtitle 'The Quiet Hunt', comes from Mikhael Gorbachev, to whose private secretary I gave a copy of *A Passion for Mushrooms* when he was eating in my restaurant. I received a thank-you letter from Mr Gorbachev, himself a passionate mushroom collector, and in it he referred to 'the quiet hunt', an expression Russians use when going out to look for mushrooms in the woods.

The present book includes a Field Guide with a huge selection of my favourite mushrooms, both edible and inedible. It ends with a discussion of cultivated mushrooms, from east and west, which are now becoming familiar and are used more and more often in cooking in many parts of the world. Finally, there are my recipes – over a hundred of them from all over the world, not just from Italy.

My passion for mushrooms, despite the many years I have now lived in Britain, remains unabated, and I always feel a strong desire to pass on that knowledge and allow others to share the joys of collecting – and eating! This book is one major result of that. In addition there is my Neal Street Restaurant, which still remains a mecca for mushroom and truffle lovers and which has now been joined by a series of Carluccio's Caffès that also offer exotic mushroom specialities. No-one, in London at least, need remain ignorant of the wonders of wild fungi.

Finally I should like to mention, and dedicate this book to, my dog Jan, who lived with me for thirteen years, giving me the best companionship one could desire, especially when out mushroom picking. The hunt was not actually that quiet with him around, though.

THE **FIELD GUIDE**
WILD
MUSHROOMS

The world of fungi, from invisible micro-organisms to 'higher' fungi with clearly visible fruit-bodies (such as mushrooms), is vast. Fungi differ from all other plants in that they do not contain chlorophyll, the green pigments by which plants synthesise carbon compounds from the sun's energy. (In fact there has been an ongoing dispute as to whether fungi should be classified as plants at all.) Instead of 'feeding' from the sun, fungi draw their nutrients entirely from living organisms – plants, or even animals – or from decaying or dead organic matter.

To be honest, if we did not have fungi, many aspects of life would be difficult. A number of fungi perform a vital role in breaking down dead matter and assisting decomposition, and this clearing-up operation also provides further nourishment for the soil, new plants that will grow in it, and thus the habitat for new generations of fungi. Conversely, some fungi are parasitic in a less helpful way, attacking living plants such as trees, eventually killing them. Dutch Elm disease, which has destroyed so many beautiful trees across Europe, is caused by a microscopic fungus called *Ceratocystis ulmi*, carried by certain beetles.

And there are many thousands of microscopic fungi that have a significant place in our lives in one way or another, in important areas such as medicine and food. Perhaps the most significant discovery was that of the fungus which was developed into the life-saving antibiotic, penicillin, while the Chinese (in their ancient wisdom) have known about the medicinal value of mushroom extracts for thousands of years. The hallucinogenic fungus ergot (*Claviceps purpurea*), which infects several of our most important cereal crops, has been known about for centuries. Poisonings were frequent during the Middle Ages, and were considered to be God's punishment for sin. Known as 'holy fire', and thought to be a contributory factor in the sudden appearances of 'witches' in the seventeenth-century American town of Salem, ergot is now used medicinally in several compounds that are closely related to LSD.

Many of our basic foods are influenced by the action of fungi: sugar is converted into alcohol in wine- and beer-making, and breads rise because of the fungus that is yeast. A mould fungus is injected into young cheese to make the world's most famous blue cheeses (the French Roquefort and the Italian Gorgonzola, for instance), and moulds are also used in the fermentation of many foods popular in the East, notably soy beans.

LEFT A PERFECT AUTUMN DAY FOR HUNTING MUSHROOMS

WHAT ARE MUSHROOMS?

But the fungi we are interested in here are not of the microscopic variety. When it comes to mushrooms, we are concerned with a single stage in the life cycle of much larger and more evolved fungi – the 'higher' fungi. The fruit-body that is the actual mushroom we eat is only part of the story.

Underlying this ephemerally visible part of the fungus is the more permanent mycelium. This is the important vegetative part of the mushroom (and should never be disturbed by inconsiderate collecting). It is formed of a complex of minute, hair-like filaments, invisible to the naked eye, called hyphae. These combine to form a cobweb-like mat that is the mycelium which, when thick enough, can be visible. This mat spreads under the soil or leaf litter, forming an ever-more complex web, and often travels several metres to grow into and through, and to gain and absorb as much nutriment as possible from, the soil and other substances. When climatic conditions such as moisture and temperature are appropriate, a new fruit-body, a mushroom, rapidly develops.

The purpose of this fruit-body is not to give us mycologists pleasure, but to serve as the reproductive part of the organism. For as the fruit-body grows and matures, it produces millions of microscopic spores (seeds). At full maturity, these spores are discharged from the hymenium (the fertile spore-producing surface), to be dispersed by the wind or in other ways. On landing upon the ground in favourable conditions, the spores will germinate, form a new mycelium, and the whole process will start afresh. (Spore prints are useful in mushroom identification, see page 14).

THE MAIN MUSHROOM GROUPS

The scientific study of mushrooms goes back many hundreds of years, and scientists throughout the centuries were keen to give names to newly discovered fungi, edible or inedible. The most useful step was in the classification of mushrooms with similar characteristics into groups. A Latin first name was given to the group – Amanita and Boletus, for instance – then a second Latin name was added to specify which particular member of the group was referred to. This second name reflects a more detailed characteristic of the individual mushroom: *Amanita caesarea*, the mushroom of the Caesar, the leader, is the edible best of the group, while the highly poisonous *A. pantherina*, which has white spots, is likened to the dangerous panther. *A. rubescens* – from the Latin for 'red' or 'redness' – is named for the pink tinge to its flesh.

It seems a fairly sensible and workable system, but confusion arises from the fact that various scientists in other countries began giving differing names to mushrooms and mushroom groups. As a result, some mushrooms now have two or more names, and are often classified as being in more than one family. In this book I have given the primary or most familiar Latin name, followed by any alternative name or synonym.

And then of course there are the local names – nicknames perhaps – which are specific to each mushroom-collecting country. The 'pre-eminent' quality of *A. caesarea* is reflected in the names used throughout Europe (see page 23), while the English for *A. rubescens*, for instance, is straightforward – it's 'the blusher'!

In the present book I have followed the example of the late Bruno Cetto, the famous Italian mycologist who wrote five masterly and comprehensive books on the subject, with descriptions and photographs of no fewer than 2,147 mushrooms.

Another primary step in the classification of fungi was to further detail the type – whether saprophytic, parasitic or mycorrhizal. Saprophytes live on dead organic matter like dying trees, decaying logs, tree-stumps, even pine cones. Parasites do exactly what one might expect: they attack and kill living trees and plants. (*Armillaria mellea*, for instance, is typical, considered a pest by gardeners and arborealists.) The fungi which are mycorrhizal live in a mutually beneficial relationship – a symbiosis – with the roots (the Greek 'rhiza' means 'root') of certain trees. They receive moisture and protection in adverse conditions, in exchange for which they give the roots of the tree phosphorus, nitrogen and other elements the tree might not be able to obtain for itself. Boletes, russulas and amanitas – as well as the highly valued truffles and matsutake – are all mycorrhizal

SPORE PRINTS

Spores are microscopic, and vary in shape and colour from mushroom to mushroom. Even without a microscope it is possible to see the colour of the spores *en masse*: all you have to do is leave the cap of a mushroom on glass or paper for a few hours. The spores will drop out leaving a 'print' clearly visible to the naked eye. (You could use a paper that is half white and half black so that the print is clearly visible whether the spores are light or dark.) Like a fingerprint, the information contained in the spore is essential for correct identification. Although the shape of the spore itself can be seen only under a microscope, the colour of the 'print', plus all the other field characteristics, will help you name the mushroom you have collected.

fungi. Many saprophytic and parasitic fungi can now be cultivated, but the unique mycorrhizal relationship is much less easy to reproduce, in nature as well as in cultivation – possibly one of the reasons why many of these fungi are so rare, so highly valued, and so highly priced!

Yet another step in fungi classification was the division by mycologists of the larger fungi into two major groups – Ascomycetes and Basidiomycetes – according to the way they produce spores.

ASCOMYCETES

Ascomycetes, or 'spore-shooters', develop spores internally within sacs called asci, from which they are violently discharged at maturity. The group comprises a diverse range of often bizarrely shaped fruit-bodies (and indeed some tubers, which actually grow underground). Here I have included only two Ascomycetes in my selection for the mycophagist (those of you who enjoy eating fungi). But as these are the highly prized morel and the even more highly valued truffle, their gastronomic importance considerably out-weighs their numerical insignificance.

BASIDIOMYCETES

The mushrooms in this category are the most numerous in the wild and in this book. These are the 'spore-droppers', which form spores externally on club-shaped cells (usually on gills or pores under a cap). These drop naturally to the ground, or are swept off and away by wind or rain. However, the spore-droppers, being such a large group, also encompass different types of mushroom. There are two principal sub-categories, gilled or pored fungi – conven-tionally mushroom-shaped with more or less convex caps and central stems – plus a motley crew of other edible Basidiomycetes.

GILL FUNGI The gilled category of mushrooms is extremely large, and includes such familiar genera as Agaricus, Amanita, Armillaria, Cantharellus, Clitocybe, Cortinarius, Laccaria, Lactarius, Lepiota, Lepista, Pleurotus, Russula and Tricholoma. They have a fruit-body which is fleshy, convex and centrally stalked. Underneath the cap there are radiating gills, the lamellae, and the spores are produced on

the hymenium, which covers the gill surface. It is vital to study the colour and mode of attachment of the gills to identify agarics properly, for instance. Some fungi in this group also have a volva – an egg-shaped membrane which encloses the small developing mushroom, and which ruptures as the developing mushroom grows. Sometimes part of the volva remains on top of the cap of the mature mushroom in the form of flakes or scales, as happens with amanitas. Another characteristic of many agarics is the veil – the membrane that in young specimens encloses and protects the gills but which, as the young fruit-body expands, is ruptured to leave a sort of skirt or ring round the stem, as in the case of Cortinarius.

PORE FUNGI The pored category of mushrooms includes the genera Boletus, Gyroporus, Leccinum, Suillus and Tylopilus. They have a fruit-body that is fleshy, convex and centrally stalked. The underside of the cap has a poroid sponge-like appearance. Instead of gills, the surface is made up of closely packed little tubes that are invisible in the youngest fungi, but when they develop, hold the spores with which the mushroom can reproduce itself. The pores differ in their density and colour from species to species, even from one bolete to another. In young boletes they tend to be cream in colour, turning to yellowish/greenish later, but they are of a reddish tone in some species. Bruising the pores also gives an indication of the type, especially if the colour changes to blue or to black.

ODDBALLS Other edible Basidiomycetes are less easy to categorise. In hedgehog fungi the hymenium covers spikes or spines (instead of gills or pores) hanging from the underside of the cap. (*Hydnum repandum* could be confused with a pale pink mushroom or bolete until one sees the spiny lower surface.) Like boletes, bracket fungi have a poroid hymenium, but differ in their woody and leathery texture, their usually fan- or shell-shaped brackets, and their occurrence on wood. *Fistulina hepatica* and *Laetiporus sulphureus* are edible examples. *Sparassis crispa* is in a category of its own. Puffballs, whose spores are formed internally rather than externally and are 'puffed' out when raindrops hit the mature fruit-body, are, surprisngly, also Basidiomycetes, but are known as Gasteromycetes.

ABOVE A NAUGHTY LECCINUM QUERCINUM!

IDENTIFYING MUSHROOMS

To identify a mushroom expertly you have to be sure of every single element. Checking physical characteristics observable in the field such as shape, colour, texture and smell is part of the procedure, as well as noting the habitat itself. (Completely accurate identification can ultimately depend on examining microscopic details such as the precise form and colour of the individual spores.) Fortunately, however, the wild mushrooms with which we are concerned are those with a clearly visible (and good-tasting) fruit-body, and if you systematically check a specimen against the descriptions in the Field Guide, you should go a long way towards establishing its identity. The surest safeguard is to consult a professional mycologist who will identify specimens accurately before you eat anything: you will often find such an expert if you join fungus forays organised by local naturalist groups or professional mycological societies. (Another alternative is to marry one, as my wife Priscilla did!)

Mycological experts themselves are slow to reach any agreement about the definitive classification of certain fungi, and this is why you will find the botanical Latin names varying from book to book (and why I have included some of the more widely used synonyms in this one). I recommend your buying two or more good books on identifying fungi (see my bibliography on page 220). Just as it is useful to have more than one to clarify the names (a giant puffball is a giant puffball whether known by the name Lycoperdon, Langermannia or Calvatia), you get a very helpful perspective on a specimen by comparing both the descriptions and the illustrations in different books.

To start you off, though, look at all the different characteristics of the mushroom you are examining, and compare them with the details in the individual descriptions. If you are taking the mushroom home to be identified, you need to gather the entire fruit-body, base and all, preferably with both young and mature specimens to compare development. Carry them home wrapped in waxed paper to preserve their freshness. Keep these unidentified specimens well away from any you may be intending to eat.

CAP Measure it, and note shape, colour and surface texture (is it shiny, scaly, and so on?).

GILLS/PORES Look to see whether the mushroom has gills or pores, their colour, how they are attached to the stems, and whether they change colour when touched.

STEM Measure its height and thickness, and note its colour and whether there is a ring, veil or volva.

FLESH The colour will be significant, as will the texture (dense, crumbly, fibrous). Does it exude milk? What does it smell like? And you can even taste most mushrooms so long as you spit out quickly and wash out with water (but not, clearly, with something like *Amanita phalloides* or those that are obviously poisonous).

HABITAT Many of the edible species of fungus favour specific types of habitat and have particular requirements in terms of host nutrient. This not only means that it is worth making forays in likely looking places with the appropriate sort of vegetation, but that habitat can be a key element in identifying an unfamiliar specimen. Some fungus species grow on living or decaying wood, others on soil or dung. Certain mushrooms have a symbiotic relationship with certain plants, often trees and shrubs. Sometimes this mycorrhizal association is with a specific tree, sometimes with more than one.

As examples, *Suillus grevillei* (the larch bolete), as its common name suggests, prefers larch trees. Leccinum mushrooms grow almost exclusively among birch. *Lactarius deliciosus* and *Suillus luteus* prefer pine trees, particularly Scots pines. *Boletus edulis* grows among oak, birch, beech and pine. Morels, one of the first mushrooms to appear in spring, prefer the edges of broad-leaved woodland, but will also be found under poplar and in gardens, orchards, wasteland and even burnt ground. If you know your trees, it helps you know your mushrooms. Field mushrooms and giant puffballs are found in open fields and meadows, and are the exceptions to the rule that mushrooms tend to prefer warm, damp, shady places. On the whole you will find most mushrooms in humus-rich soil, in places that are not too marshy, nor overgrown with thick tall vegetation.

SEASON The season varies according to the individual species. A few edible mushrooms (morels and St George's among them) appear in spring, but most appear from mid- or late summer on to autumn, and some continue after the first frosts. The right preconditions of temperature and humidity produce a flush of fruit-bodies: you can expect them to appear in warm weather following rain. Given optimum conditions – moist soil and a temperature of 18-25°C – the fruit-bodies of *Boletus edulis* can develop in four or five days, and you will know roughly when it is worth returning to the same spot for the new crop – if someone else has not beaten you to it. It is for this reason that you will often find me out hunting on a Wednesday. Mushrooming is a weekend activity for many people and the best places are often stripped bare of mushrooms by enthusiasts. By midweek there is often a flush of new growth, and the tiny specimens of the weekend are large enough to be worth picking.

THUMBSTICKS

A simple straight stick, preferably with a fork at the top, is a wonderful tool if you are a keen collector of wild mushrooms. The fork is especially important, not only as a thumb rest, but to defend yourself against encounters with snakes, and to turn over leaf litter or ferns that might just hide a new mushroom.

Hazel sticks are straight with few side branches. Find the correct height by putting your thumb in the fork – your forearm should be at a 90-degree angle, resting horizontally. (Cut the base down if too long.) Then you can decorate the stick as I have done in the photograph on page 18. It's become a major, absorbing hobby of mine!

ABOVE THE RELIGIOUS CLEANING AND SORTING OF THE SPOILS

1 Before you start, make sure that you know enough about the habitats and the mushrooms themselves, either through expert tuition or through guided forays organised by local mycological societies.

2 Preferably go with somebody, ideally an expert, and stay in contact with each other.

3 Be equipped with the right tools:
A WICKER OR WIRE BASKET This will safely transport the mushrooms and also helps to disseminate the spores while you are walking.
A MUSHROOM KNIFE to clean the stem of the mushroom on the spot, without carrying the dirt home, and to prevent the stem contaminating the gills and pores of other mushrooms in the basket. Special knives are available in Italy, with a curved blade and an inbuilt brush.
PROPER WALKING BOOTS
SOME DRINKING WATER, something to eat, and hygienic paper.
A WALKING STICK OR THUMBSTICK

4 Follow local codes of conduct and rules. These are available in every country, including Britain (where they are published by the British Mycological Society, Forestry Commission and other trusts).

5 If you intend to enter private property or secluded areas, ask for permission to do so from landowners, trusts or governing bodies, and explain your intentions.

6 Respect the environment. It is the principal source of your pleasure, so be considerate. For instance, take any rubbish home with you.

7 When collecting in large woods or forests, be sure to remember how to come out of them again.

COLLECTING AND PICKING MUSHROOMS

Every year I wait for the right conditions for the mushroom season to begin with the impatience of a small child. Although I have a good 'nose' for mushrooms, I am often a few days too early and the first trip or two into the woods may not be very productive. Not of mushrooms, at least. Instead I often come back with some consolation prizes in the form of new walking sticks to carve and decorate. Even in the height of the season my impatience has sometimes taken me to a mushroom spot in such good time that I have had to wait in the car for an hour or so before dawn breaks!

ANTONIO'S CODE OF CONDUCT

Because of the increasing popularity of collecting wild mushrooms, the authorities in most countries have intervened to regulate picking to avoid the depleting and damaging of habitats by inconsiderate, greedy or ignorant collectors. In France, Italy, Switzerland and most European countries, picking is regulated by law: local farmers can collect enough to sell to make a living, while occasional or weekend collectors have to follow strict rules (and, if these are not observed, they can be heavily fined or even imprisoned). Britain is probably the only country in Europe where collecting mushrooms is not popular, but I hope this book might help redress the balance.

I welcome the new rules emanating from Europe, as they will help preserve fungi and their habitats. And, for much the same reason, I have created my own personal set of rules. I observe these myself when collecting, and I invite other collectors and lovers of fungi to do the same.

More than once in Calabria, for instance, people have got lost and have never been found again.

8 Collect only mushrooms that you actually know and don't experiment with those that you don't. (Don't even mix unknown mushrooms in your basket with your edible ones.)

9 Collect only enough for your own immediate use, unless you encounter an enormous crop, which you would like to preserve (see pages 96–99).

10 Don't destroy any mushroom that you don't know, that you find ugly or think is poisonous. All mushrooms have an ecological purpose.

11 If you want to identify mushrooms for your own scientific purposes, take only a few specimens at a time to compare with a comprehensive, scientific field guide. Try to avoid species considered rare.

12 Don't accept mushrooms given to you as a present by somebody you don't know.

13 Collect only mature specimens, leaving the very small ones to grow on, and the very old ones to decay, in their natural habitat.

14 Never use plastic bags, or closed containers as you will spoil the quality of the mushrooms and could also alter the safety of the proteins. They will sweat, lose condition, and become contaminated with bacteria.

15 Never collect mushrooms when it is raining or immediately after rain. They will have absorbed too much water, and you will have either an unusable mess or a mushroom that will exude too much water (and flavour) when you cook it.

16 Pick, pull or cut the mushroom from the ground according to its species and my guidance. In general, try not to disturb the mycelium too much by tearing the mushroom out of the ground.

Finally, I can't emphasise enough how careful you have to be with mushrooms. Over-confidence may provide you with your last supper.

A FEW MORE TIPS

● Keep a note of your landmarks as you wander in search of mushrooms: it is easy to get disorientated.
● Once you have discovered a 'good' place, mark it on your map so that you can visit it again next season. Since the mycelium is long-lasting, mushrooms can often be found in the same place year after year.
● As you search, keep your eyes open for local clues, such as scattered caps of boletes – the leftovers from a squirrel's meal – which tell you to look for others growing somewhere in the vicinity.
● Don't just look at the ground when you are on a mushroom foray. Look up too, for you might find one of the beautiful and very edible bracket fungi.
● As you recognise more fungi you can use them as signposts. Where you see the beautiful but poisonous fly agaric, for example, look especially carefully. The cep enjoys the same environment, and is a good mushroom to start collecting. It is the easiest to recognise and the tastiest of all.
● And don't share your secret with too many friends, in case they turn into competitors.

Happy hunting!

THE EDIBILITY OF WILD MUSHROOMS

The wild mushroom is the only type of food in the world which offers equal doses of deliciousness or poisoning, depending on species. Perhaps it is this titillating frisson of danger that makes us appreciate the edible varieties even more. However, only six are lethal. The rest may be either very toxic or just mildly so, but still able to produce extreme symptoms.

To each description of a wild mushroom, I have added a word or two to describe its edibility – or the reverse.

THE DIVISION OF EDIBLE WILD FUNGI IS AS FOLLOWS:
EXCELLENT The mushrooms which are universally known as being of top quality.
VERY GOOD Mushrooms which are delicious but have a stem that may be less edible.
GOOD Good to eat, but their culinary appreciation depends on personal taste.
EDIBLE Various mushrooms containing toxins that disappear when brought into contact with heat, so they are safe only after cooking. They are inedible and toxic when raw.

THE DIVISION OF NON-EDIBLE WILD MUSHROOMS IS AS FOLLOWS:
NOT EDIBLE Mushrooms that either smell bad or are bitter, but would only spoil the dish without being necessarily poisonous.
TOXIC Mushrooms that can provoke intensive intoxication of the body. These toxins can accumulate over a long period of time.
POISONOUS These mushrooms actually poison. Symptoms are either immediate or develop within 4 hours, but only cause death in some cases. Promptly treated, they are curable.
DEADLY POISONOUS These are seriously poisonous, and ingestion usually results in death. The symptoms appear after 10 or more hours, after which organs such as the liver are destroyed. There is no antidote.

Should you ever have eaten a toxic mushroom, then you will probably begin to suffer a stomach-ache, dizziness and sweating. Seek immediate medical assistance, and if possible keep a sample of the mushroom you consumed so that the toxins can be identified swiftly.

To avoid all of the above, though, please keep to the basic rule of eating only mushrooms that you have identified to be completely safe.

AGARICUS CAMPESTRIS

Often when I talk to someone about my passion for mushrooms, I am amused to hear them say, 'Oh yes, I know all about mushrooms . . .' meaning field mushrooms, and implying that everything else is a toadstool. This blithe assurance worries me because of the possibility of a non-expert mistakenly collecting the poisonous 'yellow stainer' (*A. xanthodermus*), which can be found in the same fields and meadows, as well as in gardens and shrubberies. So when you find a colony of what looks like field mushrooms, avoid picking any with yellow stains on their stems or caps, especially if these stains are at the base of the stem and become a deeper chrome yellow when bruised. Above all, avoid any look-alikes with white gills: they could be the deadly poisonous *Amanita verna* or *Amanita virosa* (see page 27).

In the same family there is also *Agaricus augustus* – the Prince – wonderful to pick and eat, but rare.

RECOGNITION

CAP Round at first, very tightly attached to stem; becoming convex and expanding to 10 cm diameter. White, becoming cream/brown.
GILLS Adnexed, pale pink at first deepening to dark brown when fully grown. Spore print: purple-brown.
STEM Relatively thick and short, 1–2 cm in diameter and 3–8 cm tall, with slight frill-like ring.

AGARICUS CAMPESTRIS

THE AGARICUS FAMILY IS LARGE AND FAIRLY COMMON THROUGHOUT THE ENTIRE WORLD, AND IT IS FROM ONE SINGLE MEMBER OF THE FAMILY, *A. BISPORUS*, THAT ALL OUR FAMILIAR CULTIVATED 'MUSHROOMS' ARE BELIEVED TO DERIVE.

AGARICUS CAMPESTRIS

(SYN. PSALLIOTA CAMPESTRIS)
FIELD MUSHROOM **VERY GOOD**

It pleases me that this wild mushroom and its close relatives can be recognised by a lot of people, and therefore picked and eaten with safety. The field mushroom (*Agaricus campestris*) and its larger cousin, the horse mushroom (*A. arvensis* syn. *Psalliota arvensis*), can be found fairly extensively in their preferred habitat of well-manured pastures, when the summer weather has been wet and warm. Other relatives that are to be found in similar surroundings and situations are *A. bitorquis*, *A. macrosporus* and *A. bisporus*. The latter is the one I have mentioned above, the commercially cultivated button mushroom or 'champignon' that is commonly found in every supermarket and greengrocer (see page 82).

AGARICUS MACROSPORUS

FLESH White, bruising slightly pink. Taste and smell pleasant and mushroomy.

HABITAT Pastureland, especially when richly manured; occasionally in gardens or park edges. Field mushrooms usually grow scattered or in clusters, but occasionally you find them in rings.

SEASON Early summer to late autumn, especially when wet and warm.

AGARICUS ARVENSIS
HORSE MUSHROOM **GOOD**

The principal difference is in size: the horse mushroom is generally larger and more substantial, the cap growing to 20 cm diameter and the stem to 10 cm tall, with a distinctive cog-wheel-like ring. The caps of the bigger horse mushrooms are very fleshy and heavy, but the stems tend to become hollow. There is often a slight yellow tinge on the edge of the cap, so be careful not to confuse it with the poisonous *A.xanthodermus*, which becomes yellow when touched. The gills and spore print are similar to the field mushroom. The flesh smells pleasantly of aniseed. While field mushrooms are generally maggot-free, larger horse mushrooms tend to become infested. They grow singly near stables (for obvious reasons), and alongside paths. The season is the same as the field mushroom.

AGARICUS BITORQUIS
PAVEMENT MUSHROOM **GOOD**

This sturdy member of the family appears in small groups on very hard ground, sometimes erupting through tarmac, and even raising paving slabs, hence its common name. The cap is 6–12 cm in diameter, white with an inrolled margin, and the flesh has an almond-like smell. The gills are a dirty pink, finally becoming dark chocolate brown (the colour of the spore print). The stems are up to 8 cm long, white with two rings. They are found occasionally in sandy and manured soil, by roads and beneath pavements or impacted ground, from late spring to autumn. They are good to eat, but when found at roadsides, can have absorbed pollutants from the traffic (as most fungi do). Can be mistaken for many of the amanitas (*Amanita verna, A. virosa* and sometimes *A. phalloides*). Remember that all amanitas have white gills.

AGARICUS BISPORUS
BROWN CAP / CHESTNUT / PARIS MUSHROOM **GOOD**

The 'original' agaric, which is not uncommon in the wild, but is virtually the only mushroom found on sale in Britain, in its highly successful cultivated form. The cap is 5–10 cm in diameter and covered in brownish to russet fibres. The stem is up to 6 cm long, cylindrical and whitish. The

AGARICUS ARVENSIS

crowded gills are pinkish when young, maturing to reddish brown. The spore print is brown. It is found in manure heaps and garden waste, and on road-sides, but rarely in grass, from late spring to autumn. Can be mistaken for many of the amanitas, as specified above under *A. bitorquis*. See also the description of *A. bisporus* in its cultivated form (page 82).

PICKING, CLEANING AND COOKING

Cut the stems of agarics at the base with a sharp knife. Clean with just a wipe if necessary, there is no need to peel. The whole mushrooms can be used; discard older stalks if they are no longer fleshy and tender.

As these mushrooms are widely considered to be the only edible kind, it is not surprising to find them used in recipes throughout the world. They can be eaten raw in salads (especially the smaller firmer young specimens), cooked in stews and soups, baked, grilled, fried, and served with almost every type of food. They are also excellent deep-fried or reduced to duxelles and can be pickled and pre-served to serve as antipasti. Freezing and drying are not recommended, but since the very similar commercially grown species is so readily available throughout the year, this perhaps does not matter; the wild mushrooms are much tastier, though.

AGARICUS XANTHODERMUS

(SYN. PSALLIOTA XANTHODERMA)
YELLOW STAINER   **POISONOUS**

Superficially similar to *A.arvensis* and *A. campestris*, the yellow stainer (as its name suggests) stains yellow immediately when cut or bruised, and smells rather inky. Always pick out a piece of flesh from the stem base with the thumb nail. If chrome yellow,

reject. The field mushroom does not stain and smells pleasant and mushroomy (as does *A. bisporus*); the horse mushroom may have a yellow tinge, but smells of aniseed; and the pavement mushroom smells of almonds.

Although not dangerously poisonous like *Amanita phalloides* (see page 25), *Agaricus xanthodermus* can give you a painful and unpleasant time, with serious problems of respiration and digestion which manifest themselves in cold sweats and stomach pains soon after ingestion. These symptoms can be remedied if they are quickly diagnosed and treated by a doctor. Strangely enough, some people are completely unaffected.

AGARICUS XANTHODERMUS

RECOGNITION

CAP Spherical when young, becoming flat with age, and growing to a maximum diameter 15–16 cm; dirty white, becoming yellow when bruised or scraped.
GILLS Pale pink at first, becoming brown with age. Spore print: purple-brown.
STEM White, staining chrome-yellow in bulbous stem base; 1–2 cm in diameter, to 15–16 cm tall; with pronounced white ring or skirt just below cap; it is often infested with maggots.
HABITAT AND SEASON Much the same, in both senses, as the edible agarics.

IN THE AMANITA GENUS YOU CAN FIND BOTH THE SUPREMELY EDIBLE *A. CAESAREA*, WHICH I THINK IS THE MOST DELICIOUS OF ALL, AS WELL AS *A. FULVA* AND *A. RUBESCENS*, AND THE MOST TOXIC OF MUSHROOMS, INCLUDING *A. PHALLOIDES* (DEATH CAP), *A. MUSCARIA* (FLY AGARIC), *A. VERNA* (SPRING OR FOOL'S MUSHROOM), *A. VIROSA* (DESTROYING ANGEL) AND *A. PANTHERINA* (PANTHER CAP).

AMANITA CAESAREA

CAESAR'S MUSHROOM **EXCELLENT**

History tells us that *Amanita caesarea* is so named because it was the favourite of a Roman emperor, and the tradition lives on in the common names employed throughout Europe: the English 'Caesar's mushroom', the French 'impériale', the Polish 'cesarski' and the German 'Kaiserling'. The Italians, on the other hand, call it 'ovolo' because when it is very small it looks like an egg in size and colour. Even in the Mediterranean region the mushroom is fairly rare (it is found mostly in the hills of northern Italy), and because of its demand as a delicacy, the price can become astro-nomical (£60 per kilogram in the 2002 season). One of my all-time favourite dishes (tasted in Milan some years ago) consisted of raw ovoli with raw porcini (*Boletus edulis*), topped with some freshly sliced white Alba truffle. A truly unforgettable dish for a mycophagist like me!

So far this mushroom has never been found in Britain: perhaps some ardent mushroom-hunting reader can lay claim to fame by being the first to find one.

It is quite extraordinary that in this genus you can find both the deadliest and the most delicious of all wild mushrooms. Fortunately identification is easy, and there is no danger of mistaking the mature edible rarity for all the poisonous amanitas including *A. phalloides*, *A. muscaria*, *A. virosa*, *A. verna* and *A. pantherina* (but see pages 25–27).

RECOGNITION

CAP The egg-like volva splits to reveal the deep red cap; as it expands from hemispherical to convex, the cap pales through orange-red to become light orange when fully grown (diameter to 20 cm). Edges slightly cracked, and showing the yellow gills. Sometimes traces of the volva remain on the expanded cap.

GILLS Crowded, free, extremely fragile; an unmistakable rich yellow (this is the main identification characteristic – no other European amanita has yellow gills). Spore print: white to pale yellow.

STEM To 3 cm diameter and 15 cm high. Yellow, normally still with yellow ring. The stem base is encased in the bag-like volva.

FLESH Orange-yellow under the cap, becoming white towards the centre and in stem. Firm-textured. Pleasant smell; sweet mushroomy taste.

HABITAT Open deciduous woodland in warm climates, especially with oak and chestnut. Occasionally under pine, particularly in Mexico (though it is not confirmed that the New World

AMANITA
CAESAREA

AMANITA CAESAREA

AMANITA RUBESCENS

fungus is identical with that from Europe). They grow in little groups. **SEASON** In Italy and France, and other southern Mediterranean countries, from early summer to the beginning of October, especially after hot summery weather.

AMANITA RUBESCENS
THE BLUSHER **EDIBLE**

This mushroom, a close relative of *A. caesarea*, is called 'the blusher' because of the definite pink shade of its gills and stem. In fact this is the only visible difference between it and the other amanitas, which are entirely white underneath, with the exception of *A. caesarea*, where the flesh and

gills, etc. are yellow. The cap is 5–15 cm in diameter, and is brown with white spots, which are the remains of the volva. The stem is 8–20 x 1–3 cm, cylindrical, and, as it ages, it becomes hollow. The flesh is white and very tender, but it too becomes pinkish when cut and exposed to the air. There is no discernible odour. The spore print is white.

One has to be very cautious when this mushroom has just opened or is still small, because the solid egg shape is similar to all the other amanitas. The actual differences between this and its poisonous counterparts are only possible to detect when the mushrooms are more open or more mature, or when you cut it in half. The habitat is similar to

A. caesarea, although it is common under pine, and it is found from spring to autumn.

Another peculiarity of *A. rubescens* is that it can be riddled with larvae and insects very early, when it first appears. Cut the mushroom and check inside for small black points, which are the head of the larvae. Perfect stems should have the characteristic pink tinge and the flesh should be immaculately white inside.

Eastern European and Russian people are very fond of this mushroom. It is not a great culinary delight, but is considered extremely useful when all the other mushrooms have been picked and the choice has been reduced! It must be cooked before eating, and any cooking water should be discarded.

AMANITA FULVA

TAWNY GRISETTE **EDIBLE**

This extremely small and delicate member of the family grows singly in the same type of mixed woodland habitat as *A. muscaria* and *A. pantherina*. The cap is 4–10 cm across, pale orange brown, with striped see-through 'ridges' from the centre to the grooved edges. The stems are white, very long and thin (8–12 cm x 5 mm–1.5 cm), and have no ring. When you collect it, any time between button and open, just take the cap. The fragile white flesh cooks very quickly because of its delicacy, but to make a meal out of it you will have to collect a huge amount! It is found from summer to autumn.

PICKING, CLEANING AND COOKING

Just cut the mushrooms at the stem (or *A. fulva* at the cap), using a sharp knife. Don't peel the cap, just wipe the surface if necessary, and brush any foreign bodies out of the gills. In Caesar's mushrooms, if egg-shaped,

pluck whole from the ground, and simply trim off the first layer of the whitish volva. (Don't take the *very* small ones, those smaller than chicken's eggs.) Check the stem for maggots: the base in particular may be infested and can be cut away, but the upper part is usually clear. Keep all these mushrooms, especially *A. fulva* when open, separately in the basket, as they are rather delicate and could be damaged.

Because *A. caesarea* is so rare, I recommend that you eat small ones raw, but you can cook them, in sautés and stews. Always cook the other two edible amanitas. The large caps are excellent grilled, and served with freshly made pasta.

A. caesarea keeps relatively well for up to a week in a refrigerator, but eat the others straightaway.

AMANITA EXCELSA

(SYN. A. SPISSA) **NOT EDIBLE**

Although I classify it as inedible, this mushroom is considered to be edible by many people (although not of high quality). As it can easily be confused with *A. pantherina* (see page 27), I think it is best avoided if not positively identified. The word 'spissa' is from the Latin meaning 'massive' or 'huge'.

RECOGNITION

CAP 10–15 cm in diameter, dark brown to greyish ochre with greyish mealy patches.
GILLS White and crowded. Spore print: white.
STEM 12 cm long, white with a persistent ring and a bulbous, almost rooting base.
FLESH White and firm. Smells unpleasant and slightly of radish.
HABITAT AND SEASON It is fairly commonly found in broad-leaf and coniferous woodland from summer through to autumn.

AMANITA EXCELSA

AMANITA PHALLOIDES

DEATH CAP **DEADLY POISONOUS**

Most of the fatal cases of mushroom poisoning in the western world can be attributed to this mushroom. It bears no resemblance to the edible mushrooms mentioned here, but it is included because it is all too easy for it to end up in your basket of edible mushrooms, through innocence or ignorance. Even if you don't eat any, it can cause illness, possibly serious, if its spores 'infect' your other mushrooms. If ever you find yourself in this situation, then throw them *all* away, including the edible ones. Wash your hands thoroughly after even touching it. This mushroom is so dangerous that you cannot afford to take any chances.

The trouble with *A. phalloides* poisoning is that, despite years of research, there is no simple antidote. In a simplified account, after ingestion the toxin passes through the digestive tract into the liver and kidneys, which it attacks; however, it is not passed out of the body with other waste matter but is re-circulated into the bloodstream to begin its journey all over again. Symptoms (severe diarrhoea, stomach pains and vomiting) start from 6 to 24 hours after ingestion, which is already too late: although the victim may appear to recover, death from kidney and liver failure shortly ensues. The only consolation I can think of is that it is quite rare to find it in the mixed woodland where it grows from late summer to late autumn, usually with oak. Unless you are accompanied by an expert mycologist and want a specimen for studying gill structure and spores, I have to warn you – DO NOT TOUCH IT!

indisputable facts are that its toxins will attack the central nervous system, producing such effects as intoxication, hallucination, euphoria, hyperactivity, coma and possibly death. I've heard that people dry the skin and use it to gain effects rather similar to those of LSD, but caution has to be taken as there are dangerous after-effects.

The only edible mushroom with which it would be confused is *A. caesarea*. The difference in mature specimens is clear, but the danger comes in trying to identify young specimens where the caps are just beginning to emerge from the egg-like volva from which all amanitas grow. In this situation, cut one in half lengthways and check the colour of

the gills and flesh: if these are white, then it is *A. muscaria*; if they are yellow, then it is *A. caesarea*.

RECOGNITION

CAP   Grows to a maximum height of 25 cm including cap, which reaches 20 cm in diameter. Bright red with scattered spots (the remains of the volva), but these can be washed off by rain leaving the cap plain. In older specimens the cap may fade to pale orange; there is a pale orange variety in America.
GILLS   Pure white.
STEM   Pure white, scruffy, with remains of volva attached to it, and white ring just below the cap. Height as above.

AMANITA PHALLOIDES

RECOGNITION

CAP   Grows from egg-shaped volva which remains at the stem base. To 12 cm diameter, round at first, becoming flattened; silky pale green to olive colour.
GILLS   White, sometimes somewhat cream to pale green. *A. phalloides* var. *alba* is entirely white and equally devastating.
STEM   Quite tall, to 14 cm and 1–2 cm diameter, with white ring just under cap that turns green with age.
HABITAT AND SEASON   It grows in deciduous woods and forests, often with chestnuts and hazel as well as oak, but not in fields. It is rarely found with conifers. It grows singly, perhaps two to three together. The season is from August until October.

AMANITA MUSCARIA
FLY AGARIC **POISONOUS**

Amanita muscaria, or fly agaric, is perhaps the best-known poisonous mushroom, depicted by illustrators throughout the centuries to conjure up the mysterious world of toadstools. There are stories about this mushroom from all over the world, but the

AMANITA MUSCARIA

AMANITA MUSCARIA

HABITAT AND SEASON Grows from summer to autumn in mixed woodland, preferring birch and pine, and is extremely common.

AMANITA PANTHERINA
PANTHER CAP **POISONOUS**

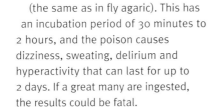

AMANITA PANTHERINA

This mushroom is likened to a panther both because of its spotted cap and because of its potential danger. In fact, it is very dangerous indeed, containing a substance called muscimol (the same as in fly agaric). This has an incubation period of 30 minutes to 2 hours, and the poison causes dizziness, sweating, delirium and hyperactivity that can last for up to 2 days. If a great many are ingested, the results could be fatal.

RECOGNITION

CAP 6–10 cm in diameter. Russet brown to milky coffee colour. It is covered with small, pure white, pyramidal, warty fragments. It can occur in a yellowish form in the USA.
GILLS Pure white, unchanging and crowded. Spore print: white.
STEM 8 cm long. White, tapering at the top with a membranous white ring and a basal bulb which often splits into two or three rings.
HABITAT AND SEASON One of the most common amanitas in parts of the USA; widespread yet uncommon in Britain and Europe. Often found in groups in deciduous and coniferous woodlands from summer to autumn.

AMANITA VERNA
SPRING AMANITA / FOOL'S MUSHROOM **DEADLY POISONOUS**

A lethal and deadly mushroom that could be mistaken for one of the agarics. It contains a substance called amanitin, which produces toxic poisons. These cause severe vomiting and diarrhoea for 12 to 24 hours, followed by a brief remission and finally the onset of kidney and liver dysfunction or failure. Symptoms appear after 8–12 hours, and death usually occurs in 4–8 days.

RECOGNITION

CAP 6–12 cm. White, silken and sometimes ochre at the centre.
GILLS White and crowded. Spore print: white.
STEM 12 cm long. White, silky smooth with a membranous ring. It also has a basal sac or volva.
HABITAT AND SEASON It has a preference for broad-leaved woods, and occurs mainly in the autumn but can appear in the spring, hence its name. It is usually found in warmer regions and is rare in Britain.

AMANITA VIROSA
DESTROYING ANGEL
DEADLY POISONOUS

The common name says all there is to be said about this beautiful but lethal mushroom. I personally regard this as more dangerous than *A. phalloides*. This is not because it is more poisonous, but because, being all white in colour, it could be confused with some white edible mushrooms by a beginner. The poison is very similar to that of *A. phalloides* and it should be avoided with the same meticulous care.

RECOGNITION

CAP White, to 12 cm in diameter.
GILLS Crowded and white (distinguishes between this and agaricus species whose gills are pink, turning brown with age). Spore print: white.
STEM White, with fibrous surface and fragile indefinite ring; to 12 cm tall, and 1–1.5 cm in diameter.
HABITAT AND SEASON In mixed or deciduous woods in big groups from late summer to autumn. Not common.

AMANITA VIROSA

There are many varied mushrooms in the Armillaria family, poisonous and non-poisonous. The most common are here, and the edible ones must be cooked before ingestion. (See also *Lentinula edodes* in the Cultivated Mushroom section.)

ARMILLARIA MELLEA

HONEY FUNGUS / BOOTLACE FUNGUS **EDIBLE**

I first started to gather *Armillaria mellea* when I was only eight, the beginning of a lifetime passion. A railwayman who worked for my father showed me how and where to collect 'famigliola', the local name for this mushroom which grows in tight little 'family' clusters. The local farmers had no objection to my tramping across their land because the mushrooms I was gathering grew at the base of young trees, and would otherwise have killed them. *A. mellea* is a lethal parasite of most trees, but in particular of the willows that divided the local fields and whose supple young branches were perfect for tying up the newly pruned vines in spring. It was a great thrill for a young boy to walk from tree to tree gathering the mushrooms, and I would return home with full baskets, proud that I was saving trees and simultaneously contributing to the family larder. My mother always used them to make a wonderful meal for us.

In autumn you can always find the inexpensive 'famigliole' at local markets in Italy and France, side by side with the very expensive porcini, ovoli and tartufi.

The name 'honey fungus' describes the colour rather than the smell or taste. The mushrooms grow in small tight clusters, with the caps very close together. The fungus spreads vegetatively by means of black rhizomorphs resembling bootlaces,

ABOVE ARMILLARIA MELLEA, CHUNKY FORM; LEFT ARMILLARIA MELLEA, SLENDER FORM

and on stumps and submerged roots.
SEASON Mid-summer to late autumn. In Britain I used to look for this mushroom starting on the 15th of October, but sometimes they are seen earlier or later than this.

ARMILLARIA TABESCENS
RINGLESS HONEY FUNGUS **EDIBLE**

This differs from the true honey fungus in that it does not have a ring on the stem. Some also say that it is bitter in taste compared to its cousin *A. mellea*. However, it is quite useful in the kitchen, and when I find it I certainly don't throw it away! The cap is 4–8 cm in diameter, and ochre brown with dark cottony scales. The gills are whitish, soon becoming pinkish brown and running down the stem. The spore print is white. The stem is 10 cm x 8 mm. *A. tabescens* is found growing in clusters at the base of deciduous trees, especially oaks, or on dead roots. From late summer to early autumn. Thought to be rare in Britain.

ARMILLARIA TABESCENS

hence the alternative name. White gills distinguish honey fungus from its poisonous look-alike, sulphur tuft (*Hypholoma fasciculare*), whose gills are dull sulphur-yellow to greenish.

A distant relation of *A. mellea* is *Lentinula edodes*, the cultivated and highly regarded shiitake.

RECOGNITION

CAP Variable 3–20 cm, hemispherical becoming flattened, with depressed centre. Pale honey-yellow to brown or ochre to dark brown, with stronger colour concentration at centre. Young specimens usually have a few rather fibrillose scales at the centre.

GILLS White, becoming creamy with age; adnate to slightly decurrent. Spore print: creamy-white.
STEM Tall and thin in relation to cap, 1.5 cm in diameter but up to 20 cm tall. White in young specimens, later becoming yellow. Becomes woody with age. Yellow cottony 'ring' just below cap.
FLESH White, with mushroomy but not particularly pleasant smell. Taste is slightly bitter and astringent. (After blanching both smell and taste improve dramatically.)
HABITAT Parasitic, growing in large clusters at the base of deciduous trees, including olive but mainly beech, willow, poplar, mulberry, etc,

ARMILLARIA TABESCENS

AGROCYBE CYLINDRICA

AGROCYBE CYLINDRICA
(SYN. PHOLIOTA AEGERITA) **EDIBLE**

This mushroom has been popular in Italy for centuries, especially in the south. It is known as the 'piopparello' or 'pioppino' because it is commonly found at the foot of poplar trees. In Britain it can be found on mulberry, elder, elm, etc., as well as poplars. The cap grows from 1 cm to 7–10 cm in diameter. Initially semi-round, becoming flatter when mature. The colour of the little heads of dark brown become paler noisette when open, but are still dark in the centre. The gills are quite tight and small, with smaller ones between them. They are whitish when young, becoming darker – to pale brown – with age. The stem is quite meaty and solid with a strong ring at the top. It is quite tall, up to 15 cm high and from 5 mm–1.5 cm in diameter. The flesh is white, smelling slightly of flour. It grows in clusters as above from springtime to autumn. This mushroom is now being cultivated.

PHOLIOTA MUTABILIS
(SYN. GALERINA MUTABILIS) **EDIBLE**

This is one of the best of the family, and is very similar to *Armillaria mellea*. The cap is 4–8 cm in diameter, brown-cinnamon, dirty, becoming ochre with age and in dry weather from the centre. The two colours distinctly zone the cap. It absorbs a lot of moisture. The gills are adnexed and tight, slightly yellow, turning cinnamon. The spore print is rust-coloured. It is not to be confused with *Hypholoma fasciculare*. The stem, up to 6 cm high and 3 mm thick, has a ring, with small scales below. The flesh is whitish, with an excellent mushroomy smell. It grows on tree stumps, in large groups, all year but especially the summer. Very common.

PICKING, CLEANING AND COOKING

Armillaria mellea is really rewarding for collectors, because it is fairly common and when you do find it, it is usually in large quantities. When very young and growing tightly together, just detach chunks of the clusters and cut off the bottom part of the stem, which is tough and inedible. When it is more mature and open, just cut off the cap because the stem will be woody. Wash if it is full of earth, and cut the stems off. You don't need to be too gentle: remember it is a parasite and endangers the trees it grows on. The same applies to the others in this family.

A. mellea is one of my favourite mushrooms to eat with spaghetti. It is delicious sautéed in butter and garlic, and excellent in stews and soups or cooked with other mushrooms (as are the other members of the family). Good for preserving as a pickle, cooked in vinegar and kept under oil or put in a jar and sterilised. None of the family is recommended for freezing (apart from *Agrocybe cylindrica*) or drying.

Do not eat any of the edible armillarias raw – they are mildly toxic – but once cooked they are perfectly safe. Blanch for at least 5 minutes at a high temperature, and discard the cooking water.

HYPHOLOMA FASCICULARE

(SYN. NAEMATOLOMA FASCICULARE) SULPHUR TUFT **POISONOUS**

Sulphur tuft is an accurate description for both colour and manner of growth. This poisonous mushroom can cause symptoms that vary from a severe stomach upset to death in medically compromised people. Fortunately, its bitter taste is an additional deterrent to eating any quantities.

Though there are other differences, the simplest and surest way of ascertaining whether a cluster of mushrooms growing on an old stump is the excellent *Armillaria mellea* (honey fungus) or this poisonous mushroom is to look at the gills. In honey fungus these are white; in sulphur tuft they are a dull sulphur-yellow, becoming green with age. There are many more mushrooms that grow in clusters on wood, in

HYPHOLOMA FASCICULARE

Hypholoma fasciculare

Pholiota squarrosa

similar conditions to those of sulphur tuft and honey fungus, and a good identification guide will describe the others in detail.

RECOGNITION

CAP To 8 cm when fully grown; yellow, with more orangey centre; sometimes having remains of veil attached to rim.
GILLS Turn from yellow to purplish green, and finally become dark purplish brown (the colour of the spores).
STEM Thin, 4–10 mm in diameter; varying from sulphur-yellow when young to rusty brown when mature; with slight, insignificant ring zone on upper part of stem.
HABITAT AND SEASON Grows in clusters on old stumps, preferring decaying wood of deciduous trees,

sometimes pine. Occasionally appearing to grow on soil, but in fact on buried stump or root, and is becoming more common in gardens, growing on wood chips. Very common; grows all year round, but most frequent in autumn.

PHOLIOTA SQUARROSA
SHAGGY PHOLIOTA **TOXIC**

This fungus can cause severe gastro-intestinal upsets that generally occur some 30 minutes to 2 hours after ingestion. Symptoms may last for up to 2 days. It could be mistaken for *Armillaria mellea* to the untrained eye. It does seem inviting, I agree, when you see a large group of this mushroom, with its wonderful colour, and its

apparently meaty flesh. But as with many things in life, beauty is not the only consideration. Leave it alone, but don't destroy it as it is pretty to look at and it's useful for insects.

RECOGNITION

CAP 10–15 cm in diameter, fleshy and shaggy with bright russet-brown upturned scales on an ochre background. The margin of the cap remains inrolled.
GILLS Crowded and pale yellow at first, then maturing cinnamon. Spore print: rust-brown.
STEM 15 x 1.5 cm. Scaly and like the cap in coloration below a membranous ring. Above the cap, smooth and pale yellow.
HABITAT AND SEASON Found in clusters on the base of living trunks, especially in the autumn. Common.

THERE ARE NOT MANY IN THE AURICULARIA FAMILY, BUT THE SINGLE
REPRESENTATIVE DISCUSSED HERE IS FOUND ALL OVER EUROPE, AND IS THE
LONGEST CULTIVATED AND MOST APPRECIATED FUNGUS IN CHINA.

AURICULARIA JUDAE

JUDAS' EAR / JEW'S EAR /
CLOUD EAR **GOOD**

A very curious mushroom
indeed. Although it is a
Basidiomycete, it doesn't have
any pores or gills in which the
spores or seeds are produced;
instead they are produced on
the surface of the fungus. This gelatinous fungus grows in the shape of an
ear, usually on stumps and branches of
elder trees. This is how it acquired one
of its common names: Judas is said to
have hanged himself on an elder tree.

The Chinese call it 'cloud ear fungus',
because it looks like the clouds
depicted in Chinese paintings, and
'black fungus', because it becomes
that colour when dry – and it dries

very successfully. When regenerated
in water from dry it absorbs so much
liquid that it completely regains its
original shape and texture. Its culinary
uses are limited because it is not so
flavoursome as other wild mushrooms.
However it has a value for its texture
and look, especially in Chinese and
Japanese cooking (in which gelatinous
textures are more appreciated than in
the West). It is the wild counterpart of
A. polytricha, the oldest cultivated
mushroom (see page 83).

RECOGNITION

CAP There is actually no cap – a cup
rather – as the shape is that of a
human ear, flat and round to oblong,
with sections inside. It is soft to the
touch, almost like membrane, because
inside it is gelatinous. It may be as

thick as a couple of millimetres while
the diameter can reach 10 cm. There
are no gills or stem. Its colour is pale to
dark wine or brown.
FLESH This is a gelatinous mushroom.
The outside colour varies from pale to
dark brown and is almost velvety,
while the inside is definitely soft and
wet. It doesn't smell particularly of
mushroom, but has a certain scent,
almost of iron, when just collected.
HABITAT It grows on dead branches
of elder trees, sometimes on elm trees,
sycamore, ornamental acers, etc., in
colonies, one attached to the other.
SEASON All year round, provided
there is enough moisture or rain.

PICKING, CLEANING AND COOKING

The mushrooms can be collected and
either used straightaway or dried. I
sometimes collect them dried, shrunken
and black and still attached to the
branches, and get them to normal size
by leaving them in water for a few
hours. Just detach them whole from
the tree by hand and cut off the little
hard bit where it was attached to the
tree. Wash in cold water; they don't
absorb much when fresh, unlike when
dried!) They very seldom have maggots.

If drying at home, the process is
very simple. Check that there are no
impurities or insects, and spread the
mushrooms on a woven flat basket
type of container to allow air through –
anywhere will do. When completely
dry, keep in a linen or cotton sack.

Great care has to be taken when
frying the mushroom in hot oil because
it may literally explode, causing the
fat to splash and possibly to burn.

I usually cook it first in stock to
give some flavour, and then I use it
together with other mushrooms either
in mixed stews or soups. It can be cut
in julienne strips and sprinkled on
salads as an exotic addition.

You can buy the dried mushrooms
from Chinese stores in case you are
too lazy to pick and dry them yourself!
Leave them in water for 30–40 minutes.

THE LARGE BOLETUS FAMILY CONTAINS, AMONG MANY, THE CEP OR PORCINO (*B. EDULIS*), PROBABLY THE PROTOTYPE MUSHROOM OF IMAGINATION – AS WELL AS THE MOST SOUGHT-AFTER – WITH ITS CURVED MEATY CAP AND PLUMP STEM. MOST MEMBERS OF THE FAMILY ARE EDIBLE, A FEW ARE TOXIC, AND ONE IS POISONOUS.

BOLETUS BADIUS

BOLETUS BADIUS
BAY BOLETE **VERY GOOD**

This relative of the more popular *B. edulis* – by no means a 'poor relation' – is very rewarding, not only for the frequency with which it grows, but also for its versatility in the kitchen. It is one of the most common edible wild mushrooms found in European countries with a moderate climate, and I used to take dried specimens with me when I went back to Italy to visit my family. (Once after a successful 'hunt', my wife and I had to build piles of them at the side of the path and pick them up later. We filled the boot of the car with them, and still left plenty for other people to gather.) My mother always found plenty of uses for it, although her local porcini had – and still have – a more intense flavour. It is called the 'bay' bolete because of its colour, that of a bay horse, and possibly also because it looks leathery when dry.

Not every year is so productive, but you very often find some of these boletes growing in woodland – especially beneath pines, where the forest floor is relatively free from undergrowth. Sometimes they are difficult to find because of the camouflage of pine needles, cones and dead branches; sometimes ferns hide the mushrooms beneath their fronds, but where these are not too dense you can brush them aside with your stick. The clue to their whereabouts has been given to me many times by the caps the squirrels leave lying on the forest floor after they have consumed the stems.

I well remember a mushroom foray in the grounds of Blenheim Palace organised some years ago by the *Observer*, Paul Levy and Roger Phillips. We collected quite a few *B. badius* there, but I had brought a big basketful of magnificent specimens with me just in case (I'd raided one of my favourite locations earlier in the day). After the foray I sautéed the mushrooms in butter with garlic and parsley, and we followed this with a wonderful apple pie cooked by the late Jane Grigson. It was a day to be treasured.

There are a couple of other boletes which are closely related to *B. badius*, and which can be collected and cooked similarly.

BOLETUS BADIUS

RECOGNITION

CAP Nearly spherical at first, almost merging with stem. Very small specimens have a deep brown velvety sheen, which becomes slippery when wet. When fully grown, cap flattens and colour pales to ochraceous

BOLETUS CHRYSENTERON

brown but retains its leathery feeling. When very old, cap tends to curve slightly, particularly at the rim, exposing more of the pores. Diameter usually 12–14 cm, occasionally larger.
PORES Cream to pale yellow in young specimens, turning yellowish green with age. In older specimens the pores can be seen quite distinctly and turn blue-green when bruised. Spore print: yellowish brown.
STEM Usually paler than cap, with vertical streaking; cylindrical, sometimes curved and tapering at base.
FLESH Firm, creamy white to pale yellow. In mature specimens, turns sky-blue when cut or touched. Delicate aroma, and the taste is mushroomy and sweet.
HABITAT Singly on soil, in coniferous and deciduous woodland.
SEASON Mid-summer to late autumn. The ideal weather conditions are three to four days after some rain which has followed a warm spell.

BOLETUS CHRYSENTERON
RED-CRACKED BOLETUS EDIBLE

This fungus is found quite commonly, but is not so culinarily valued as the other boletes (it must be cooked). The cap is hemispherical then convex, rather irregular, 3–8 cm in diameter. Very characteristic are the red cracks in the dark brown of the cap. The pores are golden yellow at the start, becoming green-yellow later, and the spore print is olive-brown. The stem is reddish, very thick, up to 10 cm high, and 8 mm–1.5 cm thick. When a little older, the entire mushroom is quite damp to the touch. The flesh is white-yellow, and under the cuticle is reddish. It smells fruity with a sweetish taste. It is found under pine and deciduous trees, also in parks, more common in the lowlands than in the mountains. It is good to eat when young, spongier when more mature. Cook it with other mushrooms.

BOLETUS PIPERATUS
(SYN. CHALCIPORUS PIPERATUS)
PEPPERY BOLETE EDIBLE

This bolete, one of the smallest in the family, is actually edible, but I think it should only be used in tandem with other mushrooms, to lend a peppery flavour (in many countries it is actually used as a condiment). The taste is really rather sharp, and it should always be cooked. The cap is 3–6 cm in diameter, orange-fawn or rust-coloured, hemispheric and sometimes slightly viscid. The flesh is a lemon yellow colour. The pores are medium sized, copper-orange, a deeper colour than the cap. The spore print is snuff-brown to cinnamon. The stem is 3–6 cm × 5 mm, concolorous with the cap. It is bright yellow inside when cut. It is often found on sandy soil with conifers, but also with beech and oak trees, and between woods and fields in groups. Common in Europe, from late summer to autumn.

PICKING, CLEANING AND COOKING

The blue discoloration of the flesh of *B. badius* is one of the reasons many people avoid eating this mushroom, believing it to be poisonous, but it is in fact quite delicious – especially if your specimens are young, with firm flesh and a fresh aroma. Remember to collect only specimens where the pores under the cap are not too spongy or dark green. You have to inspect older specimens with some care as they can contain maggots, though in general the species is remarkably maggot-free. (These large, older ones, so long as there are no maggots in them, are ideal for slicing and drying, see page 96.) Cut the stems near the base with a sharp mushroom knife. You should avoid washing them as the pores soak up water: just wipe if dirty.

B. badius can be found on the market stalls of most European countries, and its uses are very similar to those of *B. edulis*. Small specimens are delicious eaten raw, sliced very thinly for salads. They also make a wonderful accompaniment to any sort of meat or fish, and are exceptionally good sautéed in butter with garlic and parsley. They can be frozen or pickled, while dried specimens have a very delicate and subtle flavour, and can be used in all sorts of soups and sauces. *B. badius* is the only one of the three here which can be eaten raw.

A GOOD WHOLESOME CROP OF FRESHLY PICKED WILD FUNGI

OF THE BOLETUS FAMILY, *B. EDULIS* IS PROBABLY THE MOST REPRESENTATIVE, AND ALSO THE MOST VALUED THROUGHOUT THE WORLD.

BOLETUS EDULIS

CEP / PENNY BUN **EXCELLENT**

Boletus edulis represents the wild mushroom par excellence. This is what most Europeans mean when they talk about 'wild mushrooms', and it was popular enough in the pre-inflationary days of Victorian Britain to be given the appropriate nickname of 'penny bun' because of its well-baked colour and round shape. The Romans called this mushroom 'suillus', Latin for 'pig', a name echoed in the contemporary Italian 'porcino'. Some say this is because pigs like them, some that the young specimens look like fat little piglets. In Germany the common name means 'stone mushroom' – descriptive like 'penny bun' – but in Austria it is known as 'the gentleman's mushroom', while in Sweden it has the curious name of 'Karljohan' (from the king).

Some mycophiles may claim to prefer the rare *Amanita caesarea* or the morel, but the cep remains the safest to collect, the tastiest and the most rewarding in the kitchen of all wild mushrooms – quite simply, the best. Since it is commercially collected and sold both fresh and dried, it is one of the most sought-after wild mushrooms. Because of the delicacy of its flavour and its versatility, this is the mushroom that the world's leading chefs make most use of, creating many wonderful dishes.

RECOGNITION

CAP At first hemispherical, becoming flatter when mature. Usually 8–20 cm in diameter; occasionally to 30 cm. Cuticle smooth, colour varying from pale to dark brown.

PORES Closely packed and off-white at first, turning pale to dark yellowish green in older specimens, with tubular pore structure clearly visible. Spore print: olive-brown.

STEM In very young specimens stem and cap seem to merge together in almost spherical shape; later, stem grows to club-like shape, slightly broader at base, to 12.5 cm in diameter. No ring. Sometimes the stem develops larger than the cap, and tends to become riddled with maggots. Colour below cap is pale brown, becoming almost white towards base, with surface covering of white reticulum or network. To check that it is not *Tylopilus felleus* (see page 38), put a tiny bit of flesh or stem on your tongue. If it is bitter, discard swiftly.

FLESH In cap, off-white and firm; no discoloration when bruised. Stem flesh whiter, becoming woody and fibrous with age. The aroma is delicate and musty, though less intense in mushrooms found in temperate climates than in those growing in Mediterranean areas. It has a sweet, nutty and intensely mushroomy taste. (And when dried, it is the most perfumed and flavourful of all mushrooms.) Sadly, the mushroom can be attacked by another fungus, which changes the characteristics of smell and taste.

HABITAT In grass in or near mixed woodland (pine, oak, beech, birch and chestnut); usually singly, sometimes in groups of two or three. One of the

BOLETUS EDULIS

BOLETUS EDULIS

elongated. The surface of the stem is creamy with a network of lines. It grows in mixed deciduous woods, from the centre of Europe southwards. It is deemed rare in Britain. It appears from May until October.

BOLETUS AESTIVALIS
(SYN. B. RETICULATUS)
SUMMER BOLETE **EXCELLENT**

This bolete is as good as *B. edulis*, but is often riddled by maggots. The cap is 10–20 cm in diameter, pale brown with a matt surface. This is often covered with a cracked network, especially when more mature or the weather is dry, which is why its synonym is 'reticulatus'. The pores are white then greenish yellow, small and round. The spore print is olive, becoming snuff-brown with age. The stem is 15 x 2.5 cm, spindle shaped and reddish brown, covered in a fine white network from the cap to the base. The flesh is white, and has a sweetish taste. It grows mainly with beech and oak from very early summer to autumn. It fruits earlier than *B. edulis*, and is much less common.

most likely places is along a golf course, especially where the fairways are bordered with heather which in turn gives on to woodland. I have found ceps on pure sand and on bare soil – but never far from the roots of at least one of the trees that are supposed to nurture them.
SEASON Early summer to first frosts. Many Italians believe firmly that the mushrooms appear at the time of the new moon. I am much more scientific than that.

BOLETUS AEREUS
EXCELLENT

Many Italians think this is the best of the boletes, even better than *B. edulis*. The scientific name comes from the Latin for 'bronze', for from the very earliest stages the cap is a very dark brown, almost black (in Italian it is known as 'porcino nero'). The cap is 6–20 cm, convex, flattening when mature. The dark colouring has paler zones, and the surface is slightly velvety, not too dry. The pores are greyish white at the beginning, becoming yellow with maturity. The spore print is olive-brown. The stem is 7–15 x 3–6 cm, hard, massive and bulbous, becoming

BOLETUS AEREUS

PICKING, CLEANING AND COOKING

When you collect these mushrooms, hold the stem near the base and twist to ease it away from the mycelium. If you cut it free with a knife there is said to be a danger that the part left in the ground will rot and destroy the mycelium, preventing further fruit-bodies from growing in that spot. Do use your knife, though, to clean the dirt from the stem base before you put the mushroom in your basket.

Don't peel ceps and their close relations, and certainly don't wash them – just wipe off any dirt. Some people discard the pores if they have become soft. Cut larger mushrooms in half to check for maggots. If you intend drying them, don't let a few maggots worry you: they will just disappear when the ceps are sliced and dried. Dry the bits and pieces as well as the good slices, to make into savoury powder (see page 97). To avoid the larvae hatching eventually into moths (which can happen, amazingly, even after drying), keep your dried mushrooms – home-dried or bought – in the freezer.

Smaller specimens are suitable for pickling and freezing as well as cooking fresh, and may be thinly sliced and eaten raw in salads. Whole caps of mature ceps are good grilled, as in Italy. The older specimens are best sliced and fried or used in stews and sauces. Ceps are excellent dried, and give a very distinctive aroma to sauces and stews; adding a small quantity to blander mushrooms enhances their flavour immensely and is an economical way of using expensive bought dried ceps. See page 96 for some information on how to dry mushrooms.

BOLETUS SATANAS

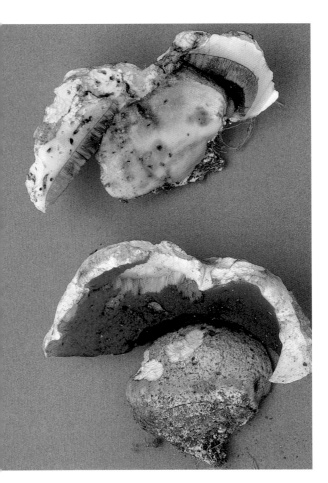

BOLETUS SATANAS
SATAN'S BOLETE **POISONOUS**

Fortunately this undesirable representative of the large family of delicious boletes is decidedly rare, and its distinguishing characteristics are so distinctive that there is little chance of making a mistake. Its appearance – especially when young, when it is very solid and bulbous – is similar to *B. barrowsii* or whiteking bolete, a form of *B. edulis* found in America growing under oaks. Another similar fungus is *B. rhodoxanthus*.

B. satanas is said by some people to be edible after a long cooking process has destroyed the toxins, but what is the point of risking severe stomach upsets when you can safely eat the other species? Generally I would advise you to leave alone any red-pored bolete you find which bruises blue. Also avoid *B. calopus*, a close relation. This bolete is not poisonous in the lethal sense, but – like *Tylopilus felleus* – it is inedible due to its bitterness, which does not disappear on cooking.

RECOGNITION

CAP At first off-white, becoming grey or greenish grey; at first round, becoming flat and sometimes cracked with age; to 30 cm in diameter.
PORES Very tightly packed, at first deep red becoming orange later, especially around the rim; turning bluish green when bruised.
STEM Enlarged below and onion-shaped; can reach 7–8 cm in diameter even when young, sometimes being fatter than the cap. Saffron-orange to bright lemon-yellow above, but red towards the base and with a red network, especially on the upper half.
FLESH Straw-colour in the cap, paler to whitish or lemon-yellow in the stem, changing to sky-blue.
HABITAT AND SEASON Grows beneath trees such as beech and oak from late summer through autumn; solitary, or in small groups of three or four.

TYLOPILUS FELLEUS
(SYN. BOLETUS FELLEUS)
BITTER BOLETE **NOT EDIBLE**

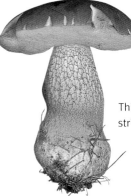

This bolete is not strictly poisonous, but it is so terribly bitter that including a whole specimen in a dish will spoil the whole thing. The possibility of mistaking it for *Boletus edulis* is more likely to occur in younger specimens, but if the mushroom is a little more mature, then the pink pores of *Tylopilus felleus* will distinguish it from *B. edulis*, which has creamy white pores. When people bring me mushrooms to identify, this is very often the most common one in their baskets.

After going through all the identification points below, as a last resort, taste a little piece of the cap (and then spit it out). If it is very bitter then it is definitely *T. felleus*, and you will have to throw it away.

RECOGNITION

CAP At first round, becoming flat later; light brown, and to 12 cm in diameter.
PORES Off-white in very young specimens, becoming pink with age and bruising brownish.
STEM Sturdy and fleshy; diameter to 3 cm at top and 6 cm at base; to 12 cm tall. Net pattern on stem surface is another major identification point, particularly in comparison with *Boletus edulis*.

T. felleus has a dark brown net pattern over a lighter background, while *B. edulis* has a white net pattern over a slightly darker background.
HABITAT AND SEASON In conifer and deciduous woods, summer to autumn.

THREE OF THE CANTHARELLUS FAMILY ARE PARTICULARLY WELL KNOWN. *C. CIBARIUS* IS PROBABLY THE MOST SOUGHT-AFTER MUSHROOM IN GASTRONOMY, AND *C. LUTESCENS* AND *C. TUBIFORMIS* ARE EXCELLENT TO EAT AS WELL.

CANTHARELLUS CIBARIUS

CHANTERELLE **EXCELLENT**

The delicate aroma of apricots and wonderful golden yellow colour make the chanterelle a beautiful and graceful mushroom. Like *Boletus edulis* and *B. badius*, this is one of the most popular edible wild mushrooms, well known to leading chefs all over the world. The French love these mushrooms particularly, epitomised in their Omelette aux Girolles. (They call *C. cibarius* 'girolle', and apply the name 'chanterelle' to the two others.) The colour, texture and shape of *C. cibarius* are unique, and in America there is a look-alike of a deep blue colour (*Polyzellus*). Can you imagine what a wonderfully exotic sight a dish with both colours would make? (Incidentally, there is also a black version, *C. cinereus*.)

My wife Priscilla is a natural chanterelle detector when we are out on forays, and usually spots them

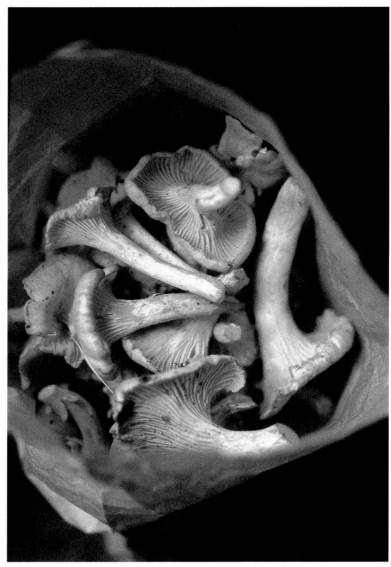

ABOVE AND BELOW CANTHARELLUS CIBARIUS

long before I do, even in autumn when the task is made more difficult by the yellow and brown leaves that have fallen from the birch trees. It is a fairly common mushroom, especially in Scotland where I believe that they sometimes literally cover the ground. I have heard of many young boys who increase their pocket money quite substantially in the season by collecting large quantities and sending them to France, where people are prepared to pay a great deal of money to enjoy them. Sometimes the woods are bright yellow with them, as they grow so gregariously, especially in Scotland

(and in Canada). I still remember with sorrow, every time I drive that way, watching my best chanterelle ground disappearing beneath the ferocious teeth of an excavator preparing for a motorway.

RECOGNITION

CAP In small specimens at first convex and minute, becoming funnel-shaped when mature, with thin and irregular rim. To 8 cm in diameter. Deep yolk-yellow to pale yellow in colour, fading with age.

GILLS Resembling irregular branching folds or veins, decurrent from top almost to base of stem. Not crowded, quite irregular. Concolorous with cap. Spore print: pale yellow.

STEM Thick and wide, tapering towards base to form narrow lower part of funnel. To 2–3 cm in diameter at base, and up to 6 cm tall.

FLESH Pale yellow, firm, with peppery taste. Fresh smell, faintly of apricots. No discolouring on bruising and usually maggot-free.

HABITAT In mixed woods, often among moss, solitarily or in groups on soil.

SEASON Summer. They love moisture, but it is better to collect these mushrooms some time after it has been raining.

CANTHARELLUS CIBARIUS

CANTHARELLUS LUTESCENS

VERY GOOD

CANTHARELLUS TUBIFORMIS

VERY GOOD

CANTHARELLUS LUTESCENS

These two Cantharellus members are extremely easy to find in most northern European countries. They are the so-called autumn alternative to the normal chanterelle (in Italian known as 'giallo' or 'finferla'). The dark brown caps are 2–6 cm in diameter, trumpet-like in shape. The stems are 5–8 cm tall, and both are yellow, bright in *C. lutescens*, less bright in *C. tubiformis*. The gills are quite pale, almost yellow in *C. lutescens*, yellow-grey in *C. tubiformis*. The flesh is not very meaty, quite thin in fact, but both are excellent to eat. *C. lutescens* has a beautiful fruity smell, unlike *C. tubiformis*. They grow abundantly and gregariously under conifers, mostly in moss, from summer to late autumn.

PICKING, CLEANING AND COOKING

Cut these mushrooms at the base with a sharp mushroom knife. They can be pulled as well, but then cut off the earthy part before putting them in the basket. Because they lose some of their flavour if washed, I suggest you clean them thoroughly with a brush when you collect them to prevent sand or grit from getting lodged in the gills.

All these mushrooms are very versatile, and the colour of the chanterelle is a fabulous decorative addition for a recipe. It is always good if eaten fresh, but also keeps well in a refrigerator for a maximum of four to five days in a basket covered with a damp cloth. It can be eaten raw, but its rather peppery taste disappears when it is cooked. In fact, it tastes at its best with scrambled eggs or in soups and stews, and is excellent for sauces. It is good for pickling, but does not freeze or dry so satisfactorily.

OMPHALOTUS OLEARIUS

chanterelles. In groups and clumps at the base of stumps of various broad-leaved trees, especially olives. Summer to first frosts. This is more of a Mediterranean mushroom.

HYGROPHOROPSIS AURANTIACA

FALSE CHANTERELLE **NOT EDIBLE**

This was originally classified as poisonous, was later declared edible, but recent findings tell us that ingestion of a large amount can cause digestive complaints. Beginners often mistake this common mushroom for the true chanterelle, *Cantharellus cibarius*. It is a worthless look-alike.

RECOGNITION

CAP   To 6 cm in diameter, varying from orange-yellow to darker orange in the centre. Margin at first inrolled, then flat.
GILLS   Concolorous with cap; decurrent, as in true chanterelle, but finer, and not extending so far down the stem.
STEM   Less funnel-shaped than in true chanterelle; concolorous with cap or slightly darker; to 5 cm tall.
FLESH   Not as substantial as in true chanterelles.
HABITAT AND SEASON   Grows in late summer and autumn in mixed wood-land, preferring conifers.

OMPHALOTUS OLEARIUS

(SYN. CLITOCYBE OLEARIA)
DEADLY POISONOUS

This poisonous lookalike of *Cantharellus cibarius* (the chanterelle) is fortunately rare in Britain (I have never seen it myself), and only occasional in central and southern Europe. In Mediterranean countries it generally grows on olive trees – hence the name 'olearius' – though when seen in America or Britain it grows on hardwood stumps. If in springtime you visit a country where olive trees grow, don't get too excited by the sight of these mushrooms: they are not chanterelles – close inspection should show you the difference – and they should be left alone.

RECOGNITION

CAP   The size of *O. olearius* is much greater than that of true chanterelles: it can reach 15 cm in diameter. From dark orange to bright yellow, as in the chanterelle. Convex in the centre, with margin inrolled.
GILLS Very tight, unlike *C. cibarius*, and concolorous with the cap. Incidentally, this mushroom may be seen glowing in the dark – mature specimens have phosphorescent gills.
STEM   Meaty, 15–20 cm tall, and tapering towards the base.
FLESH   A bit thin, saffron yellow, darkening with age.
HABITAT AND SEASON   The fact that it grows on trees is the final disqualifying factor in its comparison with

HYGROPHOROPSIS
AURANTIACA

FROM THE SAME FAMILY AS CANTHARELLUS, CRATERELLUS (ONCE ACTUALLY KNOWN AS CANTHARELLUS) HAS MANY DIFFERENCES.

CRATERELLUS CORNUCOPIOIDES

HORN OF PLENTY **VERY GOOD**

Of all the European names for this mushroom, I like the British 'horn of plenty' best. This fragile mushroom of the chanterelle family does indeed look like a cornucopia – or, perhaps, a trumpet – but it is black instead of gold. Most of the other descriptions sound too funereal to suit the mushroom. Although it is indeed grey to black in colour, it has none of the connotations of death that so many of the names suggest – 'trompette de la mort' in French, 'trombetta dei morti' in Italian. It is in fact a very good and tasty mushroom, that can be widely used in cooking. There is no edible or poisonous counterpart.

When I first introduced it on the menu in my restaurant, clients were somewhat reluctant to eat it because of its black colour. Now, however, it has become a firm favourite, especially in dishes with a delicate white fish such as halibut, sole or monkfish.

RECOGNITION

CAP Very similar to the bell end of a trumpet: deeply funnel-shaped, with irregularly lobed and wavy margins; initially pale brown, then grey and finally black. To 8–10 cm in diameter.
GILLS Almost non-existent; the forming of spores takes place on the hymenium situated on the ridged outer sides of the tubular stem. When ripe, the pores colour the stem white to grey, giving a velvety sheen.
STEM An irregular tube 1–2 cm in diameter and up to 12 cm tall, with very thin walls.
FLESH Externally grey, turning black when wet; internally darker grey. This mushroom is not very fleshy because of its thin, cartilaginous and fragile walls. A distinctive pleasant smell and particularly delicate taste and texture – in fact, it is known in some parts of Italy as the 'poor man's truffle'.
HABITAT Gregarious in leaf litter, especially in frondose woods, but preferring the presence of oak and occasionally beech. Don't forget to mark on your map where you first find them, because they usually grow in the same spot every year.
SEASON Late summer to late autumn. Don't collect it on rainy days, but wait until the sun comes out.

PICKING, CLEANING AND COOKING

The best way to collect it is to cut with a knife at the base. Pay maximum attention to cleaning these mushrooms, as small insects and other impurities find their way deep into the funnel. If they are not dislodged by shaking, it may be best to cut the mushrooms lengthways to clean them. This is one instance of a mushroom where washing is possible if the specimens are particularly dirty, but dry well with a cloth before using.

The horn of plenty is ideal for preparing sophisticated dishes requiring its black colour and delicate taste. It is delicious just sautéed in butter with parsley and chives, excellent for sauces and also very good in soups and stews. It is not recommended for freezing unless first cooked in butter. Ideal for drying and reducing to powder, which is then used to improve the flavour of sauces. It is not particularly good for pickling, nor does it keep very long in its fresh state as it tends to dry out and become rather leathery.

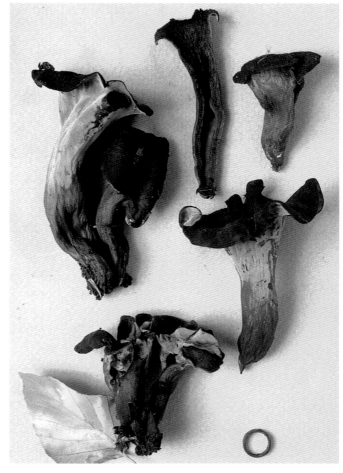

CRATERELLUS CORNUCOPIOIDES

US COMATUS

COPRINUS IS A SMALL GROUPING IN THE AGARIC FAMILY, OF WHICH ONLY ONE MEMBER, WHEN YOUNG, OFFERS GOOD EATING. THE TASTE AND FLAVOUR OF *C. COMATUS* IS NOT DISSIMILAR TO FIELD MUSHROOMS.

COPRINUS COMATUS

SHAGGY INK CAP / LAWYER'S WIG / SHAGGY MANE **GOOD**

The shape of *Coprinus comatus* always reminds me of the bearskins that the guards wear at Buckingham Palace. Once I glimpsed a glorious troop of *C. Comatus* growing in luxuriously rich grass as I was driving past the main gate of an army barracks. They looked just as if they were standing on guard. I stopped my car far too suddenly (a hazard of fungus collecting, I'm afraid), and proceeded to gather the mushrooms, much to the astonishment of the onlooking motorists behind me and the genuine soldiers on guard.

The various English names appropriately describe different characteristics. The scales on the cap indeed resemble the curls on a lawyer's wig, and the cap has a tendency to deliquesce into a black fluid, which in past ages was used as a source of writing ink.

This mushroom is a very delicate-tasting member of the Agaric family and, in my opinion, is perhaps underestimated by chefs. I have cooked it frequently over the years, with excellent results, and I find it quite versatile. Only the small specimens are of any value, while their gills are still white; once the cap and gills start to darken, the mushroom is of no use.

RECOGNITION

CAP Acutely ovate or cylindric in young specimens, growing 3–15 cm tall and 1–6 cm in diameter and closed towards the stem; the white cuticle is covered in large white scales with brownish tips, with a touch of light brown at the top. As the mushroom matures, the cap opens to a bell shape and the off-white cuticle becomes first grey then black from

ABOVE AND BELOW CORPRINUS COMATUS

too humid weather. This mushroom can go from button to deliquescence in two days, even less in warmer conditions.

PICKING, CLEANING AND COOKING

Cut the stem of small firm specimens, with the cap still closed around the stem, with a sharp mushroom knife. Mature specimens would be too mushy in texture, and the ink would colour black everything with which it came into contact. The caps quickly open out and mature once cut so do not keep them too long. To avoid this you can pull the stem from the cap. If you are not able to use them straightaway, I suggest blanching them to keep them for a bit longer. You can wash closed caps to remove the sand.

C. comatus is simply delicious however you prepare it. Deep-fry the smaller 'buttons' after dipping them in beaten eggs and rolling them in breadcrumbs. They are very good for stews, soups and sauces, and for sautéing in butter with chives and parsley. The lack of a distinct flavour/aroma means they are not really suitable for the freezing or drying processes.

the rim upwards, as auto-digestion takes place and the cap turns to an inky black pulp.

GILLS In young specimens visible only by cutting the cap lengthways. Very crowded and tightly packed. At first white, turning pink, then grey and finally black. Spore print: brownish black.

STEM Long, thin and hollow, 1–3 cm in diameter and up to 25 cm tall. White. Membrane protecting young gills remains on the stem in the form of an irregular ring, or breaks loose and falls to the base.

FLESH When very young the stem and cap form a sturdy body with very firm delicate white flesh. Smell and taste very fresh and mushroomy, not dissimilar to that of old field mushrooms. Much to the delight of the gatherer, insect larvae do not seem to infest this mushroom as the caps disappear too quickly, and the stem is hollow.

HABITAT Occasionally isolated, but usually gregarious – sometimes in huge groups. Occurs almost anywhere – on hard soil along country lanes and bridleways; where soil has been disturbed; in lawns and pastures.

SEASON Late summer to late autumn, especially in warm but not

Coprinus Atramentarius

COMMON INK CAP **TOXIC**

Although it is edible when young, I am listing this mushroom as toxic because of its violent reaction when consumed with alcohol (and this has been known to lead to death). Nausea, palpitations and hot flushes not only can occur when beer, wine or liqueur are drunk at or just after the same meal, but to some extent are likely if alcohol is taken at the next meal, some hours later. Indeed, a chemical substance with similar properties is used to treat alcoholics. I strongly advise that you avoid collecting this mushroom.

It has an inky cap just like *C. comatus*, but the two are easy to distinguish.

Coprinus atramentarius

Coprinus atramentarius

Recognition

Cap At first ovate, then conical when mature; colour greyish, brownish towards the top, growing darker with age and blackening at margin when auto-digestion takes place (as with *C. comatus*).
Gills At first white, turning grey and then inky-black with auto-digestion.
Stem To 15 cm tall; thin (only 1–2 cm in diameter); hollow.

Habitat and season Grows gregariously in tight clusters on stumps near cultivated areas, on lawns, in gardens and along roads, from late spring to late autumn.

Coprinus Picaceus

MAGPIE FUNGUS **NOT EDIBLE**

A member of the ink-cap family which is not regarded as being edible. In fact it is slightly unpleasant to eat. Young specimens may resemble *C. comatus* because of the similarity of the cap shape.

Recognition

Cap 4–6 cm in diameter, oval in shape becoming bell-shaped. White then grey, and finally black and spotted with white patches (thus the magpie connotation).
Gills White then pinkish and finally black, when they rapidly dissolve to an inky fluid. The spore print is black.
Stem 8 cm, whitish, fleecy with a woolly bulbous base.
Habitat and season It grows usually with beech from late summer to autumn in little shaded groups. It is southern in distribution in the UK, and rarely seen in the north. Occasional.

FISTULINA HEPATICA

OF THE MANY BRACKET FUNGI, OR POLYPORES, (SO CALLED FOR THE MANY PORES ON THE UNDERSIDE OF THE CAP, FROM WHICH THE SPORES ARE RELEASED), ONLY A FEW ARE EDIBLE. *FISTULINA HEPATICA* IS ONE.

FISTULINA HEPATICA
BEEFSTEAK FUNGUS / OX TONGUE
VERY GOOD

Most polypores have a destructive effect on the trees they parasitise, but there are fringe benefits. As well as being appreciated gastronomically, *Fistulina hepatica* produces a particularly fine coloration of the oak wood on which it usually grows and which it eventually destroys. This rich mahogany-red coloration is valued by furniture makers.

Bracket fungi are so named because they look like a bracket or shelf attached to the tree from which they obtain their nutrition. Hunting mushrooms does not always mean keeping your nose and eyes to the ground: although these mushrooms are sometimes found at the base of the trunk, they can grow anywhere on the host tree, so I'm afraid you will have to look a bit higher from time to time. See also *Laetiporus sulphureus*, page 53, another fine example of a bracket fungus.

RECOGNITION

CAP Can reach a diameter of 35 cm and a thickness of 6–7 cm. It is broadly tongue-shaped and when young is very soft and juicy with minute warts covering the top of the cap, which is brick-red – the whole very similar in appearance to an ox tongue. Margin rounded at first, becoming thinner and very sticky as it ages.
PORES Pinkish, closely packed. Pores visible and separate (unlike most polypores where they are fused together), bruising darker when touched. Spore print: yellowish pink.
STEM Either sessile, or attached by a short, thick almost indiscernible stem.
FLESH When cuticle is peeled away, flesh appears wet and of a brilliant red that deepens with age. Cutting reveals pale pink veinous streaks similar to some steak (hence 'poor man's meat' or 'liver'); flesh is heavy for its size and extremely succulent. Aroma pleasant, strong and mush-roomy; taste slightly sour when raw.
HABITAT Deciduous woodland; prefers oak, sometimes sweet chestnut; on living trees or stumps. Sometimes singly, sometimes in small clumps.
SEASON Late summer to late autumn. It does not need particular weather conditions because it gets its nourishment from the living tree.

PICKING, CLEANING AND COOKING

Just cut it off at the base where it is attached. As the fungus grows on trees it is usually fairly free from dirt and will just need brushing off. Don't collect sticky old specimens, which will be dry inside.

I have spent many years trying to find ways of using this mushroom in the kitchen, as it is good food, full of proteins and vitamins. Because it can be slightly sour-tasting, I once advised that it should usually be cooked to remove possible bitterness and ensure digestibility, but very succulent young specimens can be used raw in salads (see page 120). The fungus is similar to real meat in texture, being very fleshy and succulent, and so it can be prepared as such.

F. hepatica turns black when cooked, because of its acidity. Take this into account when cooking – it makes a good accompaniment to fatty or rich food such as sweetbreads or brains.

FISTULINA HEPATICA

GRIFOLA FRONDOSA

GRIFOLA IS A SUB-SPECIES OF THE MERIPILUS OR POLYPORUS FAMILY, TO WHICH THE GIANT POLYPORE AND THE DRYAD'S SADDLE BELONG (SEE PAGE 69). OF THE MANY POLYPORES, THESE ARE THE MOST DELICATE. THEY ARE NOT VERY COMMON, AND ARE UNDERGOING INTENSE STUDY FOR THE PURPOSES OF COMMERCIAL CULTIVATION (SEE PAGE 84).

GRIFOLA FRONDOSA
HEN OF THE WOODS EDIBLE

When you talk about 'chicken of the woods' (*Laetiporus* or *Polyporus sulphureus*, see page 53), one has to ask oneself if there is an equivalent 'hen of the woods'. Indeed there is, and it is one of the best wild mushrooms when young. It is also one of the most satisfying and exciting mushrooms in the wild because when you find it, it is usually large and round, and really resembles a brooding hen sitting on her eggs! The word 'frondosa', from 'fronda' ('leaf' in Italian/Latin), denotes that these special mushrooms grow from one stem, expanding in many leafy lobes one on top of the other. Because *Grifola frondosa* is a polypore, it has pores, not gills. It is found in most northern regions, in forests from Canada to Europe and Asia. The Japanese have learned how to cultivate it, as 'maitake' (see page 84), which makes them more accessible to many markets throughout the world.

RECOGNITION

CAP There isn't actually a cap, as the fruit-body consists of hundreds of leafy lobes, which grow from a many-branched nucleus attached to the tree. The cuticle, which is smooth, is of a brown to grey colour, with darker circles. It develops pale and dark stripes as it matures.
PORES White, not too tight, round and 2–3 mm long. Spore print: white.
STEM The supporting stem to the cluster of 'leaves', which grow like a fan, is of a white colour and is thick and tender when young, becoming chewy when older. It can reach a height of 30 cm and a diameter of 20–50 cm.
FLESH White and dense, slightly fibrous when old. Smells of wheat flour, becoming cheesy when old.
HABITAT On stumps or at the base of dead or dying hardwoods like elm,

broad-leaved trees, especially oak, willow and beech. It is uncommon in the US and extremely rare in Britain and Europe.

PICKING, CLEANING AND COOKING

Cut with a sharp mushroom knife, check for insects, and brush clean before cooking. They could actually be washed as well, because they take up so many impurities from the soil. Both are excellent mushrooms but should not be eaten raw. They can be sautéed in egg and breadcrumbs, stewed and even preserved. One specimen, with its multi lobes, can serve five to six people.

ABOVE AND BELOW GRIFOLA FRONDOSA

oak, beech, maple or even pine.
SEASON   Early summer to early autumn. These mushrooms don't need very wet weather to grow (although it helps), as they are drawing moisture from the tree.

GRIFOLA UMBELLATA
(SYN. POLYPORUS UMBELLATUS)
EDIBLE

This edible fungus is very similar to, and could be mistaken for, *G. frondosa*. However it is very rare, and authorities in Britain and Europe suggest it should not be collected. It is used in China as an immune system stimulant. The fruit-body – as with *G. frondosa*, this is more descriptive than 'cap' – can be up to 50 cm in diameter. A thick fleshy base gives rise to numerous umbrella-like caps each 4–6 cm. They are grey-brown in colour and covered in small scales, but fading to beige with age. The pores are angular, whitish and running down the stem. The spore print is white. The many-branched stems are white, very thin, and merging into a common base. It grows on the ground by the roots of

THE LARGE HYDNUM FAMILY HAS ONE DISTINGUISHING CHARACTERISTIC: INSTEAD OF GILLS OR PORES UNDER THE CAP, THERE ARE THOUSANDS OF LITTLE SPINES. OF ALL THE HYDNUMS, THESE TWO ARE THE EDIBLE ONES. MOST OF THE OTHERS ARE COMPLETELY INEDIBLE, EVEN EXTREMELY ACIDIC AND EMETIC, SO BE SURE TO GET IT RIGHT!

ABOVE RIGHT HYDNUM REPANDUM

HYDNUM REPANDUM

(SYN. DENTINUM REPANDUM)
HEDGEHOG FUNGUS **GOOD**

This excellent mushroom, commonly available in most European markets (although often thrown away in America), has one distinctive characteristic: instead of the gills or pores that most of the other edible mushrooms have, the spore-producing hymenophore consists of spines pointing downwards from the under-side of the cap – hence the name 'hedgehog'. As far as texture and taste are concerned, it is very similar in character to the chanterelle. It is quite common and relatively easy to find, even in seasons when other mushrooms may not be so plentiful. Because of its spines, this mushroom is one of the easiest to recognise. There are similar mushroom species with spines, but with darker colouring, making the hedgehog fungus quite easy to distinguish.

HYDNUM REPANDUM

RECOGNITION

CAP Irregular, very fleshy, brittle, convex to fat; from almost white through pale yellow to orange, depending on location. Up to 15 cm in diameter. Cuticle very smooth, not viscid, but with a suede-like quality.
SPINES Very crowded, growing perpendicular to the underside of cap, decurrent, reaching maximum 6 mm. Extremely fragile, breaking at slightest touch. Usually concolorous with cap. Spore print: white.
STEM Large, more pronounced towards the base, often eccentric to cap. Colour paler than rest of mushroom and surface as smooth as cap. To 7 cm high and 4 cm in diameter.
FLESH Fleshy and quite firm, but brittle; whitish yellow and slightly bitter in taste: when cooked, bitterness disappears and mushroom is tasty with pleasant aroma. Smell pleasant and gently mushroomy.
HABITAT Gregarious, sometimes in rings or strips, under trees in coniferous or broad-leaved woodland.
SEASON Mid-summer to late autumn in mild weather.

SARCODON IMBRICATUM

(SYN. HYDNUM IMBRICATUM)
SHINGLED HEDGEHOG /
SCALY TOOTH **EDIBLE**

Although this relation of *Hydnum repandum* is edible, it is not much sought after because it is bitter. Its cap is 10 – 25 cm in diameter, covered in coarse grey-brown scales raised at the tip, on a pale russet cap that becomes funnel shaped. The spines run down the stem, up to 1 cm long; tight, decurrent and whitish, ageing to brown. The spore print is brown. The stem is 8 x 2 cm, short, thick and whiting, becoming grey-brownish with age. The flesh is dirty white, becoming a pale sepia. Solid, but chewy. The smell is quite strong with maturity, the taste is sour and bitter. Found in coniferous woods especially on sandy soils, late summer to autumn. Abundant in North America, and in Europe, common in old pine and spruce woods.

SARCODON IMBRICATUM

PICKING, CLEANING AND COOKING

Cut at the base with a sharp knife. *Hydnum repandum* is one of the mushrooms least likely to be infested with maggots, and is easily cleaned by scraping or a light brushing. It can be kept in the refrigerator for a few days.

Younger specimens are very rewarding, as the whole mushroom can be used, including the spines; in older specimens the spines should be removed, as they can add to the bitterness. Both should always be cooked before eating, to remove any hint of bitterness. They can be eaten by themselves, stewed or fried in butter with onions, and also with other mushrooms. The flesh of *H. repandum* is firmer than that of the chanterelle, making it good for drying and using later in sauces and soups. It is also excellent pickled, and once cooked may be frozen. *Sarcodon imbricatum* is not a mushroom for gourmets, but is useful cooked in a mixture.

THERE ARE NOT MANY MEMBERS OF THE LACCARIA FAMILY, BUT OF THE MANY SMALL EDIBLE MUSHROOMS YOU MIGHT FIND WHEN MUSHROOM HUNTING, THIS IS THE BEST FOR ME.

RECOGNITION

CAP Very small, 1–8 cm in diameter. Bright amethyst-violet in colour, but fading with age and drying to a pale lilac-buff. Sometimes scurfy at the centre.
GILLS Distant and irregular, at first bright violet, but becoming powdery white with age. Spore print: white.
STEM 8 cm x 7 mm, concolorous with the cap. The base is covered with lilac down.
FLESH Tender and delicate in young specimens. The taste is sweet; there is no significant smell.
HABITAT Coniferous and deciduous woods, usually with beech, in many small groups. (*L. laccata* will be found everywhere there are trees, from sea coasts to mountain tops, where it grows with dwarf willows.)
SEASON Late summer to early winter. Very common.

LACCARIA AMETHYSTEA

AMETHYST DECEIVER **GOOD**

This is a much underrated mushroom so far as cooking is concerned, perhaps because of its colour, but it is one which gives me great pleasure, both in collecting and cooking. It is very small and delicate, but I actually love it for its colour! It is said to 'deceive' because the fruit-body changes colour as it ages. Alternatively, you could use *L. laccata*, a reddish brown relation, which is edible.

ABOVE AND BELOW LACCARIA AMETHYSTEA

PICKING, CLEANING AND COOKING

Just cut at the base, and brush off any soil. I usually use both *L. amethystea* and *L. laccata* as an addition to salads – where they can be eaten raw – or for any dishes I want to embellish. They lack culinary quality and so are best used in a mixture of mushrooms but *L. amethystea* especially goes well with the yellow of chanterelles.

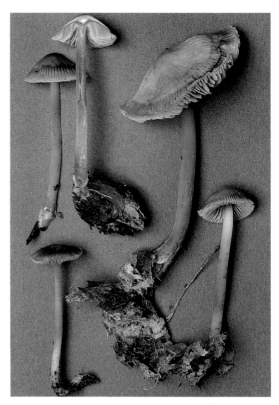

MYCENA PURA

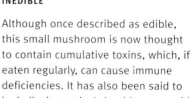

MYCENA PURA

INEDIBLE

Although once described as edible, this small mushroom is now thought to contain cumulative toxins, which, if eaten regularly, can cause immune deficiencies. It has also been said to be hallucinogenic. I should try to avoid it. It can resemble *Laccaria amethystea*, but is generally much paler.

RECOGNITION

CAP 2–5 cm in diameter. Purple to pale lilac and lined at the margin when wet.
GILLS White fading to pink. Smelling of radish. Spore print: white.
STEM 6 cm x 6 mm, concolorous with the cap. It is also tough, leathery and hairy at the base.
HABITAT AND SEASON Gregarious in all types of woodland. Growing in leaf litter and moss from summer to winter. Very common.

As the names 'Lactarius' and 'milk cap' suggest, the members of this genus exude a milky substance when broken or cut; this liquid may be white or coloured, or it may turn wine-coloured or orange, depending on species.

RIGHT AND BELOW Lactarius deliciosus

LACTARIUS DELICIOSUS
SAFFRON MILK CAP **EXCELLENT**

Two major features distinguish *Lactarius deliciosus* from other members of the family: the milky fluid it exudes immediately becomes a deep red-orange, and the saffron-orange flesh turns green when bruised.

There are many other edible species of Lactarius, especially in America (around 200), ranging from purple to indigo-blue in colour, but in Europe *L. deliciosus* is one of the few considered excellent and worth collecting. Many people, including the French, Germans, Poles, Swedes and Russians, feel passionately about this mushroom. I love it for its nutty taste and firm texture, but above all for the brilliant colour, which looks wonderful in special dishes. Timothy Neath, my 'Scottish man', supplies me in season with wonderful specimens of milk caps, ceps, wood blewits and chanterelles – and occasionally sends me some lovely candles, made with pure beeswax taken from his very own hives.

When collecting, take extra care not to confuse this mushroom with the poisonous *L. torminosus* (see overleaf).

RECOGNITION

CAP At first convex, with a small depression at the centre becoming larger and deeper as the margin, which is initially rolled, expands to form a large shallow funnel. Smooth cuticle first orange-saffron (often with concentric narrow zones alternating lighter and darker saffron, which fade with maturity); later paler and rather dull; tending to turn green when bruised. Diameter to 15 cm.

GILLS Same colour as cap, turning green when bruised. Very crowded, slightly decurrent, fragile. Spore print: pale yellowish.

STEM Hollow, relatively short and thick, to 7 cm in diameter. Colour paler than cap or gills, and flecked with orange depressions, especially towards base; also discolouring green.

FLESH When cut or broken all parts exude a milky latex, which rapidly turns carrot-orange in contact with air. Slight bitter taste (disappears on cooking); the milk is slightly sweetish. It smells of fruit and acid, boiled sweets in fact!

HABITAT Among short grass in coniferous woods, often nestling beneath pine needles (with stem hidden and only the characteristic 'zoned' cap visible). Occasionally solitary; usually gregarious.

SEASON Late summer to late autumn.

PICKING, CLEANING AND COOKING

This mushroom has an al dente texture and a not-too-distinctive flavour. To my palate it is delicious, given some attention in its preparation. Cut with a sharp mushroom knife. First of all, check for maggots: older specimens may be infested, so cut these lengthways down the stem for closer inspection and cleaning. These mushrooms are firm enough to rinse in water if they are particularly dirty or gritty. Next, blanch for 2–3 minutes to remove any bitterness.

After this, use the blanched mushroom raw in salads; steam, stew or fry; or use in sauces for pastas, meat and fish. It freezes well. The Russians preserve this mushroom in salt (see page 97).

LACTARIUS TORMINOSUS

LACTARIUS TORMINOSUS
WOOLLY MILK CAP **POISONOUS**

Of the many Lactarius species some are edible, many are inedible due to their taste, and some are distinctly poisonous. Mistakes are made between *L. deliciosus* and its poisonous counterpart *L. torminosus* – but the key differences are easy to spot. There are parts of northern Europe and of Russia where this mushroom is eaten after special treatment, but I recommend you to play it safe and leave it alone, if you don't want to suffer a severe colic.

RECOGNITION

CAP The most obvious difference between *L. torminosus* and *L. deliciosus* is the woolly, fluffy filaments covering the cap of the former. The latter is smooth. The cap can reach 12 cm in diameter. The general colour is pinkish orange, while the general tone of *L. deliciosus* is orange. There are the same concentric circles of dark and pale.

GILLS White. Spore print: cream.

STEM Flesh coloured, and roughly same size/height as *L. deliciosus*. The primary difference is that the stem and flesh of this mushroom, when cut, exude a milk which is and remains white (and is reddish orange in *L. deliciosus*). It is peppery in flavour (if you wanted to taste it!).

HABITAT AND SEASON Grows singly in birch woods, not conifers as its edible counterpart, from summer to autumn.

LAETIPORUS IS A BRACKET FUNGUS, GROWING ON LIVING TREES. FORTUNATELY, THE WORD 'SULPHUREUS' APPLIES ONLY TO THE COLOUR OF THIS SPLENDID FUNGUS, NOT TO ITS TASTE!

LAETIPORUS SULPHUREUS

(SYN. POLYPORUS SULPHUREUS) CHICKEN OF THE WOODS / SULPHUR POLYPORE **VERY GOOD**

Like *Fistulina hepatica*, this is a bracket fungus, a member of the polypores, and it parasitises older trees, from which it gains its nutrients. So, when you go mushrooming, always remember to look up as well as down! Years ago I employed an Italian to pick wild mushrooms for me. On one occasion he found a wonderful specimen in rather a precarious situation, suspended from a huge willow bough overhanging a lake. He had to borrow a boat and a ladder in order to collect it – a hair-raising experience, since the boat was small and he was large. We managed to pick the fungus, though, and greatly enjoyed it later on.

It is called 'chicken of the woods' because of its tender white flesh, which is similar – when young – to chicken meat in texture.

RECOGNITION

CAP Brilliant sulphur-yellow, the cuticle very smooth and suede-like when young, becoming leathery later. Sessile, attached by growth to bark of host tree. Shape at first bud-like, later fan- or bracket-shaped; sometimes singly but often in tiered clusters that assume grotesque shapes and proportions. Fully mature specimens can reach 70 cm in diameter and weigh up to 22 kg, although they are too tough to be edible at this stage.

PORES Visible only under magnification; concolorous with or slightly paler than cuticle, depending on age; bruising darker. Spore print: white.

FLESH Extremely succulent, with fibrous structure similar to chicken meat. Young specimens exude moisture when squeezed (you sometimes see droplets of liquid – known as 'fungal guttation' – exuding from surface, giving an aura of extreme freshness); flesh becoming white and crumbly with age. Aroma very mushroomy, sometimes even pungent; taste usually excellent, though sometimes sour.

HABITAT Deciduous woodland: prefers oak and willow; common on wild cherry and yew. Sometimes singly, sometimes in small clumps.

SEASON Late spring to autumn. This mushroom continues to grow despite a lack of rain and appears fresh and succulent even in dry spells, as it is taking moisture from the host tree.

ABOVE AND BELOW LAETIPORUS SULPHUREUS

PICKING, CLEANING AND COOKING

Cut away the base of *L. sulphureus* where it was attached to the tree, since splinters of bark are occasionally absorbed into the fruit-body and must not be eaten.

Large slices from a tender specimen can be grilled or used as cutlets. When the specimen is more mature and the colour deepens to orange-yellow, it is excellent for soups, stews and pickling – but is not recommended for freezing (unless first cooked in butter). Although I haven't tried it, it is said to be a good spice when dried and then reduced to a powder (see page 97). It is better to cook this mushroom, as some people could be allergic to it raw.

LECCINUM
VERSIPELLE

THE BOLETES OF THE LECCINUM FAMILY CAN BE VERY CONFUSING FOR
BEGINNERS, BUT ONCE YOU HAVE CRACKED THE RELATIONSHIPS OF NAME,
COLOUR AND SHAPE, YOU ARE DEALING IN FACT WITH THE SAME TYPE OF
MUSHROOM.

LECCINUM VERSIPELLE

(SYN. BOLETUS VERSIPELLUS /
B. AURANTIACUS) ORANGE BIRCH
BOLETE **GOOD**

This family is still confused in the
minds of mycologists, who tend to
give different Latin names to the
same mushroom. *Leccinum versipelle*
is the most commonly found and
known, and many experts say that it
is synonymous with *L. aurantiacum*.
Others say it is synonymous with
L. testaceoscabrum and even with
L. quercinum. See what I mean!
Anyway, the main similarity is that
every single one is edible, and I
love them all. Although they are not
exceptionally good culinarily, they are
extremely satisfying to pick because
they are solid, large and heavy.

Above you can see all the aspects of
L. versipelle, and on the right, in my

hand, is an example of *L. quercinum*
(*L. testaceoscabrum*).

L. scaber, the common birch bolete,
or carpini, is the poor relation of the
family, but nonetheless also useful.
This comes in many different colours
from pale grey and brown to dark
brown, and it is slightly smaller.

In America *L. testaceoscabrum* is
mostly known as *L. manzanite*, while
L. versipelle is known as *L. insigne*
(the aspen bolete).

If any mushroom can be considered
to have a 'phallic' image, the young
specimens of Leccinum possess this
quality *par excellence*, sometimes
even assuming grotesque proportions!
You can usually spot the orange cap
of *L. versipelle* from quite a distance,
and on parting the grass to pick it,
you may be surprised by the length of
the solid stem. In a good season my
basket can be full in minutes, and the
problem for me then is to carry them
back to the car, since they are very
heavy indeed.

If you discover a secluded place
that people rarely visit, you may find
mature specimens with caps as large
as 30 cm in diameter. These are
usually so soft and spongy (and so
infested with insect larvae) that the
only useful thing to do is to break
them up into pieces and scatter
them around in the hope of assisting
in the dissemination of spores.
I have a fabulous place for hunting
this mushroom, which likes to grow
beneath birch trees.

Poles and Russians in particular
love this mushroom and cook it in
many ways; some of them even
prefer it to *Boletus edulis*.

RECOGNITION

CAP Hemispherical at first, growing
to maximum 30 cm in diameter and
becoming largely convex. At first very
solid and a rich reddish orange,
becoming quite soft and paler orange
on maturing.

PORES Minute in young specimens,
dark grey to ochraceous, becoming

paler later but also very spongy. Spore print: yellow-brown.

STEM Almost as distinctive as cap: off-white with brown or black scabrous scales. To maximum 5 cm in diameter and 25 cm tall, tapering towards cap. *L. scaber* is smaller altogether.

FLESH Both cap and stem in young specimens are very firm, almost hard, but tender. When mature, the flesh of the cap becomes white and slightly spongy, and the stem becomes more fibrous, both turning greyish blue when cut. The smell is freshly mushroomy and the taste pleasant.

HABITAT Usually solitary, sometimes in groups, among rich vegetation beneath birch and oak trees.

SEASON Early summer in humid weather to end of autumn.

PICKING, CLEANING AND COOKING

Cut with a sharp mushroom knife. Always peel the stem with a sharp knife and discard the scales. Check for any insect larvae present, and discard any older specimens whose pores have become watery.

As the Leccinums are fairly moist and lack a particularly intense aroma, I would not suggest drying them. They are, however, good for freezing from the raw state, and they pickle well, though the colour turns dark grey. Above all, I recommend them sliced and fried or sautéed in butter and garlic, or stewed; they are also extremely good for soups and sauces. Don't worry if the mushrooms turn almost black after cooking – they will still be delicious. They are good 'bulking' mushrooms, useful for quantity rather than quality.

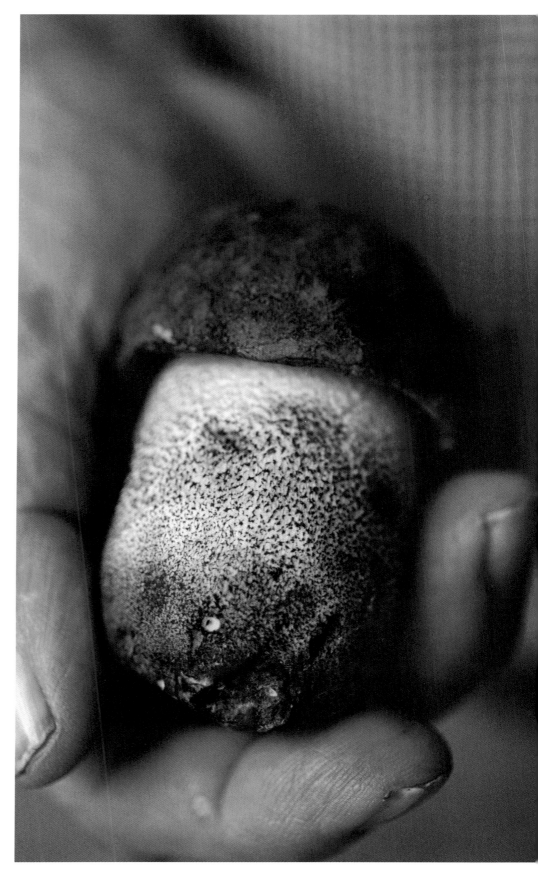

A NICE PLUMP EXAMPLE OF
LECCINUM QUERCINUM

some gastric upsets in sensitive stomachs, so it is best to keep to the simple parasol, *L. procera*.

RECOGNITION

CAP At first ovate, with a veil sealing the rim to the stem. When the cap opens the veil breaks away and remains loosely on the stem as a whitish brown ring. Fully grown cap has concentric brownish scales around the centre, where there is a definite nipple or umbo, and underlying colour is whitish. To 25 cm in diameter.
GILLS Free and crowded, white, very broad (accounting for two-thirds of the cap's thickness); resembling pages of an open book. Spore print: white.
STEM To 30 cm tall and 2 cm in diameter (4 cm at bulbous base). Ridiculously thin, apparently not strong enough to support the cap, but tough, because woody and fibrous, and hence inedible. Initially greyish, becoming white later with brownish scales or snake-like markings. Veil remains loosely on hollow stem as large double ring.
FLESH Thin flesh of cap is white, at first firm, becoming soft with age. No colour change on cutting or bruising. Pleasant smell and taste.

ABOVE AND BELOW LEPIOTA PROCERA

LEPIOTA OR THE PARASOL MUSHROOM IS PROBABLY THE TALLEST OF THE LOT, AS ITS STEM CAN REACH 30 CM. THE WORD 'PARASOL' DESCRIBES IT PERFECTLY!

LEPIOTA PROCERA

(SYN. MACROLEPIOTA PROCERA)
PARASOL MUSHROOM **VERY GOOD**

While the Italian name for this mushrooms means 'drumstick', after the similarity between the young specimens and the drumsticks that drummers in brass bands use, all the other countries name it 'parasol', after the mature specimens, which look just like huge sunshades or parasols. Considering the differences in the weather, and the British love of brass bands, I would have thought the Italian and British names would be more apt if reversed.

The parasol mushroom is an agaric with a distinctive appearance, and is quite easy to find and to recognise. It is one of the best and tastiest of the edible mushrooms, and is quite safe to collect if you follow the exact description. You need to distinguish it from its relative *L. rhacodes* (see opposite), which has more woolly scales on top of the cap, a shorter stem and red-staining flesh. This species is believed to have caused

HABITAT Solitarily on soil, sometimes in small groups; in drier parts or margins of deciduous woods (with no particular tree preference); also open fields, gardens, hedgerows.
SEASON Periodically from mid-summer to autumn.

LEPIOTA RHACODES
(SYN. MACROLEPIOTA RHACODES)
SHAGGY PARASOL / WOOD PARASOL **GOOD**

This parasol mushroom is regarded as edible and good, but it is known that some people have an allergic reaction, which can cause a minor gastric upset. It differs from *L. procera* in that when the stem is cut, the flesh reddens immediately. The cap is 5–15 cm in diameter. It has a woolly texture, eventually leaving a beige brown central patch surrounded by slightly reflexed concolorous scales, which gives it a shaggy appearance. The gills are white but bruise red and also turn red with age. Spore print: white. The stem is 12 x 1.5 cm, with a broad basal bulb, which is creamy white becoming orange to red when cut. It has a double membranous ring. It is often seen in coniferous woodland and occurs from summer to late autumn.

PICKING, CLEANING AND COOKING

Cut with a sharp mushroom knife. This mushroom is usually free from any insect larvae – unless the specimen is too old for picking anyway. When cleaning, just brush away any residual earth or sand from the cap. Avoid washing, since it readily absorbs water and this dilutes the flavour.

The stem is too tough to be edible, but depending on the stage of growth, the cap can be cooked in many different and delicious ways. When it is small and still closed (at the 'drumstick' stage), it can be dipped in batter and fried; it looks something like a small Scotch egg! When it has opened into a sort of cup, it is ideal for stuffing prior to stewing. When it is completely flat like an opened parasol, it can be coated in beaten egg and breadcrumbs and then fried, making a tasty meal in itself.

Parasol mushrooms are not particularly good for pickling or preserving, so I suggest that you eat any you find fresh.

LEPIOTA CRISTATA
STINKING BABY PARASOL
POISONOUS

This mushroom produces an amanitin-like poison that takes from 5 to 15 hours to incubate. Symptoms may include muscular cramps, sweating and intestinal congestion, and the duration is not properly known. Many of the small lepiotas are poisonous, and for that reason all, except those you have very firmly identified, should be avoided.

RECOGNITION

CAP 2–6 cm in diameter, mainly white with a reddish central patch and similarly coloured concentric scales.
GILLS White and well spaced. Spore print: white.
STEM 5 cm x 4 mm. White and becomes vinaceous red at the base. There is also a slight ring on the stem.
FLESH Thin and white, with a very strong and pungent smell of latex or rubber.
HABITAT AND SEASON Found growing in woods, garden refuse, leaf litter and soil. From summer to autumn. Very common.

LEPIOTA CRISTATA

MEMBERS OF THE LEPISTA FAMILY
ARE PALE TO DEEP VIOLET IN
COLOUR, AND TASTE MEATY WITH
A WONDERFUL AROMA THAT MAKES
THEM QUITE SOUGHT AFTER.

LEPISTA NUDA
(SYN. TRICHOLOMA NUDUM)
WOOD BLEWIT **EDIBLE**

Mushrooms do not contain any of
the chlorophyll that gives plants their
green colouring, but they do have a
wonderful assortment of other colours
instead. *Lepista nuda,* or wood blewit,
is one of the commonest and most
exquisite edible wild mushrooms in
Britain, and its colours range from
bluish lilac and violet to pale brown
and buff. It is a very satisfying mushroom because it grows abundantly,
is quite easy to recognise and is
excellent to eat. This is *after* cooking,
however, which is why I have classified
it as only 'edible': avoid the temptation
to enjoy the beautiful colour raw in
salads, because *L. nuda* contains a
toxic substance that can cause gastric
upsets if eaten in large quantities.
This mild toxicity is removed during
the cooking process, after which the
mushroom is perfectly safe and
absolutely delicious.

LEPISTA
NUDA

LEPISTA NUDA

These mushrooms often grow in
large groups over a wide area, so you
can gather a substantial amount very
quickly – though fallen leaves in the
deciduous woods make them more
difficult to find. Their season is later
than that of many other mushrooms,
continuing well into the winter.

They are now cultivated quite
easily and commonly (see page 88).

RECOGNITION

CAP At first convex, expanding
irregularly until the margin curls up
exposing the gills. To a maximum
12 cm in diameter. First lilac-coloured,
then brownish. The cuticle is very
smooth, giving a moist impression
even in dry weather.
GILLS Free or slightly sinuate,
crowded, darker than the cap, soon
fading and becoming buff. Spore
print: pinkish.
STEM Surface at first lilac-speckled
or fibrillose, becoming pale with age.
When cut, darker at the edges and
paling towards the centre. To 3 cm in

diameter (tapering slightly towards top) and 10 cm tall.

FLESH In young specimens thick and firm; violet, becoming more greyish with age. When cut the flesh in older specimens has the appearance of being impregnated with water. Pleasant, fruity almost perfumed aroma; extremely tasty.

HABITAT In small or large groups, sometimes covering a wide area, in deciduous woodland, hedgerows, sometimes gardens, and often on compost heaps.

SEASON Relatively late, sometimes starting at the end of September and continuing into December or even into the New Year, despite frosts.

LEPISTA SAEVA
(SYN. L. PERSONATA)
FIELD BLEWIT **EDIBLE**

L. nuda's close relative, the field blewit, can – as the name suggests – be found in fields, meadows and well-manured pastureland, often growing in rings or little groups. It is more difficult to find than the wood blewit. It differs in having a very pallid, cream to brown cap; only the stem is a brilliant violet, hence its other common name of 'blue leg' ('pied bleu' in French). It is more or less the same size as its relation, in height and cap diameter. Its season is slightly earlier, from autumn to early winter. The taste is very similar – and, like the wood blewit, it must be cooked before eating.

PICKING, CLEANING AND COOKING

Cut at the base of the stem with a sharp mushroom knife, and clean before putting in your basket. Sometimes leaves stick to the caps, so wipe them if necessary. Blewits are usually fairly insect-free and clean, but check the stems particularly for any signs of infestation. Discard the tougher stems of older specimens. Since blewits tolerate cold weather,

they will keep well in the refrigerator for a few days.

Both lepistas are excellent mushrooms: the very thick, moist flesh means that a satisfying meal can be made from just a few specimens. They are wonderful by themselves, simply cooked by the time-honoured method of stir-frying in butter with a little garlic and parsley. You can use them in stews or sauté them with other mushrooms, and they are particularly good in sauces accompanying meat or fish. They freeze well after initial cooking, and are very good for pickling and for preserving in oil. I usually dry them in my purpose-built mushroom-drying machine (see page 96). In fact, these mushrooms are of the few that can be used in any culinary process – but do remember that they do need cooking.

MUSHROOM HUNTING WITH MY THUMBSTICK AND BASKET

TO THE LYCOPERDON OR CALVATIA FAMILY BELONG THOSE MUSHROOMS THAT HAVE NEITHER GILLS NOR PORES, BUT INSTEAD EXPEL THEIR TINY SPORES IN THE FORM OF A CLOUD COMING FROM THE INSIDE. JUST A LIGHT SPRINKLING OF RAINDROPS CAN START THE PROCESS OFF.

LYCOPERDON GIGANTEUM

(SYN. CALVATIA GIGANTEA)
GIANT PUFFBALL **VERY GOOD**

The photograph shows the typical open fields where puffballs grow, and indeed when they grow, they do so in great profusion. However, they sometimes grow in more unexpected places. Years ago, I was walking through an autumnal Hyde Park – in the very centre of London – with my dearly loved dog, Jan, when I glimpsed what I thought was a white football partly hidden among some shrubs near the path. There were no children around who

LYCOPERDON GIGANTEUM

might have lost it. My attention was then drawn to a smaller ball next to the big one, which immediately gave me the clue that maybe this was a giant puffball. And, of course, this is what it turned out to be: a superb example of *Lycoperdon giganteum*, whose habitat, according to the books, is open fields.

And once on the M25, the circular road around London, I saw that the middle section between the opposing lanes was covered with thousands of puffballs. I mentioned this shortly

afterwards in an interview with a newspaper, and was thereafter severely reprimanded by the police. Apparently people who had read the story were slowing down to look at the puffballs, and threatening to cause accidents. Needless to say, the M25 has since expanded, and the prolific puffball ground is now covered with tarmac.

Of the many species of edible puffballs, the giant one is obviously the most rewarding as well as the most distinctive; one prime specimen is enough to provide a good meal for the whole family. The other species such as *L. perlatum* and *L. pyriforme* need to be collected in far greater amounts, since each specimen seldom amounts to more than a mouthful. All the puffballs are good to eat while the flesh is firm and white, but the smaller ones need to be distinguished from the common earthball, *Scleroderma citrinum* (see opposite), which is toxic, and *Amanita phalloides* (see page 25) in the unopened-egg stage. To check the latter, cut open: in the amanita, the outline of the gills and cap will be seen, whereas the puffball is solid.

RECOGNITION

The giant puffball has neither cap, gills nor stem; it is a Gasteromycete, with a subglobular fruiting body measuring up to 80 cm in diameter, its spores developing internally and 'puffing' out of the top when mature. It is attached to its mycelium by a sort of fragile root which eventually breaks, leaving the puffball free to be blown about the fields by the wind, disseminating its millions of spores. It looks like a ping-pong ball at first, grows to the size of a tennis ball, and finally attains the size of a football, at least – a truly sporting life.

The outer skin, or exoperidium, is

quite firm and slightly leathery in texture, initially white and turning brown with age. The flesh – technically known as the 'gleba' – is also white and firm at first, then yellow and finally completely brown and powdery. Spores: dark yellowish brown. The smell of the fresh is wonderfully mushroomy, like a field mushroom but slightly stronger-tasting. The smell becomes bad as the fungus ages.

HABITAT On well-manured fields, in gardens and parks; on grass or among shrubs and nettles. It grows singly rather than in clumps, but is very gregarious.

SEASON Late summer to late autumn.

LYCOPERDON PYRIFORME
PEAR-SHAPED PUFFBALL **GOOD**

A small puffball that is edible when young. It smells slightly of latex or rubber, which tends to put collectors off eating it, and it tastes rather bland. The fruit-body is 3–5 cm in diameter. The surface can resemble coarse sandpaper, and it is beige in colour, fading to a light brown. The inside flesh, or gleba, is white becoming ochre; it is porous, and I think rather similar to marshmallow in texture and consistency. The spore powder is olive-brown. It is always found in large compact groups growing on rotten trunks or buried wood, from August to November.

LYCOPERDON PERLATUM
PEARL PUFFBALL / GEMMED PUFFBALL **EDIBLE**

This small puffball is only edible if the flesh, or gleba, is still pure white when the fungus is cut in half. It becomes yellow then olive-brown with age, and if the latter colour, it will be unfit for eating. It is regarded as being only mediocre in taste. The fruit body is 4–6 cm in diameter, club-shaped and

LYCOPERDON PERLATUM

SCLERODERMA CITRINUM

(SYN. S. AURANTIACUM / S. VULGARE)
COMMON EARTHBALL **TOXIC**

I am including this common mush-room so that you will not collect it thinking you have found a truffle or a puffball. Though it is not deadly poisonous, it can cause digestive problems and is best avoided.

RECOGNITION

Earthballs seem to grow everywhere, either solitarily or in small groups. When young they are quite tempting, compact and fleshy. On maturity the flesh inside turns black – the colour of the spores, which are released when the outer skin or peridium cracks open. It is impossible to confuse them with *Lycoperdon giganteum*, the giant puffball, which is pure white in colour and far greater in size than the 10 cm maximum which *S. citrinum* attains. The small edible puffballs mentioned above are more similar in size but they tend to be pear- and club- rather than globe-shaped. Confusion with truffles should be equally impossible, since truffles are hypogeal fungi – they grow under-ground – while earth-balls are epigeal and grow on the surface.

HABITAT AND SEASON   They grow in dry sandy soil, from summer to autumn, associated with trees.

white, becoming brownish with age. It is covered with pyramidal spines surrounded by a ring of tiny warts, which rub off to leave a mesh-like pattern. The spore print is olive-brown. It is found on the ground in woods and pastures from June to November. It is gregarious and very common.

PICKING, CLEANING AND COOKING

Just turn a large fungus on its base to remove, then lift gently. To tell if it is still good, tap on it. If there is a good deep and full sound, it is still edible. If it sounds hollow, the fungus is probably too old – and anyway you would see the millions of spores scattering as you handled it. The surface may need wiping to remove grass and earth; otherwise all the cleaning that needs to be done is to trim away the point at the base where the puffball was attached to its 'root'. The same applies to the smaller varieties.

In Italy *Lycoperdon giganteum* is prepared in the same way as veal cutlets and, funnily enough, the flavour is quite similar. The firm flesh is wonderful to eat when it is sliced and deep-fried or grilled, as well as in soups. It is not good for drying, but can be sliced or cubed and pickled. Do remember, only the young specimens with firm white flesh can be eaten. The little puffballs can be sautéed together with other mushrooms.

SCLERODERMA CITRINUM

ABOVE AND BELOW MARASMIUS OREADES

the mushrooms grew where fairies used to dance in circles! In Italy the circles are thought to be more sinister, made by witches . . .

However formed, by fairies, witches or Mother Nature, this tiny mushroom is a very enjoyable one to seek and collect, provided you are able to find enough to make at least one meal.

Curiously, the mushroom ring is formed, and very visibly, in grass that is darker in colour than that in the surrounding area. This is because the mycelium (the 'root' part of the mushroom, which lies below ground and which spreads at the rate of a couple of centimetres every year), gives the grass a darker colouring.

It is possible to confuse this type of mushroom with many others, one of which is the poisonous *Clitocybe rivulosa* (see opposite). But the most important thing to remember is the growing pattern: in *Marasmius oreades* you will find a perfect half or full circle, while the others are much more irregular in growth.

RECOGNITION

CAP   From 1–6 cm in diameter, firstly convex and bell-shaped when young, later becoming teat-shaped, with little knobs in the centre. From cream to brown, darker towards the centre. It becomes paler when dry, darker when the weather is more humid.
GILLS   Concolorous with the cap, distant and free from each other, and

MARASMIUS, OR THE FAIRY RING CHAMPIGNON, IS IN A GROUP ALL BY ITSELF, ALTHOUGH THERE ARE MANY SIMILAR SPECIES WHICH DO NOT ACTUALLY GROW IN CIRCLES, AND ARE INEDIBLE, IN SOME CASES TOXIC.

MARASMIUS OREADES

FAIRY RING CHAMPIGNON **GOOD**

When you come across one of these mushrooms, to find more, all you have to do is go down on your knees and trace the arc of a circle from it. For, in the same way as the St George's mushroom (*Tricholoma gambosum*), clouded agaric (*Clitocybe nebularis*), the field mushroom (*Agaricus campestris*) and a few others, this mushroom grows in circles. These are called fairy rings in ancient mythology, for people imagined that

MARASMIUS OREADES

not regular. Spore print: white.

STEM   Very thin, almost out of proportion with the size of the cap, but is full, not hollow. Mostly inedible, it measures from 4–6 cm tall, and 2–3 mm in diameter.

FLESH   Beige at first, then hazelnut or whitish. The flesh has a sweetish taste and pleasant smell.

HABITAT   Grows as described above, in groups, usually circles, in grass-land, parks, fields that have not been cultivated for some time. It is easy to recognise.

SEASON   From spring to autumn.

PICKING, CLEANING AND COOKING

Cut just underneath the cap with your sharp mushroom knife, as the stem is not good. Brush and wipe to clean. Try to avoid picking it soon after rain, as it will be full of water. And beware when buying: to increase weight they are often sprayed with water. It is an excellent mushroom to eat, and can keep for a few days in good conditions. Stewed, braised, or briefly sautéed, it is used to accompany delicate dishes of meat or fish. It can also be used mixed with other mushrooms for sauces or salads when cooked. It is not recommended for preserving or freezing, although it dries very well, and regenerates in water back to its original size.

CLITOCYBE RIVULOSA
DEADLY POISONOUS

It is possible to confuse *Marasmius oreades* with *Clitocybe rivulosa*, which is common from late summer to autumn and also grows in rings

(although these are irregular), but which is deadly poisonous. It is very common in Canada. But because of the different habitats, and to an extent different seasons, the two should be fairly easy to differentiate.

RECOGNITION

CAP   3–4 cm in diameter, elastic but not very fleshy. Flat with slight depression in the centre. Dirty white, with occasionally the teat shape so characteristic of *Marasmius oreades*.

GILLS   Very tight, decurrent, white with slightly pinkish flecks. Spore print: white.

STEM   The same height as the diameter. Fibrous, cylindric and straight.

FLESH   Pale and watery. Smells of grass, no significant taste.

HABITAT AND SEASON   In sandy soil on grassy ground, also in parks and gardens. Summer to autumn. Uncommon.

CLITOCYBE RIVULOSA

DRIED MUSHROOMS OF THE MORCHELLA FAMILY CAN REACH UP TO ABOUT £200 PER KILO, BUT GOURMETS ARE PREPARED TO PAY THIS PRICE BECAUSE THEY ARE SO INVALUABLE IN THE PREPARATION AND FINAL FLAVOURING OF MANY WONDERFUL DISHES.

MORCHELLA ELATA
(SYN. M. CONICA) MOREL
EXCELLENT

This much sought-after mushroom, as well as its close relation *M. esculenta*, commands a very high price on the world's markets, and is not always readily available. Like the truffle, it belongs to the category of fungus known as the Ascomycetes, and instead of having gills or pores, the spore-bearing hymenium lines the inside of the pits or honeycomb-like depressions of the cap. It is one of the first mushrooms to appear in early spring, sometimes by late March if it is mild. Italy, France, Switzerland, the American Mid-west, Tibet and Kashmir, all with climates with a well-regulated seasonal cycle of cold/mild/hot/mild, are where morels grow best. The state of Minnesota even has its own Festival of the Morel to welcome the arrival of this valuable member of the fungus world.

This mushroom has rather fond memories for me. In the mid-1990s, a friend who was heading a charity operation not far from Katmandu, in Nepal, asked me if I might be interested in morels that were being collected and dried by local villagers, and sold to an Indian middle-man for a very low price. I said yes, and that I would pay a price ten times that of the middle-man for as many as they could give me. As a result I received in London about 120 kg dried morels packed in five purpose-built tin containers – and I am still using them today! The village is still waiting for me, their benefactor, to visit them, as apparently my money – about £7,000 – was the most they had ever seen all in one go, which led to the mayor

being re-elected, and some consider-able affluence for all. I would love to go to see for myself, but shall wait for more peaceful times.

I remember finding some morels among great stands of cane as a small boy at Castelnuovo Belbo (actually, I was never *that* small). I soon came down to earth when I got home, where my mother and brothers subjected my collection to a thorough scrutiny to make sure that what I had gathered was the true morel. Experienced eyes can easily distinguish it from the poisonous *Gyromitra esculenta* (false morel), which also grows in spring, by the shape of the cap, which is fairly symmetrical in the edible morel, and

distinctly lobed and contorted in the false one.

M. elata and *M. esculenta* are the two very best species of morel. They differ slightly in their shape, colour and size, but their general characteristics are the same. If you cut a morel in vertical section, you will see that the cap and stem grow together forming a single body.

RECOGNITION

CAP Made up from many cup-like depressions or pits, giving the appearance of a rather irregularly open-pored sponge. Lining these depressions are the asci – microscopic

MORCHELLA ELATA

sacs in which the spores are produced. Conical, dark brown in colour, becoming darker with age; the pits have a fairly regular lengthways orientation; up to 5 cm in diameter and up to 10 cm tall.

STEM Pale off-white; cylindrical and hollow, slightly more swollen towards the base. 3 cm in diameter and up to 5 cm tall.

FLESH Both cap and stem look and feel cartilaginous and fragile, but the flesh is crisp and moist to the touch. Pale brown in the cap and white in the stem. I believe the culinary attraction of this mushroom (and *M. esculenta* below) has to be attributed more to the appearance, texture and preparation than to its intrinsic taste and smell – which are just pleasantly and delicately perceptible.

HABITAT Prefers sandy soil with underlying chalk; given this criterion, little groups can be found in open shrubby woodland, on wood edges and banks, in pastures, orchards, wasteland – and, curiously, on burnt ground. Armed with this knowledge, a few years ago some ultra-passionate morel 'hunters' from Provence deliberately set fire to woodland in the hope that the following spring they would see the cherished fruiting bodies popping out of the scorched earth. They did!

SEASON Late March to May, depending on weather, which should be a cold winter followed by a nice warm spring. In mountainous regions, when the snow goes, the morels appear.

MORCHELLA ESCULENTA

MORCHELLA ESCULENTA
(SYN. M. ROTUNDA) **EXCELLENT**

The cap of this mushroom has the same characteristics as *M. elata*, but is more rounded, with the pits irregularly arranged. A creamy yellow colour at first, becoming pale brown or buff with age. It is usually larger than *M. elata*, reaching up to 15 cm tall. (As with all mushrooms, the measurements vary according to location: in America, naturally, they grow bigger!) The stem is off-white, similar to *M. elata*, but reaches 5 cm in diameter and up to 9 cm tall. It looks more spongy, but is also crisp and firm; flesh colour is paler than that of the surface. The flesh, habitat and season are the same as for *M. elata*.

PICKING, CLEANING AND COOKING

Cut at the base of the stem with a sharp mushroom knife. Morels are not usually infested with any insect larvae (although slugs love them), but I would check the hollow inside, which may harbour insects or other unwanted material. Try to keep them clean when you collect them by cutting away the base, which tends to be full of sand, so that this does not find its way into the wrinkles of the caps when the specimen is placed in your basket. If sand does get into these folds (and some will probably be there anyway), then a longer and more thorough cleaning job is in store for you. Use a brush: washing is not really recommended, but may be used as a last resort.

I have already described this mushroom using many superlatives. It can be served with any type of food. I would stress, though, that it should always be cooked; when eaten raw it proves indigestible to some people, even poisonous. My best recipe is morels stuffed with foie gras (see page 128), but otherwise you can just sauté them with a little cream, and use them in egg, soup,

MORCHELLA ESCULENTA

risotto and pasta dishes. In Finland they are delicious served with venison. This is one of the few mushrooms that regenerate very well from the dried state, and dried ones can be used in exactly the same way as fresh ones. (I find they taste strangely of bacon!) Although they are expensive, dried morels are becoming more readily available in stores if you are not lucky enough to pick and dry your own. They need 20 minutes' soaking in lukewarm water; you may have to cut off the stem base – and remember to strain any sand out of the soaking water. (Keep this as it will contain some of the morel flavour – but, like the morels themselves, it should be cooked.) Morels also preserve well by sterilising in water, and by pickling and freezing. (Keep your dried morels in the freezer, as I did those from Nepal, to avoid any larvae developing.) Obviously, however, the best way to use them is fresh.

GYROMITRA ESCULENTA

GYROMITRA ESCULENTA
FALSE MOREL / LOREL **POISONOUS**

The difference between this and the true morel is in the shape of the cap, which in *Gyromitra esculenta* consists of folded lobes and in morchella species is made up of pits or hollows, and is usually more symmetrically shaped. As the epithet 'esculenta' implies, some Europeans consider these mushrooms edible and regularly eat them after boiling them thoroughly or drying them, but cases of poisoning occasionally occur among apparently seasoned consumers. In the raw state these mushrooms are certainly very poisonous, so don't take any unnecessary chances and experiment.

RECOGNITION

CAP Made up of brain-like meandering folds and lobes, hollow; colour varying from pale tan to deep brown. Sometimes irregular in shape.
STEM Hollow; usually white; to 7 cm high and 2.4 cm in diameter. Altogether the mushroom can grow to 12 cm high, and of course in the USA (where else?) they can grow up to 20–30 cm high!
HABITAT AND SEASON Grows solitarily or in small groups, usually under conifers but sometimes under hardwood, in the spring.

ABOVE AND BELOW PLEUROTUS OSTREATUS

PLEUROTUS OR OYSTER
MUSHROOMS ARE FAMILIAR TO ALL
OF US BECAUSE THEY ARE WIDELY
AVAILABLE CULTIVATED. TO
FIND THEM IN THE WILD IS
A REAL TREAT, AS
THE COLONIES
ARE SO
BEAUTIFUL.

PLEUROTUS OSTREATUS
OYSTER MUSHROOM **VERY GOOD**

Named after the oyster because of its
shape and its greyish blue colour,
Pleurotus ostreatus is one of the few
mushrooms that have been found
suitable for cultivation (see page 89).
The domestic version of the oyster
mushroom can be found in supermarkets, although I still prefer the wild
version, which has a stronger taste.

Its relative *P. cornucopiae* takes its
name from its resemblance to a horn
of plenty. Although the two mushrooms
are different in shape and colour, I
have purposely put them together here
because of their very similar general
characteristics and culinary uses.
Breaking through the bark of fallen
trees and stumps, these
typical parasitic fungi
grow down into the
structure, absorbing
the life-giving substance,
until the wood is
reduced to worthless
matter. Be careful with
identification, however:
there are other similar
mushrooms growing on
stumps which are
inedible or poisonous.

RECOGNITION

CAP   Flat and round;
lateral, resembling a shell or tongue.
Upper surface varies in colour from
blue-grey when small to pale brown
when fully grown; also from pale cream
to noisette. Skin quite shiny. To 16 cm
in diameter.
GILLS   Pale cream, not very crowded,
decurrent. Spore print: lilac.
STEM   Excentric to lateral, or almost
absent.
FLESH   White and very tender in small
specimens, becoming tougher. Taste
and aroma indistinct.
HABITAT   Parasitic shelves and
colonies attaching to fallen and
decaying trees, mostly beech, in parks
and countryside. Often hidden by grass
or nettles, so remember to carry a stick.
SEASON   Early summer in warm
conditions to first frost (I have even
found some in December).

PLEUROTUS CORNUCOPIAE
VERY GOOD

This is distinctly funnel-shaped, and
grows more upright than laterally. It
has a more pronounced stem than in
P. ostreatus, reaching 20 cm when
several fruiting bodies are grouped
together forming a cluster. The cap is
round and concave to the centre,
forming the shape of the cornucopia.
The colour of the top varies from
white to pale brown, depending on
location. The flesh is white and the

PLEUROTUS
CORNUCOPIAE

spore print pale lilac. Habitat
as for *P. ostreatus* with a preference for
oak and elm. Be careful. The cap can
appear immaculate, but open it up to
check for maggots.

PICKING, CLEANING AND COOKING

Cut off in clumps from the tree. When
cleaning, inspect the larger and older
ones carefully. Sometimes you will find
maggots in the stems: if so, simply cut
them off and enjoy the caps. And the
stems actually become a bit tough as
they age.

These are not superior mushrooms
in the culinary sense – they do not
have an outstanding flavour – but they
are versatile when cooked fresh, and
their availability in cultivation makes
them useful for adding that extra
mushroomy something to a dish. Sauté
them with garlic and butter, deep-fry
them dipped in egg and breadcrumbs,
or use them in soups. They are worth
preserving only if you pickle them in
vinegar before bottling them in olive
oil (see page 99). Unless very small,
they become too tough when frozen,
and they lack the flavour to make
them dry well.

When buying cultivated oyster
mushrooms, choose the smaller
specimens – they are less watery.

POLYPORUS GIGANTEUS

POLYPORUS GIGANTEUS

(SYN. MERIPILUS GIGANTEUS)
GIANT POLYPORE **GOOD**

The word 'polypore' always describes, in the mycological sense, a mushroom with millions of pores, which are easily visible beneath the cap or tongue. Living up to its name, this is indeed a giant mushroom, a bracket fungus like *Fistulina hepatica* (see page 46). However, it grows on the stumps of fallen or felled trees, rather than further up the trunks, although I've also found one at the foot of a living beech tree. It grows in clumps of layers or lobes of great size, and one mushroom alone can weigh up to 80 kg! Often I have had great difficulty in transporting it because of its size – but then I am collecting it for decorative rather than culinary purposes. For it is only edible when young and tender, becoming fibrous and inedible when older. In some mushroom books it is considered inedible, probably due to its toughness, but it is not poisonous, and I think it can be excellent.

RECOGNITION

CAP   The mushroom grows in various flattish and round lobes, with a very strong stem attached to the tree. When young, the lobes exude a brown liquid, and this is when you should collect it. After this the lobes become much thinner, larger and woodier. The caps have concentric marks of a darker brown colour than the rest of the mushroom, lighter at the edges.
PORES   Situated beneath the lobes. When the fungus is mature you can spot a rust-coloured dusting of spores on the ground beneath. Spore print: white.
STEM   Tough and inedible. It attaches itself to the base of the tree.
FLESH   A pale cream colour. When you cut into the flesh, you can see it is fibrous, consisting of many filaments pressed together. The taste is very mushroomy. The smell is slightly sour,

MEMBERS OF THE POLYPORUS (OR MERIPILUS, AS MY FRIEND ROY WATLING PREFERS TO CALL THEM) FAMILY ARE ONLY EDIBLE WHEN YOUNG, AND ARE HUGE WHEN FULLY GROWN. THE PHOTOGRAPHER AND I FOUND A GIANT POLYPORE IN OCTOBER 2002, WHICH MUST HAVE BEEN ABOUT 60 KG! UNFORTUNATELY WE HAD JUST MISSED ITS EDIBLE STAGE.

POLYPORUS GIGANTEUS

but this disappears when the fungus is cooked. The surface tends to discolour to the touch, becoming streaky black (as do your fingers when you work with it).

HABITAT It grows on the stumps of dead trees like beech, oak or other large trees, usually at the base. Many groups of clusters, but all coming from one big stem attached to the wood.

SEASON July to October.

POLYPORUS SQUAMOSUS
DRYAD'S SADDLE **EDIBLE**

The word 'squamosus' derives from 'squame', or 'scaly', and the cuticle is formed of alternating concentric circles in different colours of brown and cream. The underside is cream, becoming brown with age. The English name of 'dryad's saddle' refers to the shape of the fungus, which is said to resemble the saddle a wood nymph might use.

The fungus is also known as 'scaly polypore'. One day, when we were visiting the Italian Embassy for a reception, my wife noticed a huge specimen of this fungus hanging from a sycamore tree beside our parking space in Belgrave Square (of all places). Pity I couldn't pick it!

This polypore, like all the others, is only edible when young. With age it becomes leathery and fibrously woody. The cap grows flat and round, up to 60 cm in diameter. The colour is dark yellow with brown flakes growing in an irregular circular way (the 'scales'). The outside of the mushroom is very thick, becoming thicker towards the centre where it disappears into the stem. This is very short, black-crusted at the base, and very strongly attached to the tree, from which it has to be cut to be collected. The pores are white at first and quite tight, becoming yellowish and darker with age. The tubuli are from 2 mm – 1 cm long, becoming shorter towards the stem. Spore print: white. The flesh is fibrous and whitish, becoming tougher with age, when it becomes inedible. It smells strongly of cucumber, and the taste when cooked is very pleasant. It attaches itself to stumps of fallen and dead trees, eventually transforming these into humus. Huge clumps or clusters, but also singly, in spring and summer, rarely autumn.

A close relative of this mushroom is now being cultivated.

PICKING, CLEANING AND COOKING

Just cut off at the piece attaching the fungus to the tree with a sharp knife or a little pruning saw, and brush well before putting in your basket. These mushrooms will never be a first choice for gourmets, but are extremely pleasant when young and tender. When they are being used for culinary purposes, it is best to mix them with other mushrooms, as they do not have a lot of flavour on their own. The giant polypore turns black once it is handled – as do your hands – so wash your hands with salt and lemon juice afterwards. Use in stews, or deep-fry or sauté, and you can also pickle them. They don't freeze very well, but both of these polypores can be dried very successfully and reduced to a powder (see page 97), particularly when mixed with more aromatic mushrooms.

ABOVE AND BELOW POLYPORUS SQUAMOSUS

RUSSULA VIRESCENS

OF THE HUNDREDS OF RUSSULAS, I HAVE CHOSEN TO FEATURE THE MOST EDIBLE AND THE MOST POISONOUS. IN BETWEEN THESE THERE IS AN INCREDIBLE VARIETY OF SIZES AND COLOURS, MOST OF WHICH ARE INEDIBLE.

RUSSULA VIRESCENS
GREEN-CRACKED RUSSULA
EXCELLENT

This is the most delicious and sought after of all the russulas. The Spaniards particularly value them, and in season you can find them in all the markets. I must admit to never having collected a russula in the wild, but then I have never really paid much attention to the family – until now. I think this will probably be the mycological and culinary study of my future, to find out which russula is really the best. I hope that in the process I don't make any mistakes, for there are some unpleasant and toxic ones out there as well.

RECOGNITION

CAP Not exactly nice to look at. Very meaty, 5–15 cm in diameter, very solid. Slightly hemispheric then round, and flattienng with a depression in the middle. Very warty. Grey-green, speckled and cracked with a white background.
GILLS Very tight, fragile, white-cream in colour, and sometimes tinged brown or reddish. Spores white, as is the spore print.
STEM Full but spongy, cylindric, and irregularly white/brown. 2–9 cm high.
FLESH White, sometimes blushing, and thick and solid. Has a very light smell and a sweet taste.
HABITAT Mixed woods, especially chestnut and oak, and in grass. More or less common, depending on region.
SEASON End of spring to autumn.

RUSSULA CYANOXANTHA
THE CHARCOAL BURNER
VERY GOOD

A good edible member of the family, and it is prized in Europe – but, sadly, it is also prized by maggots! The cap is 5–12 cm in diameter, with a large colour range from green, steely blue to violaceous or lilac, often with a mixture of all of these. The gills are soft and elastic to the touch, not brittle like most other russulas; also oily to the touch. Colour varies from white to pale cream. Spore print: white. Stem pure white and 7 x 1 cm. The flesh is white and bland. Found under broad-leaved trees of all kinds from summer to late autumn. Very common.

PICKING, CLEANING AND COOKING

Cut the stems with a sharp mushroom knife. Because russulas are quite fragile, don't transport them along with other mushrooms: they are very prone to get dirt in their gills. Never wash them, simply wipe the caps with a damp cloth. If they are big, cut in quarters or, as they do in Spain, use the cap only (and grill it). Generally, just briefly sauté in butter, as they are very tender. It is best not to preserve them, but to eat them fresh.

RUSSULA CYANOXANTHA

RUSSULA EMETICA

RUSSULA OCHROLEUCA

RUSSULA EMETICA
THE SICKENER **POISONOUS**

This member of the Russula family gets its second name from the Greek, and I think its meaning is quite obvious. The 'sickener' has another poisonous relative, *R. mairei*, which has the common name 'beechwood sickener', because of its affinity with beech. Great care has to be taken with red mushrooms, and russulas in particular. They are mostly inedible and occasionally poisonous as this one is. Unless they have yellow gills and stems, not white, it is best to leave them alone.

RECOGNITION

CAP 3–10 cm in diameter. Bright cherry red or scarlet with a shallow depression in the centre. It is sticky when moist.
GILLS Fairly distant, white fading to pale cream. Spore print: whitish.
STEM 7 x 1 cm. White, cylindrical and somewhat swollen at the base. Often rather soft.
FLESH White.
HABITAT AND SEASON Found typically with sphagnum moss on wet ground under conifers. Common, from summer to late autumn.

RUSSULA OCHROLEUCA
COMMON YELLOW RUSSULA
NOT EDIBLE

This mushroom may look fantastic and many people consider it to be edible, but I personally think it is of very little culinary value. I have included it here primarily to show just how varied the family is. Its name translates from the Greek, meaning 'white to ochre yellow'.

RECOGNITION

CAP 8–12 cm in diameter. The colour ranges from bright yellow to a dull shade of ochre, sometimes developing an age-related greenish tinge.
GILLS White, contrasting with the yellow of the cap. Spore print: white to pale cream.
STEM 7 x 1 cm. At first white, greying with wet conditions and age.
FLESH White, with a hot taste.
HABITAT AND SEASON From late summer to autumn under broad-leaved trees and conifers. Very common.

ABOVE AND BELOW SPARASSIS CRISPA

'SPARASSIS', 'BRAIN', 'CAULIFLOWER', 'WIG', AND SO ON. THERE ARE HUNDREDS OF NAMES FOR THIS CURIOUS FUNGUS. HOWEVER, I KNOW FOR CERTAIN THAT, WHATEVER IT MIGHT BE KNOWN AS, IT ENJOYS A GREAT DEAL OF ROYAL APPRECIATION!

SPARASSIS CRISPA
CAULIFLOWER FUNGUS **VERY GOOD**

Whenever I am walking through pinewoods during the autumn, I keep an eye on the base of the trunks, which is where this peculiar mushroom usually chooses to grow. If you find a large specimen (and they can grow very large), it will be enough to make a complete meal. It really does look like a cauliflower, and is quite as interesting in its culinary uses. Keep a keen look out for this mushroom, since you are very unlikely to find it for sale in shops and markets – it is only of value to the connoisseur!

There is no cap in the normal sense of the word; the mushroom consists of a short, strong stem and many cartilaginous flat lobes, reminiscent of a 'brain coral', hence the name 'brain fungus'. The fruit-body can grow in quite a short time and can envelop in its flesh anything lying nearby. Often when cutting one open I have found pine needles and even small pine cones incorporated in the flesh. This fungus is now being cultivated.

RECOGNITION

FRUIT-BODY   Usually subglobular, very variable in size: 20–50 cm in diameter. Flat irregular lobes coloured cream to pale noisette, darkening with age.
SPORES   White or pale yellow. Spore print: whitish.
FLESH   Fragile, more consistent towards centre. Smell pleasant; taste sweet and nutty.
HABITAT   Singly, in coniferous woods, at tree bases and on stumps.
SEASON   Late summer to late autumn.

PICKING, CLEANING AND COOKING

Just cut at the base with a sharp mushroom knife. Pick only specimens that are creamy white (cauliflower colour); any that have turned yellowish will be tough and indigestible. Cut into sections to check for dirt, insects and foreign bodies. A good wash before cooking is – for once – recommended.

Sparassis crispa is very versatile indeed to cook with. I have fried it, preserved it in oil, frozen it and dried it (and it is one of the handful of mushrooms that reconstitutes really well from dried), all with excellent results. It is very good for soups, either fresh or dried, and can be used in all sorts of stews and, of course, on its own. Used together with other mushrooms, it adds a certain sophistication to a dish through its appearance, texture and flavour.

SUILLUS LUTEUS

THE GENUS NAME OF THESE MUSHROOMS COMES FROM THE LATIN FOR PIG, 'SUILLUS'. THEY ARE FOUND MOSTLY UNDER PINE OR LARCH TREES, HENCE THE ITALIAN NAME OF 'LARICINO'.

SUILLUS GREVILLEI

(SYN. BOLETUS ELEGANS) LARCH BOLETE / TAMARACK JACK / LARCH SLIPPERY JACK **GOOD**

SUILLUS LUTEUS

(SYN. BOLETUS LUTEUS) SLIPPERY JACK **GOOD**

The characteristics and culinary properties of these two mushrooms are so similar that I am discussing them together here, although they are distinct in appearance. Both grow under conifers of different types, and both have a slippery cuticle (hence the name 'slippery jack'), so mind where you put your feet! Neither exactly reaches the high point of culinary distinction, but both are plentiful and rewarding used in soups and stews together with other mushrooms.

The powers that be have decided to classify boletes such as these with glutinous caps in the genus Suillus – though they are still listed under Boletus in many books.

RECOGNITION

SUILLUS GREVILLEI

CAP   Hemispherical when young, closed underneath by a veil, later flattening to a maximum 10–12 cm in diameter. As the mushroom develops the veil detaches itself from the cap and remains on the stem in the form of a ring or skirt. The cuticle is viscid with gluten when moist, shiny when dry. Yellow-orange when young, paler yellow later.

PORES   Spongy and very absorbent. Lemon-yellow and slightly decurrent. Spore print: olive-brown.

STEM   Golden yellow above the pale yellow ring, becoming darker yellow below with a brownish patterning. Grows to a maximum 3 cm in diameter and 10 cm tall.

FLESH   Soft and tender, lemon to

SUILLUS GREVILLEI

chrome No distinctive aroma or taste.

HABITAT   Exclusively under larch. Singly and in little groups.

SEASON   Summer to late autumn.

SUILLUS LUTEUS

The cap is the same as *S. grevillei*, differing only in colour: chocolate-brown when young, brown to violaceous later. The pores are spongy and very absorbent, paler yellow and adnexed. The spore print is ochre-brown. The stem is the same height as *S. grevillei*, and is concolorous with pores above the ring (which is whitish and pale purple beneath) and yellow-brown to brown below it. The flesh is soft and tender, pale yellow to white. No distinctive aroma or taste. The habitat is usually with Scots pines, particularly near footpaths and banks, singly and in little groups. Season is from summer to late autumn.

A similar mushroom to *S. luteus* is *S. granulatus*. It has larger pores than *S. luteus*, and grows in the same situation, but is worthless, although not poisonous. Another is *S. bovinus*. Both these mushrooms appear from the end of spring to autumn.

PICKING, CLEANING AND COOKING

Cut with a sharp knife halfway down the stem. The caps are so viscid that any grit, leaves, pine needles, etc that comes into contact with them will adhere in the basket, so I recommend removing the cuticle and ring as soon as you pick them. Both mushrooms are generally relatively maggot-free.

Their lack of distinctive flavour and moist flesh puts them in the 'useful' rather than the 'sought-after' category. They are not good for preserving, since they freeze well only when cooked, are too moist and slight in flavour for drying, and the spongy flesh is not firm enough for pickling. Enjoy them in season, when plentiful; they are best fresh, used alone in soups and stews or added to a mixture of other mushrooms.

TRICHOLOMA AND INOCYBE ARE PUT HERE TOGETHER TO STRESS ONCE AGAIN THAT, ALTHOUGH THEY DO NOT GROW IN THE SAME SITUATION, OR BELONG TO THE SAME FAMILY, MISIDENTIFICATION CAN OCCUR.

TRICHOLOMA GAMBOSUM

(SYN. CALOCYBE GAMBOSA / TRICHOLOMA GEORGII)
ST GEORGE'S MUSHROOM
EXCELLENT

This excellent wild mushroom is one of the first mushrooms of the season. It is known as 'St George's mushroom' in English because it usually appears around St George's Day, the 23rd April (although it's actually better a week or so later). However, in Italy it is called 'marzolino' from Marzo, March, because there, further south, it comes up earlier in the year. The German name, 'Mairitterling', suggests that it is a

TRICHOLOMA GAMBOSUM

treat to be expected in May, but it is around in other seasons. This mushroom is most popular in Italy, I think, as it grows so plentifully in the lush pastures of the Alpine foothills.

It's also rather popular with me. Once, on one of my many diets in spring, I was so hungry that I was tempted to eat anything that came my way. A basket of St George's mushrooms was what came my way,

and I ate the lot raw, about 225 g! They saved the day, satisfying my hunger and yet not letting me put on any weight!

It is one of those mushrooms that likes to grow in circles like the fairy ring champignon (see page 62) and others. The mycelium in fact spreads just beneath the soil in a circular way, moving and enlarging the circle every year by a couple of centimetres. The grass is darker and often longer as well, which is what should alert you to the mushroom's presence.

RECOGNITION

CAP Compact, off-white in colour, sometimes split and with split edges. Can reach up to 5–15 cm across.
GILLS White and crowded. Spore print: white.
STEM One of its Latin names, 'gambosum' (like a big leg) refers to the stem, which is bulky at the foot, thinning towards the cap. It also thins with age. White, and 2–4 x 1–2.5 cm.
FLESH Soft, dense and dirty white, with a slightly mealy and cucumber scent. A very subtle flavour.
HABITAT The best places to find these mushrooms are fields and grassy areas where the grass has not been disturbed by cultivation. Racecourses are ideal, as are parks and roadsides. Look for greener, lusher grass in rings.
SEASON April and May. It requires water, and becomes slightly darker in colour when wet because of absorbtion. Pick when the weather is dry.

PICKING, CLEANING AND COOKING

Cut the mushroom at the base of the stem, and brush clean of soil and grass before putting in your basket. It shouldn't harbour any unwanted insect life. Trim the ends of the stems. Slice or use whole, fried in butter or olive oil with a little garlic and parsley or chives. They can be included in

pasta sauces, or cooked and dressed in a salad. They can also be pickled.

Throughout the year, this mushroom is imported from Romania, Hungary, Turkey and other regions where they grow, so a good supplier should be able to find you some.

INOCYBE PATOUILLARDII

INOCYBE PATOUILLARDII

RED-STAINING INOCYBE
DEADLY POISONOUS

This mushroom must be avoided altogether, as it is extremely poisonous. It is similar not only to *Tricholoma gambosum*, but also to small field mushrooms. However, the cap becomes slightly redder in colour, longer and more shiny with age. There is still a possibility of confusion, though, despite its habit of growing with trees and in woods. It's primarily because the seasons are so similar that mistakes can be made. Be very careful indeed.

RECOGNITION

CAP 2.5–8 cm in diameter, colour initially whitish to cream, later on tinged reddish and shiny.
GILLS Tight, becoming freer with age. White. Spore print: white.
STEM 4–6 cm long, plum, cylindric, quite straight and strong with filaments. At base bulbous white becoming pinkish.
FLESH White, smell faintly unpleasant and sweet when young, becoming ranker with age.
HABITAT AND SEASON In mixed woods, usually deciduous, alongside paths, also in parks. May to July.

THERE ARE MANY HUNDREDS OF SIMILAR TRUFFLES OR TUBERS IN THE WORLD – IN PLACES AS FAR APART AS CALIFORNIA, NEW ZEALAND AND CHINA – BUT ONLY THESE PRECIOUS THREE HAVE THE FLAVOUR AND AROMA WHICH HAVE ENSURED THEY ARE THE MOST HIGHLY PRIZED OF ALL.

TUBER MAGNATUM
WHITE ALBA TRUFFLE
EXCELLENT

TUBER MELANOSPORUM
BLACK PERIGORD TRUFFLE
EXCELLENT

TUBER AESTIVUM
SUMMER TRUFFLE **GOOD**

The only time a professional truffle-hunter will take someone with him is when he is absolutely certain that his location will remain a secret. As I was only seven or eight years old and incapable of divulging the route, my father's friend Giovanin offered to take me with him on a truffle hunt. Giovanin appeared wearing big gumboots and a real hunting jacket with a large game pocket. He had with him a stick, a funny-shaped digging tool and a small mongrel called Fido.

I clearly remember my impression of the November woods, with the leafless branches reaching out into the fog. Something about the mysterious atmosphere fascinated me, and I have been a fanatical mushroom hunter ever since. Suddenly Fido became excited and started running up and down, his nose to the ground, sucking in the scent of the truffles like an animated vacuum cleaner. When he stopped abruptly and began clawing at the ground, Giovanin had the sign he'd been waiting for: Fido had found a truffle. Giovanin gently pushed the dog aside, dug a small hole with his special tool and lifted out a wonderful specimen of *T. magnatum*. He brushed the earth from the truffle and put it gently in his pocket. Only then did Fido receive his reward of a small biscuit.

On another occasion, Giovanin gave me a truffle to take home. I was hooked and still am. I call truffles 'food of gods, kings and pigs'. Some truffles contain a chemical resembling the male pig's sex hormone, and the riper the truffle the stronger and more attractive (for the female pig) the scent. The Romans used pigs to locate truffles, but it was hard to prevent them from eating them; the trained dogs used nowadays are easier to handle and can be dissuaded from eating their find.

Something of the same mystery still attaches to truffles. Although France and Italy have increased supplies for commerce by developing techniques of treating the roots of young oaks with black truffle spores, it is still left to nature to produce what is and always has been the mushroom most sought after by gourmets. As this cultivation is difficult, and requires much hands-on attention, the prices are still high. I was once asked to appear on a television programme dealing with the latest scientific innovations and use my expertise to assess the merits of a synthetic black truffle from Switzerland. After examining and tasting the product I had to state that if this was man's attempt to emulate nature then he had failed dismally: the soft liquorice-like substance was devoid of any taste or smell, and could at best be used for decorations on pâtés.

Brillat-Savarin called the black or Périgord truffle the 'black diamond', which could 'make women more tender and men more agreeable'. Aphrodisiac qualities have been attributed to the truffle throughout history. I personally think that the difficulties involved in finding something so rare and exquisite trigger off a demand which inflates the price to an unaffordable level, and this very process becomes a stimulation – almost a sensual experience. The fact that this delicacy sometimes reaches palates that cannot appreciate it is an old human story, applying not only to truffles but to most exotic foods.

Of the many different varieties of truffles in the world, three are the most esteemed and precious: *T. magnatum* (the white Alba truffle); *T. melanosporum* (the black Périgord truffle); and *T. aestivum* (the summer truffle). The aroma of the first of these is very pungent indeed. I once had a phone call from the Customs and Excise Officers at Heathrow Airport warning me that a parcel of perishable food that had arrived for me from Turin was suspected of containing 'something that had gone off'. It was beyond the imagination of the poor officials that white truffles could possess such a penetrating aroma. When I collected the package even the police dogs were looking slightly disturbed by the smell.

Knowing of my obsession, a colleague of my wife's once promised to bring me back some truffles from Saudi Arabia, where apparently they grow in profusion in the desert. When they arrived my heart stopped at the sight of a big plastic bag full of large white truffles. On closer examination, however, my heart stopped again – this time with disappointment. Although these tubers are prized locally, for me there was no smell or taste at all! All that glisters is not gold. And infiltrating the market now are tuber species from China, which are much less sought-after.

RECOGNITION

Truffles are Ascomycetes – 'spore shooters', like the morel – with roundish fruit-bodies, which develop underground in mycorrhizal association with certain trees (why they are so difficult to 'cultivate'). The folded hymenium appears as a marbling of fine veins in the flesh, and the spore-producing asci are situated in the darker part of the flesh. The intense aroma of the ripe spores attracts animals to the fruit-body, which they grub up and eat, dispersing the spores by means of their droppings. Flies are important too, if a nuisance. Flies which try to deposit eggs near, on or in truffles, can disperse spores on their bodies, and larvae, once hatched, can release spores as they move on or in truffles. I have never actually seen the so-called truffle flies in clouds above a hidden truffle – one of the clues to a truffle's presence, so it is said – but they must exist, as the larvae certainly do.

TUBER MAGNATUM

T. MAGNATUM

It grows in symbiosis, only in Italy, with oak, hazel, poplar, beech, the best in the Langhe area of Piedmont, of which the town of Alba is the centre (hence 'Alba truffle'). Other white truffles, but which have less smell, are found in the Marches, Emilia-Romagna, Umbria and even Calabria. An irregular potato-like tuber, it has smooth skin from creamy yellow to pale hazel; the flesh is from pale cream to pale brown, marbled with white veins. (It occasionally has bright red spots, especially when growing with hazel or poplar, and these are highly valued by connoisseurs.) The flesh is solid, hard and brittle – it will break in pieces if dropped on a hard floor. Specimens can reach 12 cm in diameter and weigh 500 g, but most are around 30–50 g. The season is from late September, reaching the best harvest time in November. Provided the soil is not frozen, these truffles can be found until the end of January. A well-trained dog can detect the scent of a mature *T. magnatum* from 50 metres away, even if the truffle lies up to 50 cm underground. Attempts to grow *T. magnatum* commercially have failed.

Once in my restaurant, I was standing near the door with a platter full of white truffles. A customer and his guests, leaving after a good lunch, asked what they were. 'Truffles,' I replied, and one of the guests promptly took one, popped it in his mouth and ate it. His face was a picture – the flavour is quite different to that of white chocolate! – and I refrained from telling him he had just devoured £80 worth.

T. MELANOSPORUM

The most famous are those of the Périgord region of France, but this black truffle is also found in Provence and around Spoleto in Umbria and Norcia in the Marches. The French, because it is the only truffle in their country, think it the best in the world. This causes quite a degree of awkwardness between France and

TUBER MELANOSPORUM

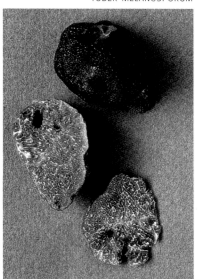

Italy because, as we all know, it is generally acknowledged that the white Italian truffle is the most aromatic and therefore the most valuable. It grows from mid November to March in symbiosis with oak: the roots of young trees are treated with spores before planting, ensuring a supply for commerce in these areas of France and Italy. (Interestingly, it also grows in countries where there are vines. In New Zealand, for instance, they are commercially producing the black truffle in plantations, and having good economic success.) The subterranean fruit-body is irregularly round, with a rough black skin made up of hundreds of polygonal 'warts'. The flesh is very solid and brittle, with a pleasant smell. It is marbled brown with white veins which disappear when the flesh turns black on cooking. It grows to a maximum diameter of 7 cm and weighs 40–50 g. Rare examples reach 100 g.

TUBER AESTIVUM

T. AESTIVUM

The 'summer' truffle usually grows between June and November, but has also been found through the winter, until March. Similar in appearance to *T. melanosporum*, but with a skin covered in pyramidal black warts. The flesh is a solid brown, with white veins which disappear on cooking, and has a very delicate aroma. It is round, to about 3–4 cm in diameter and 20–30 g in weight. Found in England on chalk soils, it usually favours beech. We don't use trained dogs here, but the keen eyes of keen humans when a fraction of the warty skin of a truffle growing just below the surface is visible above ground. The luckiest person in England is without doubt Jenny Hall in Dover who has found some 150 examples of this tasty tuber in her own garden beneath an oak.

PICKING, CLEANING AND COOKING

Very rarely will any of us find a truffle to 'pick'. Only the summer truffle comes anywhere near the surface of the earth in order that you might identify it. The other two are hidden beneath the earth, and you will need a highly trained dog to find them. (In Italy, there is huge rivalry between truffle hunters, and I'm afraid dogs have been poisoned by their masters' competitors.) It is this dog that will smell the truffle and will probably enthusiastically dig for it. Many is the time I have received a contingent of truffles, one or two with claw marks on them!

During the season you can often find me at my restaurant cleaning truffles, which I do with an almost religious reverence to avoid any waste. I never wash white truffles for fear of losing some of the aroma, but use one of those little brushes with brass bristles intended for cleaning suede. They can be used for cooking, but are usually served raw.

Considering the high price I prefer to 'shave' them with a 'mandolino' raw over the food (pasta, risotto, salads etc.). When you buy them, make sure they are firm and heavy – and that any holes made by insects have not been filled with earth to make up the weight again, an important consideration when the price is (in 2002) £3 a gram!

White truffles are delicate and can be kept for a maximum of only seven days after collection. I suggest you buy a small quantity and use straight-away. In the restaurant, where I need larger amounts, I keep them wrapped singly in tissue paper in a tightly closed plastic box in the refrigerator.

TRUFFLE HUNTING

Never leave any type of truffle in an open container in the refrigerator: the aroma will permeate all the other food around – unless, of course, you want everything to taste of truffles! (For instance, eggs kept beside a truffle will be wonderfully flavoured, even through the shell, and are magnificent scrambled for breakfast!) The best Piedmontese fonduta – a fondue-like mixture using fontina cheese – is finished off with shavings of white truffle.

Black truffles keep much longer than white ones – up to 14 days when refrigerated. The tough warty skin has to be washed and scrubbed with a brush to dislodge earth. Edible raw, shaved over foods like the white truffle, but usually used with cooked food such as in sauces, on pâtés, under the skin of roasted birds – all methods which retain the maximum flavour.

The summer truffle is usually used to impart the 'feeling' of a truffle, mostly in decoration. You could use it with

some success, though, in combination with some truffle oil – as I'm afraid many restaurants do.

If you have to transport a truffle at any time, put it in an airtight container with some raw rice to absorb moisture, but don't leave it for too long, or the truffle will deteriorate. When it becomes wet and soggy, it is of no further use and must be discarded.

No truffle takes kindly to being preserved. Freezing and drying are ineffective because the aroma is lost; bottling in water retains the texture but also allows most of the aroma to disappear. A paste of white truffles is now produced commercially in tubes and jars for using in sauces or as a spread. One enterprising Italian company makes a natural essence of truffle, which I use for sauces and to flavour salad dressings. There is also an expensive truffle oil, which is good for salads, but is mainly used to brush on meat before grilling.

CULTIVATED MUSHROOMS

Although mushroom cultivation is now world-wide, the name 'exotic' has been applied to all those of a different shape, colour, taste and flavour to the common button mushroom. In fact it's not too incorrect to call these mushrooms 'exotic', as their cultivation started in the Far East and was then exported to the West.

Once it had been recognised that mushrooms were not only good for medicinal purposes, but also as a foodstuff, attempts were made to cultivate more crops than the brief season of nature allowed. Many mushrooms resisted – and some still do – but very early attempts were successful with certain species. The first mushroom to be cultivated was probably *Auricularia polytricha*, as early as 600 AD. The next was *Flammulina velutipes* (enoki) in 900 AD, followed by *Lentinula edodes* (shiitake) in 1000 AD. These were all Eastern efforts, and the mushrooms are primarily used in Eastern cuisines to this day. In the West, successful cultivation of *Agaricus bisporus* started in the 1600s in France, then the technique was taken to other European countries, and thence to America.

Mushroom-growing technology then advanced significantly, especially after World War Two, since when ideas have been shared between East and West, and cultivated mushrooms have become an important part of our lives.

A very sophisticated technology is needed to cultivate these mushrooms economically. Specialised plants and factories have been created so that the growth, packing and distribution is of guaranteed quality. Each type of mushroom is grown in a different way. The major task was to recreate the ecological and biological conditions in which the mushrooms would flourish. As a mushroom is a fruit-body that grows underground or on or under the bark of trees, using the juices, which include cellulose, to gain nourishment and growth, various 'food' compounds were investigated. Nowadays, straw, sawdust, manure, wood chips and logs are first pasteurised and then injected with the relevant fungus spores. The mushrooms are then grown under controlled conditions of heat and humidity, eventually being collected by hand when mature. The technology is actually quite complicated, but it is improving all the time.

Twenty years ago I didn't regard cultivated mushrooms as proper mushrooms, but my view has now changed considerably. International gastronomy has taken this special ingredient – the cultivated mushroom – on board, recognising that it provides wonderful food. But then I think all mushrooms are wonderful. I still maintain, though, that it is much more fun to go hunting for the wild ones.

LEFT CULTIVATING OYSTER MUSHROOMS CAN RESULT IN COLOURS NOT FOUND IN NATURE

MATURE AGARICUS BISPORUS (PORTOBELLO)

AGARICUS BISPORUS
CHAMPIGNON / PARIS MUSHROOM /
BUTTON MUSHROOM

It was in the 1600s that French melon-
growers discovered that their unused
melon beds were good mediums
for growing mushrooms. They later
grew them in caves, where climate,
temperature and other considerations
could be controlled. (So many
mushrooms were produced in the
Paris region that in the trade small
mushrooms are known as 'champignons
de Paris' to this day.) There were

mushroom-producing
quarries in England too,
around Bath, at the
end of the nineteenth
century, and the great
Carême, chef to the
Prince Regent, admired
the preparation of the
English mushrooms on
sale locally.

During the last 50
or so years, there has
been a huge increase in
production of *A. bisporus*
world-wide, the total
reaching millions of
tonnes. Britain, the
Netherlands, Italy,
France, the USA and
China are but a few of
the countries to have
benefited from the
latest technology. The
mushrooms are usually
eaten fresh, but they
are also canned.

Nowadays special
mushroom 'houses'
are used, and trays of
specially formulated
compound/compost are
used for the growing
medium. (In fact, you
can buy equipment for
growing mushrooms
at home!) The yield of
27 kg per square metre
of soil or compound,
recorded in the
Netherlands, shows how prolifically
these mushrooms can grow.

However, it is in China, particularly
in the south, that some 70 per cent
of the world supply of *A. bisporus* is
produced. The cultivation there
is much more of a family business,
whilst in the West we have large,
technologically perfect plants in
which to cultivate mushrooms.

A.bisporus can grow to the size
of 2 cm in a couple of days after
appearing from under the compost,
depending on the temperature and
general conditions.

BUTTON Mushrooms with a stem no
higher than 2 cm and the cap 3–6 cm
in diameter. The membrane (ring)
is still closed and there are no gills
visible. It is white, and please remember not to peel it as some people do!
CAPS Mushrooms that have
advanced to the next stage of growth,
measuring 2.5 cm high, with a cap up
to 7 cm in diameter. They are already
open, and the ring shows under the
cap, as do gills of a pinkish colour.
FLAT OR OPEN Mushrooms where
the cap is totally developed, from
5–7 cm in diameter, and the stem is
not higher than 3 cm. The visible gills
are starting to become brown.
PORTOBELLO/PORTOBELLA When the
mushroom is left to grow continually,
and separately, it becomes what the
Americans call 'Portobello'. This is a
mushroom with a stem of 4–5 cm
long and 2–3 cm wide, with an open
cap of up to 12 cm in diameter. The
gills are brown-black.

COOKING

All types have a pleasant mushroomy
smell and are sweet in taste. None
should ever be peeled.

The different types are used in
many different ways, starting with
the button, which may be eaten raw,
due to its texture and taste. It can
also be used in stews, fried, sautéed
whole, or sliced, pickled or preserved
in oil. It works well in risottos when
accompanied by dried ceps (funghi
porcini) to give more flavour.

Caps have more flavour than
buttons because they are more mature.
They can be used in similar ways to
buttons, but have the advantage of
size, in that they can be stuffed with
various ingredients. They taste better
cooked than raw. They are also used
finely chopped to stuff meat, or in
sauces.

Flat or open mushrooms can be
sliced and eaten as the cap but, like
the Portobellos, are best fried,
brushed with oil and grilled, or
baked, with or without a stuffing.

AURICULARIA POLYTRICHA
WOOD EAR / TREE EAR / KIKURAGE

According to Chang and Miles, in their masterly *The Biology and Cultivation of Edible Mushrooms* (Academic Press, New York, 1978), *Auricularia polytricha* is the first mushroom in history to have been cultivated. This was in China about 1400 years ago. Its natural wild counterpart growing in the West is *Auricularia judae* (see page 32). Like the wild counterpart, *A. polytricha* is a gelatinous fungus, ear shaped and ranging from a pale to dark brown colour. It reaches a diameter of 15 cm and is about 8 mm thick. It has a very smooth surface, almost velvety and very soft to the touch.

Naturally, it grows in hardwood forests on various types of trees from which it draws nutrients. This natural habitat has been recreated using special logs or even sawdust, with the addition of other elements. The

AURICULARIA POLYTRICHA (WOOD EAR)

Chinese, for instance, allow oak poles to rot for a year or so, then erect them into a sort of shed. The spores are introduced, and over the next two years or so the fungi grow all over them. At this point they are harvested, because the wood will have become too rotten to continue acting as host.

This mushroom is seldom sold in its fresh form in the West, but it is available in dried form from most Chinese or Japanese shops. Even in China the mushroom is mostly sold in its dried form, which means it has become an everyday, readily available product. The dried form has the advantage of regaining its original shape and size when soaked in water and does not lose any of its proteins or vitamins. In fact, the Chinese believe this mushroom has properties that make the blood more fluid, and doctors prescribe it to counter-act the effects of arteriosclerosis.

COOKING

I don't think this mushroom tastes particularly good, but its peculiar gelatinous texture is greatly appreciated in the East. I use it mainly in stews, braises and soups, because when heated in fat, for example when fried, it tends to expand and cause an 'explosion'. If the fat is very hot, this could be dangerous. After poaching or braising, it can be cut into strips and used in salads.

FLAMMULINA VELUTIPES (ENOKI)

FLAMMULINA VELUTIPES
(SYN. COLLYBIA VELUTIPES)
ENOKI / ENOKITAKE / WINTER MUSHROOM / VELVET SHANK

In most cases, cultivated mushrooms are quite similar to their wild or natural versions, but not in the case of *Flammulina velutipes*. In the wild, this winter mushroom grows in clumps on deciduous logs (sometimes pine), throughout the winter until spring. It has a velvety stem (hence the English name 'velvet shank') up to 10 cm tall, and a sticky yellow to orange cap that can grow to 5 cm in diameter. It is found in temperate parts of the northern hemisphere and it is called 'enoki' because in Japan (its main area of cultivation and consumption), it grows on the enoki, or Chinese hackberry, tree. However, with Japanese expertise, the cultivated version has developed differently. It is also stunningly pretty, but much smaller and thinner. Encouraged to grow in clumps, it resembles little bundles of short spaghetti with very small caps of 5 mm, and thinner and longer stems of up to 12 cm tall.

The clumps of mushrooms have a deep, musty smell, and the taste is sweet and nutty. To obtain the immaculate white, almost porcelain-like colour, the mushrooms are kept in the dark during cultivation and forced through a narrow aperture in a jar containing sterilised sawdust of various decomposing hardwoods which have been injected with the spores of the fungus. The jars often have a stiff collar to keep the tiny stems growing upright. Growth can take as little as a week from sowing to sprouting of the fruit-body. The clumps are packed in bundles of 115 g and wrapped in cellophane.

In Britain and the rest of Europe, mushroom growers are starting to experiment with this mushroom, with some success, but there is still a long time to go until major production.

COOKING

Enoki are usually eaten raw as an embellishment to salads, and I would recommend combining them with the dark purple *Laccaria amethystea* (see page 50) to have a real taste sensation. I have created recipes that lean on Japanese tradition, but I have also veered back towards the Italian, which involved enveloping a clump of enoki in Parma ham and flavouring them with olive oil and lemon juice. In Japan, enoki are mostly used in soups because they make soups look so beautiful.

GRIFOLA FRONDOSA (MAITAKE)

GRIFOLA FRONDOSA

MAITAKE / HEN OF THE WOODS / DANCING MUSHROOM

The food industry, always in search of something that is commercially viable, has managed to isolate the spores of the wild *Grifola frondosa* (see page 47), and cultivate them on a chip and wood compound imitating its natural habitat (oak mainly). Masters in this field are the Japanese, and they have given the name 'maitake' to the very successfully cultivated variety, which has a taste and texture much loved by the Japanese. It has been cultivated for the last ten years or so, with a production of 60,000 tonnes a year.

The wild variety is indisputably more valuable than the cultivated because of its better flavour. However, the disadvantages of insect infestation and other impurities make the cultivated variety more acceptable. Another reason for the enormous success of the cultivated mushroom, apart from its texture and taste, is the fact that it reportedly has many health properties.

Indoor cultivation produces much smaller examples than the wild (see page 47). In indoor cultivation, glass containers with narrow openings – or plastic bags with holes – are filled with chips of wood and treated saw-dust, which are impregnated with the spawn where the mycelium eventually forms. After 60–120 days the fruit-body starts to grow. In order to have a continuous output, large quantities of containers and bags have to be inoculated and rotated. The yield potential is 225–450 g mushrooms per 2.25–3.2 kg sterilised, enriched hardwood sawdust.

Outdoors, cultivation is left more to nature. Logs and hardwood stumps are innoculated and buried, which is more productive than leaving them to rot naturally. How wonderful and profitable it would be if all the old stumps of pine worldwide were inooculated with maitake! Although outdoor cultivation is more vulnerable to insect infestation, in general this mushroom does not seem to be too badly affected.

COOKING

When used in Eastern cooking, the maitake adds a touch of refinement and delicacy. It is excellent when fried with scrambled eggs or sautéed by itself or with garlic and chilli, and is ideal for soups. I usually treat it as a vegetable to accompany dishes of meat or fish. I have also combined maitake with pasta, with very good results. Any of the Eastern dishes that I give in this book could use maitake as their main mushroom ingredient, but in fact it can actually be used to replace practically any mushroom.

HERICIUM ERINACEUM

POM-POM / YAMABUSHITAKE / BEAR'S HEAD MUSHROOM

This cultivated mushroom is popular in America, and is slowly appearing in European markets as 'lion's mane fungus'. It is already well known in the Far East, where it is highly sought after for its medicinal properties. It has been given lots of names, including 'bear's head', 'monkey's head' and 'sheep's head', but I like 'pom-pom' best, as it reflects its funny shape. It has also been called 'hedgehog mushroom' (not to be confused with *Hydnum repandum*), because of the many white spines of which it is formed.

Completely white in colour, the fruit-body – rather like a fluffy snow-ball or huge knitted pom-pom – can reach up to 40 cm in the wild once fully grown, and the colour goes from white to yellow, then to pale brown. I have seen it only once in the wood-lands of Britain, but it is popular and fairly common in the rest of Europe, in North America, China and Japan. It grows on dying or dead trees, such as

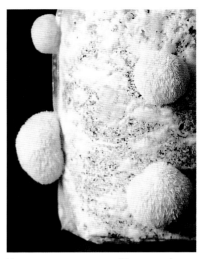

HERICIUM ERINACEUM (POM-POM)

walnut, beech, maple and other broad-leaf trees, stumps and logs.

But the mushrooms are also cultivated indoors, in polythene bags full of treated woodchips and sawdust, which develop this mushroom from incubation to fruiting in 20 days. The mushrooms are forced through small holes in the plastic to form the desired round shape and are then easily collected and packed. It is interesting to note that 2.25 kg of wood mixture produces a 450 g cluster. They are also cultivated in narrow-topped containers in Japan.

It has been discovered in China that the pom pom contains a compound able to combat cancer, and also senility. Tablets made from these mushrooms are available in China.

COOKING

Per 100g of fresh mushroom, 31g consist of protein, 4 g of fat and 17 g of carbohydrate, which along with other elements and vitamins, makes it culinarily attractive.

Cultivated mushrooms need no cleaning, but this one should be quartered before use. It is very much appreciated when cooked with other mushrooms, especially shiitake, presenting a contrast in colour and texture. It is said to taste of lobster or aubergine.

HYPSIZYGUS TESSULATUS

(SYN. LYOPHILLUM SHIMEJI)
BUNA-SHIMEJI / BEECH
MUSHROOM / HON-SHIMEJI

A latecomer in the cultivated mushroom market, *Hypsizygus tessulatus* is considered by the Japanese and Chinese to be a gourmet delicacy.

There has been great confusion about what to call it in the last couple of centuries, with scientists all giving it different names. A Japanese company has registered the name 'Hon-shimeji'. It reminds me of the first stage of *Armillaria mellea*, the honey fungus (see page 28). It grows naturally on various species of trees like beech, elm, cottonwood, willow, oak and other hardwoods in Europe, Asia and North America.

Cultivation takes place in containers, sometimes glass jars, which are filled with wood chips and treated sawdust. The idea is to force the growth through a small aperture, to encourage a tighter cluster of mushrooms with a longish tapered stem and a small hemispheric cap. The cap starts off grey, then becomes paler with age. The stem is up to 6 cm long and is white, as are the gills. The mushrooms are excellent when the caps are still closed. I truly believe this to be one of the mushrooms of the future.

COOKING

The texture, fragrance and taste are totally delicious and the mushroom can be prepared in many interesting ways. To use, just cut off the compressed bottom of the clustered stalks. I combine the mushrooms with all sorts of ingredients. I have even pickled them in vinegar and preserved them in oil. As they are so fresh and aromatic, they may be used as an antipasto. Fried or boiled and flavoured with olive oil, garlic and chilli, they also make an excellent sauce for pasta.

LENTINULA EDODES

(SYN. CORTINELLUS SHIITAKE)
SHIITAKE / WINTER MUSHROOM /
BLACK MUSHROOM

A distant relation of *Armillaria mellea* (see page 28), this mushroom must be the best-known of all the exotics. It is featured in the menus of most Chinese and Japanese restaurants, together with the wood or tree ear fungus (see page 83). Occasionally I have seen these mushrooms claimed to be ceps or porcini on Western restaurant menus, because the meaty slices of the cap have a dark brown colour and a tender texture similar to that of the cep, but without the inimitably decisive flavour. Sadly this can happen when chefs and customers are not particularly knowledgeable about the real thing.

The cultivation of shiitake is of great importance to all of Asia, not only for its edibility, but also because it is believed to be very useful in the battle against cancer, especially in Japan where it is formally recognised as a medicine. In fact in the West, drug companies and the medical press have started to recognise

ABOVE AND BELOW LENTINULA EDODES (SHIITAKE)

that many mushrooms, wild and cultivated, contain substances which may be beneficial to health. A great deal of money is being invested in this, as well as in the improvement of cultivation techniques.

In the wild, this winter mushroom grows on trees such as beech and oak, in temperate areas. They are known as 'shii' because they commonly grow on a type of oak, the 'shii' tree ('take' means mushroom). In cultivation, they use blocks of sterilised sawdust impregnated with the spores of the fungus, which are put into plastic bags with holes in to allow the clusters of mushrooms to grow. Logs are also used, and after soaking are left outside to sprout their valuable fruit-bodies, while the plastic bags are kept in humid, temperature-controlled rooms. This latter method has proved to be much more profitable for continual production, which now runs into

OPPOSITE
HYPSIZYGUS
TESSULATUS
(BUNA-SHIMEJI)

millions of tonnes yearly, competing with *Agaricus bisporus* in popularity.

The cap grows up to 25 cm in diameter and is hemispheric at the beginning, expanding to convex and then flat. When small, the mushrooms are dark brown in colour, becoming paler as they grow. The cap is rolled, which gives a lovely shape when cut into slices. Caps with white fissures on them are considered the best culinarily in Japan. These fissures are obtained by letting air into the growing room: as the caps dry in the air, they crack. The gills are white and quite tightly packed, becoming irregular with age, and they bruise to a light brown colour when touched. The spores are white. The stems are rather tough, and not usually eaten.

The mushrooms are available fresh in most supermarkets and food shops, but the Chinese actually prefer the dried version, which is readily available, and very flavoursome once regenerated in water to its original size.

Cooking

I use this mushroom when an exotic flavour is required in recipes. The best marriage between shiitake and *Auricularia judae* is to be tasted in the recipe on page 188. It can be fried, stewed, stuffed, braised or eaten in soups. There isn't a more versatile mushroom, and I've even managed to pickle it with good results. Try it!

Lepista nuda
WOOD BLEWIT

'Wood blewit' is the name given to *Lepista nuda* in England, whether it is wild or cultivated, although the wild one is much darker in colour than the cultivated, starting off dark violet and gradually fading to brownish purple. The cultivated mushroom is one of the few mushrooms that is violet in colour, apart from the wild

LEPISTA NUDA (WOOD BLEWIT)

L. saeva, which is purple.

In my restaurant we use this mushroom quite a lot. It is cultivated in France, Holland and Britain and is very easy to grow. Its natural habitat is in or around decomposing piles of sawdust, in conifers amongst the leaves – even on piles of compost. In cultivation, these conditions are imitated; treated horse manure and straw compost are inoculated then kept in total darkness for 25–60 days. Germination occurs within a fortnight. For 24–52 weeks, mushrooms

continue developing every 10–14 days.

They are gilled mushrooms, with a deformed cap. The stems are quite large at the base, with a dry texture. When fresh they are totally violet, becoming paler with age, with the stem always remaining violet.

Cooking

It is mostly sautéed, together with other mushrooms, due to its inherent lack of flavour. It is good in sauces, and can also be deep-fried in breadcrumbs.

PHOLIOTA NAMEKO

NAMEKO / GLUTINOUS PHOLIOTA

Similar to *Flammulina velutipes* (the Japanese enoki mushroom, see page 83), this mushroom is said to withstand winter temperatures. It grows naturally on logs of oak and beech in the cool, northern parts of China, Taiwan and the islands of North Japan. It is not known in Europe or North America.

Having discovered that the nameko is an excellent decomposer of hard wood, cultivation is taking place out of doors by burying oak, beech and poplar logs under the earth before inoculating with the spores of the fungus. It requires a high humidity but not too high a temperature. The fungus grows in clumps, and is collected when the stem is 5–8 cm tall, and the cap from 3–10 cm in diameter.

The nameko is highly prized in a culinary sense in Japan, immediately after matsutake, shiitake and enoki. It does not enjoy the same sort of popularity here – as yet – because it has a layer of slime on its cap, which makes it rather sticky. This remains until maturity, and puts Westerners off it a little, although it disappears on cooking. I hope that some day we

PHOLIOTA NAMEKO (NAMEKO)

can appreciate it more in Europe and America, as it has a good texture and taste. I certainly intend to give it a try when I can get my hands on more than the few Mr Uchida manages to bring me back from Tokyo (and which I used to make the nameko miso soup on page 113).

COOKING

The Japanese use this mushroom in soups, not just for embellishment, but also for that certain 'je ne sais quoi' which appeals to the Japanese palate. You can also occasionally find it preserved in plastic bags in Chinese supermarkets. This type can be used in soups and stews.

PLEUROTUS
OYSTER MUSHROOMS

The Pleurotus mushroom family is perhaps the least exotic now of all the cultivated mushrooms, because it is so widely available everywhere. This is due to it being relatively easy to grow, and for this reason many people choose these mushrooms with which to start a cultivation business. There are four types of Pleurotus mushroom, which all descend from the wild *P. ostreatus* (see page 67). All grow in the wild in small clumps, using the cellulose of hardwood trees, and other decaying woods. None of these mushrooms is very fussy about where it obtains its nutrition, and once it was discovered that it was a most prolific grower, it was then cultivated artificially. It is useful as a food for hungry populations because of its valuable protein and vitamin content.

The composts prepared for cultivation are in plastic blocks or containers, and are of wood by-products or straw, which have been previously pasteurised and tested. The mushrooms can thrive on sawdust, cereal, straw, corn and corncobs,

coffee residue, banana fronds, cottonseed husks, soy pulp, paper, and various other materials containing liquid and cellulose. One benefit is that, after the crop, the compost can be used for other purposes such as animal feed. Another is that the cultivated variety does not have to be checked for larvae and maggots, because it is produced under controlled hygienic conditions.

P. CITRINOPILEATUS
Golden Oyster / Tamogitake

This has a brilliant yellow colour and is very fragile and tender. It imparts a nutty flavour when cooked. It descends from the *P. cornucopiae*, the funnel-shaped natural one, which is white with very elongated gills (see page 67). It is native to the subtropical regions of China and southern Japan. The spores are pale pink, and the fleshy cap can grow in the shape of a tongue up to 10 cm in diameter.

P. DJAMOR
Pink Oyster / Takiiro Hiratake

Also known as 'salmon oyster', 'straw-berry oyster' and 'flamingo mushroom'. The brilliant pink colour fades as the mushroom grows, but it is still very attractive. It grows in a similar way to the yellow variety, although its evolution is still being studied by mycologists. The wild variety is collected in Thailand, Singapore, Sri Lanka, Malaysia and other nearby countries. It is cultivated in polythene bags filled with sterilised compound – as listed above – which is impregnated with the mycelium.

P. OSTREATUS
Oyster Mushroom / Hiratake

According to Salvatore Terracina, a Sicilian farmer, the largest *P. ostreatus* he managed to collect weighed nearly 19 kg. It sounds almost unbelievable, but it's true!

The cultivation of this mushroom takes place in controlled rooms, in polythene bags full of treated straw

PLEUROTUS CITRINOPILEATUS (GOLDEN OYSTER MUSHROOM)

and wood chippings. The display of these clusters growing out of the bags is no less impressive than in nature (if you forget the plastic containers). The taste and flavour of the cultivated variety is slightly different from the wild, but is still very attractive and produces good dishes. The mushrooms bought in shops and supermarkets are usually cut at the base of the lateral stem, showing the white gills. It is rather delicate, and therefore doesn't have a long shelf-life, so take note of the sell-by date when purchasing.

P. ERYNGII
King Oyster

This mushroom grows mainly in Europe, is easy to cultivate and, because of its impressive size and solidity, is called the king oyster. It fully deserves this name because it is the most substantial of them all, as well as the most tasty. In the south of Italy it is called 'cardoncello', and grows in late summer to autumn on hardwood trees.

Cultivation is easy – on hardwood sawdust and chips or straw – and the results are stunning. The cap ranges in diameter from 3–12 cm, and is very solid, as is the large stem. It grows in impressive clusters, becoming a broad funnel shape first, then getting flat. It has a greyish colour, and white, firm, thick flesh.

COOKING

Culinarily all pleurotus mushrooms are similar despite the differences in colour, although once cooked the colours fade. None of them needs washing or peeling, just slicing, or they can be left whole if small. All in all they are good mushrooms, full of vitamins and proteins. They can be eaten raw in salads, or cooked in most other ways (stir-fried and used in salads or served as a vegetable, fried in breadcrumbs, in quiches, or in duxelles). Large flat oysters can be fried, sautéed, stewed or braised. The eryngii can be cut into slices and grilled.

STROPHARIA RUGOSOANNULATA (KING STROPHARIA)

STROPHARIA RUGOSOANNULATA
KING STROPHARIA / BURGUNDY MUSHROOM

This massive and excellent mushroom is grown in Europe and other parts of the world with equal enthusiasm, particularly in America. Its size has led to it being given yet another name, 'Godzilla mushroom'!

It is mostly cultivated out of doors, using hardwood chips, straw or sawdust. This method of cultivation was discovered by pure chance, when somebody in America transplanted the mycelium off a tree stump into a private garden where woodchips and sawdust were being stored. (Perhaps the only mushroom that can be successfully transplanted!) It has a good yield, and the clusters are beautiful to look at, but it grows very slowly, over 8–10 weeks.

The stem is white, with a meaty, reddish brown cap that measures from 4–13 cm in diameter. The gills are also white but become grey as they age.

COOKING

The king stropharia can be used in all the recipes in this book, either as a substitute or as the main mushroom. The cleaning is simple, just cut off the stem at the base. They do not have maggots or insects. They are wonderful just sautéed in butter or cooked as part of a mixed stew. If you have bigger examples they can be cut in half, brushed with oil and then grilled.

TRICHOLOMA MATSUTAKE
MATSUTAKE

For the Japanese this is the finest of all mushrooms. It is so greatly appreciated that a kilo of good wild specimens can fetch up to £800. (This is still quite a way from the white truffle, which – in late 2002 – was priced at £3,000 per kilo!) I have never seen this mushroom growing wild, as it is rarely found in Europe, but I have had the pleasure of tasting one or two examples brought to me by an enthusiastic Japanese customer. The husband of a Japanese friend of mine, Miho Uchida, recently brought some back from Tokyo, so that I was able to have the photographs taken specially for this book.

This mushroom, together with the truffle and others, belongs to the mycorrhizal type which requires a symbiosis with the roots of certain trees. These types of mushroom are much more difficult to cultivate than the saprophytic or parasitic ones, which grow from dead matter, or attach themselves to living trees and organisms. The difficulty in growing matsutake and similar fungi is being continually researched, because it concerns the most highly prized mushrooms in the culinary world. As a result, cultivation is limited, and prices are very high!

The matsutake grows in a similar way to the fairy ring champignon, in circles around certain types of pine, usually the Japanese red pine ('matsu' means pine, and 'take' means mushroom). The size of the circle increases every year by 10–15 cm. The mushroom itself grows up to 12 cm high in the wild, with a very strong stem. The hemispherical cap is between 4–20 cm in diameter when open, initially cream on the outside edges, red-brown with streaks in the centre. In cultivation, the cap is red-brown, a little flaky and still closed. It is always collected as soon as its head pops out of the earth, because this is the best time to enjoy it – tender and sweet, rather than open and a bit tougher.

The European counterpart is called *Tricholoma caligatum*. It grows in coniferous woods in a similar way, but it tastes slightly bitter compared to the superb flavour of the Japanese variety.

COOKING

The matsutake has a nutty, sweet taste, and the delicate fibre of the stem makes it ideal for grilling when cut in half. It is also good in soups and other delicate dishes.

TRICHOLOMA MATSUTAKE (MATSUTAKE)

THE RECIPES

Wild mushrooms are vitally important in the food chain. You only have to look at the histories of medicine and cooking in the East to realise how valued these little miracles of nature are. They have been a source of food and health in China and Japan, for instance, for thousands of years. In the West, Alexander Fleming was the first to scientifically appreciate the health potential of fungi when he discovered penicillin, but since then huge efforts have been, and are still being, made to isolate and extract other useful compounds believed to exist in many fungi.

But it is as food that fungi are most appreciated. The definition of 'edibility' is, of course, something of a moveable feast. A handful of mushrooms are universally acknowledged to be gastronomically superb in flavour; a lot more are praised or dismissed according to the opinion of the person who is passing judgement. This is partly a question of taste in the most literal sense, partly, perhaps, a cultural matter. In Italy, for instance, people will ignore delicious mushrooms in their single-minded quest for ceps, even regarding with suspicion the agarics. These, which include the field and horse mushrooms, are probably the only ones many British people will actually recognise and eat.

Local markets all over Europe sell wild mushrooms in season – gathered by professional collectors whose supply is systematically checked before appearing on the stalls and in the shops. Many European governments appoint specially trained officers to inspect mushrooms before they are sold. There is also an industry collecting desirable species such as ceps for the busy commercial concerns that dry and preserve wild mushrooms.

Mushroom appreciation is full of contrasts and contradictions. On the one hand, wild mushrooms are often considered as peasant food, to be eaten by more sophisticated people only to supplement dietary shortages during wartime. On the other, city people pay dearly now for the privilege of eating this same 'peasant' food in restaurants. In some communities, the autumn hunting season involves the whole family in the gathering of sufficient mushrooms to preserve for the winter, and people go to some lengths to render edible mushrooms that others would consider toxic. And of course, alongside all the delicious mushrooms, there are those that are unpleasant to eat, those that are toxic, and those that are downright poisonous. The Field Guide (see pages 10–79) should help you with identification of these.

LEFT HONEY FUNGUS READY FOR THE KITCHEN, AS IS ANTONIO WEARING HIS APRON – A BIRTHDAY PRESENT FROM HIS GREAT FRIENDS VALÉRIE AND FABRICE MOIREAU

A SUCCESSFUL DAY'S HARVEST READY TO BE CLEANED

THE FOOD VALUE OF MUSHROOMS

Most mushrooms consist of approximately 90 per cent water but also contain important minerals – potassium salts and phosphates – plus varying quantities of vitamins B1, B2, D and E. In nutritional terms, the key qualities of a mushroom are its low calorie content (only 42 per 100 g), its low fat (1–2 per cent) and its protein (3–9 per cent, comparable with meat and milk). But it is texture and flavour (and in certain cases a unique aromatic quality) that make mushrooms generally so indispensable in cooking.

The most sensible way to approach eating wild mushrooms is with caution, and this doesn't only refer to the need to identify them accurately. Even those acknowledged to be edible can cause gastric upsets since their micro-structure makes them less digestible than many other plants and their mycosine content affects the stomach juices, making the juices take longer to break food down. So never over-indulge with mushroom eating: it is best to limit portions to 115–140 g. Even good edible mushrooms can become indigestible if not treated or prepared properly. The rule is to eat them as fresh as possible and to choose only the best specimens. Deterioration that results in the production of damaging toxins can take place when mushrooms are badly stored (and that includes transporting them from the gathering site to the kitchen in a plastic bag). And they can deteriorate after cooking as well, so eat immediately and do not reheat more than once.

Some mushrooms are inedible unless cooked or blanched before cooking: the Field Guide indicates which these are. And finally, many mushrooms react badly with alcohol, so limit alcohol consumption when eating most wild mushrooms.

DEALING WITH YOUR MUSHROOM HARVEST

A common autumn spectacle in Italy is of a group of people sitting around a table piled high with mushrooms, sorting and cleaning them. Mushrooms don't improve once they have been gathered, and even if you have picked

The mushroom world may be full of contrasts, but it is also full of changes. Wild mushrooms are now becoming much more popular in countries like Britain, where once they were considered virtually inedible. And the science of mushroom cultivation has grown enormously in the last decade or so. In the East they have been cultivating selected species for hundreds of years (see page 81), but now many more fungi are being grown commercially. With truly wild mushrooms, we are subject to location, season and weather vagaries, while their cultivated cousins can be grown in suitable conditions almost anywhere in the world, and throughout the whole year. This avoids expensive transport costs (although I will always have to import my precious white truffles from Italy!), and guarantees fresh quality. I truly believe that fungi are becoming more and more important in our lives, and that they can be regarded as the food of the future.

only a few handfuls, you should perform this ritual as soon as you get home to avoid the disappointment of finding that they have gone soggy overnight, or that the maggots have had a feast in your stead.

The ritual involves having someone knowledgeable check the identity and edibility of each specimen. Then there is the cleaning, inspecting and sorting into size and type. (See the Field Guide for more detail.) And finally, there is the challenge of assessing the best way to make the culinary most of each mushroom. Sometimes a special find calls for a particular accompaniment and you must buy a piece of prime fish or meat to make a meal. Sometimes a tiny amount of a good mushroom needs eking out. Sometimes (perhaps most often), you have a miscellaneous assortment that, while not gourmet material, is at least versatile. Sometimes there is enough to sort out some for preserving. So what do you choose?

Imagine you have come back from the woods with a small basketful of mixed fungi. If they are extremely fresh and tender you might make a *fritto misto* or eat them in a salad, but if they look a bit tired, then soups, stews and casseroles are a good idea. For more elderly specimens, drying is the best bet. You might have found a nice big cauliflower fungus or a cluster of honey fungus. After you have put aside enough for a sauce to accompany a plate of pasta and perhaps cooked some for a stew, cook the rest in vinegar to preserve as an antipasto.

Imagine your basket contains a substantial number of a single species – ceps if you are very lucky. Sort them out according to whether they are small and firm (incidentally, the most expensive to buy), medium, big and young or big but old. Do your cleaning and maggot-excising. Once you can see how much good mushroom material you have, you can explore the options for eating them.

● Small ones in prime condition – slice raw in salads
● Small and medium – sauté for immediate use or for freezing; or freeze, sliced or whole; or slice and preserve in oil
● Big and young (pores still creamy) – grill whole, or slice and use as above
● Big but elderly – slice for drying, or for immediate cooking
● Bits and pieces, old and young – dry for powdering, or cook into duxelles or extract.

MIXED SAUTÉED MUSHROOMS

COOKING METHODS

Although my recipes specify *how* to cook the mushroom ingredients in all cases, I include these notes to help explain *why*, as well as to offer a summary of processes for you to draw on to develop your own recipes.

FRYING I do this in oil, or butter, or a mixture of both. A mixture helps prevent the butter turning brown, or I use oil first and add butter later to give sauces a nice taste and a shiny, creamy look. When you sauté mushrooms briefly in very hot fat, add seasoning at the end. Garlic should on no account be allowed to brown, and salt will make the mushrooms exude water and alter their taste. The purpose of frying is to cook the outside of the mushroom so it is nice and crisp, sealing in the flavour, and it is a good thing to do so straightaway, since it is the first stage of any number of recipes. Mushrooms treated like this keep for a few hours or can be frozen.

SAUTÉING This uses a lower heat than frying and is good for combinations of fresh and dried mushrooms. Flavour is exuded with the juices, making a delicious sauce.

GRILLING This is good for substantial mushrooms – big caps of cep, Caesar's mushrooms, parasols, the agarics, slices of giant puffball and chunks of ready-blanched cauliflower fungus.

BLANCHING This is sometimes a useful precaution for preserving young ink caps in their closed stage, for example, but is sometimes a necessary measure to remove the toxins present in raw mushrooms.

DEEP-FRYING This is a favourite of mine. Dip mushrooms in beaten egg and then in breadcrumbs and deep-fry. This seals in the flavour and gives an appetisingly crisp texture to the outside.

MICROWAVING I do not recommend this for cooking mushrooms, but it can be useful for reheating dishes – but once only.

PRESERVING METHODS

The art of preserving food is as old as humanity itself. Prehistoric hunters dried and salted their foodstuffs, and these early methods are still used today, particularly with wild mushrooms. Later, pickling and bottling or canning offered additional methods of preservation, and most recently freezing has opened up new possibilities. Different mushrooms call for different approaches. The various methods maintain, enhance or even transform the natural qualities of the original, and your choice depends both on the means available and on how you want to use your preserves.

Speaking personally, no matter which way I preserve mushrooms, I always enjoy them and continually find new ways of using them. From the anonymity of the convenient frozen blocks of mushrooms in the freezer to the rows of glass jars packed with dried and pickled delights which turn my larder into a mycophagist's Aladdin's cave, preserving enables me to serve and enjoy wild mushrooms all the year round.

ABOVE PICKLED BUNA-SHIMEJI
IN OIL

TOP PICKLED PORCINI IN OIL

DRYING

Until recently, anyone entering our house in autumn was assailed by an intense smell of wild mushrooms, and confronted in every room by sheets of newspaper spread with thin slices of drying ceps. Then, in Switzerland, I came across a machine purpose-built for drying quantities of mushrooms and now I can dry 3 kg mushrooms in about 2 hours.

Drying captures and preserves the taste, aroma and texture of mushrooms, but very few retain their shape after they have been reconstituted by soaking in water – morels, cauliflower mushrooms and shiitake are exceptions.

WHAT TO DRY

Not all mushrooms are suitable: the fibrous texture makes some stringy and tough, while others lose their aroma. The best results come from the following.

BOLETUS EDULIS (CEP) This has the perfect texture for slicing and drying, intensifies in taste when dried, and reconstitutes quite well. Considering the price of the fresh mushrooms, it is no wonder that just a little amount of bought dried ceps (funghi porcini) is expensive.

BOLETUS BADIUS (BAY BOLETE) Although the flavour is less intense than that of the cep, the texture is similar and it dries equally well. Since it is a common mushroom, I dry large quantities and find it very useful.

MORCHELLA ELATA AND M. ESCULENTA (MORELS) Probably the most expensive to buy dried and much sought after. Haute cuisine – especially French and Swiss – makes abundant use of morels. They can be dried whole and the dried reconstitute well, with a good taste and texture, but relatively little aroma. Look out for dirt at the stem base in bought ones.

CRATERELLUS CORNUCOPIOIDES (HORN OF PLENTY) Ideal for drying because of the absence of watery flesh and the increase in aroma when dry. They reconstitute well, and are also extremely easy to reduce to powder.

SPARASSIS CRISPA (CAULIFLOWER FUNGUS) Ideal for drying (it needs slicing) because of its good texture and slight aroma. When reconstituted, it regains the cartilaginous quality of the fresh fungus, so is ideal for soups and dishes requiring some texture.

Suitable but not so highly recommended are *Agaricus campestris* (field mushroom), *Auricularia judae* (Judas' ear), *Hydnum repandum* (hedgehog fungus), *Marasmius oreades* (fairy ring champignon), the polypores and shiitake. Sadly, the least successful of all is *Cantharellus cibarius* (chanterelle), which becomes tough and tasteless. The only thing it retains is its charming colour.

How to dry
● Never wash the mushrooms. Brush or cut away parts that are dirty or sandy.
● Use only mature, not overripe specimens. The odd insect larva doesn't matter – it will vacate its habitat once the mushroom is sliced.
● Small mushrooms can be threaded whole on string (with space between for air to circulate) and hung up to dry. For larger, fleshy mushrooms, cut cap and stem into 5 mm slices.
● In warm climates, lay mushroom slices on gauze-covered mats and place in an airy spot in the sun – they should dry in a day. Where colder and more humid, dry indoors, on clean newspaper covered by a clean cloth. Leave in a well ventilated room, on top of a radiator or in an airing cupboard, turning occasionally. They can be dried in a fan oven at a very low temperature with the door slightly open. If using a conventional oven, keep the door open and put a fan in front to ensure air circulation.
● Store the perfectly dried mushrooms in airtight jars or plastic bags.
● Make mushroom powder from dried mushrooms using a mortar and pestle or a food processor. Keep in an airtight jar and add to soups, sauces and omelettes, or incorporate in savoury butters and fresh pasta dough.
● If buying best quality dried mushrooms, inspect to make sure they contain whole slices, not scrappy bits. Keep in fridge or freezer.

To RECONSTITUTE Soak in lukewarm water for 15–20 minutes before preparing as directed in the recipe. Dried shiitake take about 30 minutes: discard the stem, which is usually tough and dirty. Use the soaking water – after straining through a fine sieve – for added flavour or as stock. Dried mushrooms may be added as they are when cooking soups and some sauces; they revive during the long, slow cooking.

CEPS THREADED ON A STRING FOR DRYING

SALTING
Salting is still widely used to preserve food in Poland and Russia not only for meat and fish, but also for vegetables, including mushrooms. The process simply consists of embedding the mushrooms in plenty of salt, which gradually dissolves into a preservative brine. Saffron milk caps and ceps are two that are traditionally salted, but any young firm mushrooms are ideal. Once you have cleaned the mushrooms thoroughly (without, of course, washing them), remove any grit, check for maggots and cut in slices if they are large. Allow 55 g sea or rock salt per 1 kg mushrooms. Alternate layers of salt and mushrooms in non-corrosive containers

A HARVEST OF FRESH MORELS

FREEZING FROM RAW Good to freeze raw are:
● The agarics (though I wouldn't bother, as the cultivated ones are sold all year round).
● All the boletes (Boletus and Leccinum, of which the cep and bay bolete are the best).
● Chanterelles and horn of plenty. The latter, however, are very fragile after freezing.
● Hedgehog fungus, after its spikes are removed.
● Morels.
● St George's mushroom.
● Giant polypores and chicken of the woods.
● Wood and field blewits.

Saffron milk caps freeze perfectly after blanching. Other mushrooms need cooking before they freeze successfully.

Choose only small and maggot-free specimens, and clean thoroughly. If necessary, blanch in boiling salted water for 30 seconds or so, then drain well and leave to cool completely on a clean cloth. Put 8 or 10 at a time in a transparent plastic bag and seal, extracting as much air as possible. Put in the freezer and keep frozen at 18°C or more. Or open-freeze the mushrooms on a tray, then bag them up. Remember to date and label the bags.

Thaw either by deep-frying in hot oil or by boiling in water. To deep-fry, drop the frozen mushrooms into a deep-fryer for a few seconds (this seals the outside and thaws the inside, but be careful not to let the oil bubble over). Alternatively, plunge them into boiling salted water for a few minutes until they are soft. Drain, slice and use as if fresh.

FREEZING IN BUTTER My own favourite way of freezing boletes in particular is to cook them in butter, which helps protect them against 'frost-bite'. Use plenty of butter – 250g unsalted butter per 1kg mushrooms. Gently fry 150g finely chopped onions in 115g of the butter until golden, add the sliced mushrooms and cook for 2–4 minutes. (If the mushrooms are wanted later for sautéing or frying, omit the onions.) Take the dish off the heat, add the remaining butter and leave it to melt. Cool, put into plastic freezer boxes with lids, labelled with the date and type of mushrooms, then freeze.

To thaw, leave the block at room temperature for an hour. The mushrooms and butter can be used together to provide a ready-made basis for soups and sauces, or can be used separately, after the mushrooms have been drained from

with lids. Start and finish with a layer of salt. You can add more layers of mushrooms and salt later, as you find the mushrooms. Press the contents down with a weight, and cover closely. Check occasionally, to ensure they are still covered with the salt solution. To use, rinse well and cook without additional salt.

FREEZING

Since they may be up to 90 per cent water, mushrooms are not difficult to freeze: the problems arise when you come to thaw them. Experiments over the years have taught me which mushrooms can be frozen raw without becoming tough or 'frostbitten', and which need blanching before freezing. I have also evolved reliable ways of thawing.

the thawed butter. Mushrooms frozen in this way are ideal for risottos. You won't be able to tell the difference from fresh.

FREEZING DUXELLES I give a recipe for this mushroom basic on page 105. Duxelles is the standard way of beginning sauces and soups, and produces a ready-made filling for stuffed pasta. I freeze the mixture in an ice-cube tray, then put the cubes in a plastic bag in the freezer. (The amazing advantage is that you don't have to thaw the whole block of mushrooms when you only want a little to flavour a sauce – exactly as I recommend for stock.)

PICKLING

Whether the mushrooms are to be kept in brine or olive oil (brine is cheaper), they must first be boiled in a vinegar solution so they retain their texture and appearance. But since a traditional Italian antipasto must include something piquant and vinegary to tease the appetite, these delicacies are just what are needed. Commercially, you will usually only find pickled ceps, but almost all the edible mushrooms in this book are suitable for pickling. I quite like to serve a mixture.

Choose only the most tender specimens, because they are likely to be maggot-free, and clean them thoroughly. For once you can use water to rinse the mushrooms. They reduce in volume by about half when pickled. Store them in sterilised screw-top jars, using smaller jars in preference to larger ones since, once opened, the contents need to be consumed quickly. See page 102 for the recipes.

MUSHROOM EXTRACT

A useful way of coping with either a mixture of small quantities of different mushrooms or a glut of any one kind is to make this concentrate.

Clean the mushrooms, chop finely, just cover with water and simmer until they have exuded as much as possible of their natural juices. Strain off the liquor. The mushrooms themselves will now be pretty tasteless, but could be used to make up a quantity for pickling, if you don't want to eat them. Add to the liquor a sprig of rosemary, some sage leaves, a few bay leaves, some black pepper and a lot of salt. (I further reinforce the mushroom flavour by adding some dried mushrooms and garlic.) Boil until the liquid starts to thicken, then strain into a clean bottle and store in the fridge. Use a drop here and a drop there to flavour all sorts

A JUICY MORSEL OF WOOD BLEWIT

of dishes, and it will disappear in no time! Alternatively, you can freeze it in cubes.

THE RECIPES

I hope you enjoy cooking my recipes. As with everything in cookery, nothing is set in stone. You may decide that you need more salt here or more chilli there, or you may want to make more substantial adaptations and improvements. Alternatively, you may use my ideas as a starting point for your own experiments. I leave it to your imagination and, I hope, pleasure – but please remember my warning, one which you will find everywhere in this book, do not experiment with any mushrooms about which you are unsure. *Buon appetito!*

CHAPTER ONE

SOUPS, SAUCES AND PRESERVES

In this chapter, I give you recipes for soups, sauces, preserves and other basic preparations necessary for producing delicacies based on mushrooms. They use mostly cultivated mushrooms, which are highly sought after and many of which are produced in the Far East. These mushrooms are increasingly to be found in Oriental shops and good greengrocers. In this chapter, soups are very much to the fore, and all are very interesting and delicious. In Europe we use mushrooms in soups as well, but mainly in sauces and stews. The sauces here are basic, but do not forget about those hidden within recipes for pasta, fish and meat throughout the rest of the book. These are just as good, and may be used in many contexts. In fact, by combining various of my ideas or suggestions, you will probably be able to develop excellent new recipes. And last but not least, here you will find many ways of preserving your wild mushrooms.

Pickled Mushrooms in Brine

Mushrooms pickled in brine have to be mixed with some oil before serving to make them more palatable and to reduce the sharpness (although the taste of the vinegar can be softened by adding extra herbs).

FILLS 1 x 1KG JAR

2 KG FRESH MUSHROOMS
SALT TO TASTE

BRINE
1.2 LITRES GOOD WHITE WINE
    VINEGAR
600 ML WATER
1 TBSP SALT
1 SMALL SPRIG ROSEMARY
A FEW BLACK PEPPERCORNS
5–6 BAY LEAVES
1 MEDIUM ONION, QUARTERED
2 GARLIC CLOVES

Clean the mushrooms, then slice or cut according to size.
Combine the brine ingredients in a large, non-corrosive pan and boil for 15 minutes. Meanwhile, cook the mushrooms separately in salted water for 8 minutes. Drain the mushrooms, then add to the vinegar and boil for a further 5 minutes. Remove the mushrooms with a sterilised spoon and fill your jars with them, leaving some space for the liquor. Let the liquor cook for a further 10 minutes, then strain and set aside to cool. When completely cold, cover the mushrooms with the strained vinegar liquor. Cover the jars carefully and they will keep for a few months in a cool place.
To serve, drain the mushrooms well and toss in a few drops of olive oil.

Pickled Mushrooms in Oil

This second method of pickling, the usual one in Italy, is slightly more expensive, since after pickling in vinegar, the mushrooms have to be immersed for keeping in good olive oil (never extra virgin, that is too strong). However, the results are so delicious that it is well worth it.

FILLS 2 x 1KG JARS

2 KG FRESH MUSHROOMS
OLIVE OIL
2 MEDIUM-SIZED DRIED HOT
    CHILLI PEPPERS (OPTIONAL)

BRINE
1.2 LITRES GOOD WHITE WINE
    VINEGAR
600 ML WATER
2 TBSP SALT
5 BAY LEAVES
10 CLOVES

Clean the mushrooms, then slice or cut according to size.
Combine the brine ingredients in a large, non-corrosive pan and bring to the boil. Add the mushrooms and boil, allowing 5 minutes for small mushrooms and 10–12 minutes for larger ones. Drain and, without using your hands (because the mushrooms are now sterilised), spread on a very clean cloth to cool and dry for a few hours. Put a few mushrooms into a sterilised jar, pour in a little oil to cover them and (using the same spoon for each operation) mix gently so that the oil reaches all parts of the mushrooms. Add more mushrooms and more oil in the same way until the jar is full. If you wish, you can pop in a couple of red chilli peppers for added flavour. Close the lid tightly and keep for at least a month before use (and for up to a couple of months thereafter). Once opened, however, a jar should be used up fairly rapidly.
Occasionally I find a few pinpoints of mould on the mushrooms after some months. If I catch them early enough the situation can be retrieved. I throw away the oil, boil the mushrooms in pure vinegar for a minute or so, then store in fresh olive oil as before.

RIGHT PICKLED MUSHROOMS IN OIL

BASIC STOCK

Home-made stocks will immeasurably improve many dishes, do not cost much and only require a little patience. For chicken stock, use a whole chicken, or pieces (thighs and drumsticks are good). For beef stock, use the same weight of a stewing cut (not the best rump or fillet!). Mincing the meat or poultry makes for greater flavour. For fish stock, the preparation is similar, but substitute the meaty ingredients with white fish pieces, bones and heads, and cook for 1 hour only (but see also page 184). For vegetable stock, simply omit the meat. You may use chicken, meat, game, fish or vegetable stocks freshly made, or after a day if kept in the fridge. You can also freeze them in a suitable container, or in an ice-cube tray, then pack the cubes in a plastic bag.

MAKES 2 LITRES

1.5 KG MEAT/FISH PIECES AND BONES
1 LARGE ONION, QUARTERED
4 MEDIUM CARROTS, DICED
2 CELERY STICKS, DICED
3 GARLIC CLOVES, LEFT WHOLE
10 BLACK PEPPERCORNS
2 BAY LEAVES
1 SMALL BUNCH PARSLEY
200 G BUTTON MUSHROOMS, SLICED
  AND DRIED BRIEFLY IN A MEDIUM
  OVEN
1 SPRIG MARJORAM

Put the meat or fish pieces and bones into a large pan and cover with 3 litres cold water. Bring to the boil quickly and boil for a few minutes. Skim off the foam and reduce the heat to simmering point. Add the remaining ingredients and cook for 1½ hours.

Strain the liquid through a fine sieve and if further reduction is needed – to intensify the flavours – cook a little longer to allow evaporation. When cool, use or freeze for later use.

MUSHROOM SAUCE

This Italian sauce can be used in many ways and is utterly delicious. It is good for flavouring pasta, rice and polenta, but can also top crostini or flavour meat or fish dishes. It is best when made with fresh or dried ceps, but you can also use giant polypore or chicken of the woods. The sauce can be frozen.

MAKES 500 ML

300 G SMALL FRESH CEPS
15 G DRIED CEPS (FUNGHI PORCINI),
  SOAKED IN WARM WATER
2 GARLIC CLOVES, FINELY CHOPPED
4 TBSP OLIVE OIL
2 TBSP FINELY CHOPPED PARSLEY
2 MINT LEAVES, FINELY
  CHOPPED
1 TBSP TOMATO PASTE
SALT AND PEPPER TO TASTE

Clean the fresh ceps, then cut into small cubes. Drain the dried ceps after 20 minutes, reserving the water, then chop finely.

Fry the garlic in the oil until transparent, then add the fresh and soaked dried mushrooms. Fry for about 10 minutes over a medium heat. Season to taste. Add the parsley, mint, tomato paste and 4 tablespoons of the reserved cep soaking water. Warm through, and the sauce is ready.

If you use this sauce for pasta – especially – sprinkle with a little grated Parmesan before serving.

Dried Morel and Truffle Sauce

This is one of the best sauces to be used either for roasted meat or game, or even to flavour risottos and pasta dishes. In this recipe of Italian origin I used the dried morels that I got from Nepal (see page 64), as I still had some left from the original purchase!

When reduced in a sauce, the morels give a full, smoky flavour. My favourite way of serving this sauce is to pair it with handkerchief pasta (see page 160). The sauce can be frozen.

Serves 6

60 G DRIED MORELS
55 G SUMMER TRUFFLE
55 G BUTTER
2 SMALL SHALLOTS, FINELY CHOPPED
400 ML CHICKEN STOCK
 (SEE OPPOSITE)
125 ML DOUBLE CREAM
10 DROPS TRUFFLE OIL
SALT AND PEPPER TO TASTE

Soak the morels in warm water for 20 minutes, then trim off the base of the stems, and chop the mushrooms finely. Clean the summer truffle and, at the last minute, cut it into 3 mm slices, then dice.

Melt the butter in a casserole dish, add the shallots and soften. Add the morels to the casserole with the stock, and cook for 8–10 minutes. Leave to cool and then add the cream, plus some salt and pepper. Process in a blender then, lastly, add the truffle oil and fresh truffle dice. Warm before using.

Wild Mushroom Duxelles

Duxelles are actually nothing more than minced and flavoured mushrooms that have been deprived of most of their moisture. They can then be used as a filling for many dishes, such as ravioli, stuffed mushrooms, squid or pockets of puff or other pastry, or they can be added to sauces, stews and soups. You could also use this tasty treat on toast or bruschetta. It may most famously be of French origin, but it is now used all over the world.

Makes about 175 G

250 G FRESH WILD MUSHROOMS (CEPS, MORELS, CHANTERELLES, BAY BOLETES) OR 200 G BROWN CAP MUSHROOMS, PLUS 15 G EACH OF DRIED CEPS, MORELS AND SHIITAKE
55 G BUTTER
3 TBSP FINELY CHOPPED SPRING ONION
1 GARLIC CLOVE, FINELY CHOPPED
1 TBSP FRESH BREADCRUMBS
2 TBSP COARSELY CHOPPED PARSLEY
SALT AND PEPPER TO TASTE

Clean and trim the fresh mushrooms as appropriate. Chop the brown caps coarsely if using. Soak the dried mushrooms in warm water for 30 minutes, then squeeze and finely chop. (Save the water for a later use.)

To cook, melt the butter in a pan over a low heat and fry the spring onion and garlic for a few minutes to soften. Add the mushrooms and breadcrumbs and stir-fry for a few more minutes. When the moisture has almost gone, add the parsley and some salt and pepper to taste, then cook for a little longer. Cool, then refrigerate for up to 5 days. Although I usually say not to eat reheated mushrooms, cooked and flavoured in this way they are quite useful. The duxelles can also be frozen.

Mushroom Minestrone

The famous Italian thick soup, or minestrone, uses all sorts of mixed vegetables, so I used mixed mushrooms instead to give a collection of flavours, textures and colours – a celebration of nature. This recipe is useful for when you come home with only a few specimens of each mushroom – or you could use cultivated ones. Some dried mushrooms can always come to the rescue if need be. For vegetarians, just omit the cubes of Parma ham and use vegetable stock.

Serves 6

1 KG MIXED WILD MUSHROOMS
1 ONION, FINELY CHOPPED
200 G PARMA HAM, DICED
6 TBSP OLIVE OIL
2 GARLIC CLOVES, FINELY CHOPPED
5 FRESH BAY LEAVES
1 SMALL SPRIG ROSEMARY
3 TBSP CHOPPED PARSLEY
500 ML VEGETABLE OR CHICKEN STOCK
   (SEE PAGE 104)
300 G COOKED BORLOTTI BEANS (THEY
   COULD BE FROM A JAR OR CAN)
6 SLICES GOOD ITALIAN BREAD,
   TOASTED FOR BRUSCHETTA
   (OPTIONAL)
FRESHLY GRATED PARMESAN
   (OPTIONAL)
SALT AND PEPPER TO TASTE

Clean and prepare the mushrooms as appropriate. You could use chicken of the woods, wood blewits, hedgehog fungus, chanterelles or ceps.

Fry the onion and diced ham in the oil until the ham has taken on some colour, then add the garlic and herbs. Add the cleaned mushrooms and the stock and cook for 10 minutes. Add the cooked beans. Bring to the boil again, and cook for 3–4 minutes. Remove the bay leaves and rosemary, and season the soup. Put a toasted bruschetta in each soup bowl if using, and pour the soup on top. Sprinkle with Parmesan if liked. Buon appetito!

Mushroom and Pearl Barley Soup

This soup from the Slavic countries used to be a delicacy for poor people and gypsies. I like the idea of these humble ingredients being brought together to produce a simple dish. The original recipe used double cream, but I have substituted thick soured cream to give another dimension. If you cannot find soured cream, then use thick double cream mixed with a little lemon juice. Serve with toasted bread.

Serves 4

4 TBSP PEARL BARLEY
40 G DRIED CEPS
3 GARLIC CLOVES, CRUSHED
2 TBSP FINELY CHOPPED SHALLOT
A PINCH OF FRESHLY GRATED NUTMEG
6 TBSP SOURED CREAM
SALT AND PEPPER TO TASTE

Soak the pearl barley in enough water to cover for a few hours. Soak the ceps in warm water for 20 minutes. Drain both well, reserving the mushroom soaking water, and coarsely chop the mushrooms.

Put the barley, mushrooms, garlic and shallot into a pan. Season with salt, pepper and nutmeg. Cover with water, add the mushroom soaking water and cook until the barley is tender, about 10–15 minutes.

Just before serving, taste for seasoning, then stir in the soured cream.

TUSCAN SOUP WITH SAFFRON MILK CAPS

The original Tuscan dish is made with ceps, but the addition of the saffron milk caps, with their nuttiness and colour, makes it new and interesting. Both mushrooms are freely and freshly available in autumn, but should you have only the saffron milk caps, then you can add the ubiquitous dried ceps for flavouring. In this case, increase the amount of saffron milk caps to 600g.

SERVES 4

500 G SAFFRON MILK CAPS
200 G FRESH CEPS OR 40 G DRIED
  CEPS, SOAKED IN WARM WATER
  FOR 30 MINUTES
4 GARLIC CLOVES
4 TBSP EXTRA VIRGIN OLIVE OIL
400 G TOMATO PULP (FRESH OR
  CANNED)
600 ML CHICKEN OR VEGETABLE STOCK
  (SEE PAGE 104), HOT
4 SLICES BREAD (PREFERABLY
  TUSCAN), TOASTED
6 BASIL LEAVES, TORN
60 G PARMESAN OR PECORINO
  CHEESE, FRESHLY GRATED
SALT AND PEPPER TO TASTE

Clean the fresh mushrooms thoroughly and slice them finely. Rinse the dried ceps, if using, and save their soaking water.

Chop 3 of the garlic cloves and put in a pan to fry in 2 tablespoons of the olive oil. When they start to colour (but not too much), add the tomato pulp and, if fresh, cook for 10–15 minutes (less for canned). Add the mushrooms, stock and soaking water and cook until the mushrooms are tender, about 8–10 minutes. Check for salt and pepper.

Rub the remaining garlic clove gently over each slice of toast and brush with olive oil. Add the basil to the soup and cook for 1 minute. Place the toasts in 4 deep plates and cover with soup, dividing the ingredients evenly. Add the grated cheese and serve.

Pumpkin and Cep Soup

Pumpkins and mushrooms both arrive in autumn, and this is the ideal time to make this heart-warming, USA-inspired soup. However, should you not be able to find fresh mushrooms, you could use dried ceps with fresh cultivated varieties such as blewits. The ceps recreate that inimitable 'wild' flavour. The pumpkin gives colour and a floury texture to the soup, as well as flavour, and I recommend that you serve it in the pumpkin shells for maximum effect. Scoop out the flesh to use in the soup, discarding the seeds. Keep the 'lids', and for safety, cut a tiny sliver off the base of the pumpkins so they stand upright.

Serves 6

300 G FRESH CEPS, OR 55 G DRIED CEPS
   PLUS 300 G CULTIVATED BLEWITS
6 SMALL PUMPKINS, HOLLOWED OUT
   (YOU WANT 800 G RIPE FLESH)
1 MEDIUM ONION, FINELY CHOPPED
85 G BUTTER
2 TBSP OLIVE OIL
PLAIN FLOUR FOR DUSTING
150 ML DRY WHITE WINE
CHICKEN OR VEGETABLE STOCK (SEE
   PAGE 104), AS REQUIRED
2 TBSP FINELY CHOPPED ROSEMARY
1 TSP MARJORAM LEAVES
SALT AND PEPPER TO TASTE

Clean the fresh ceps or blewits, and slice. If using, soak the dried ceps for 20 minutes in warm water, then drain, retaining the water for use another time. Cut the soaked ceps into strips. Cut the pumpkin flesh into cubes.

Fry the onion in the butter and olive oil until soft. Dust the cubes of pumpkin with flour and fry in the same fat until golden. Add the wine, stir-fry a little to evaporate the alcohol, then cover with stock and bring to the boil. If using dried ceps, add them now, otherwise add the fresh variety after 15 minutes and cook for a further 10 minutes. Press down on some of the cubes of pumpkin to 'mash' them and obtain a thick soup. Add half of the herbs and some salt and pepper. Serve in the small pumpkins with their lids on (standing in soup plates for safety) and sprinkle over the rest of the herbs.

Holstein Mushroom Soup

I lived in this part of Germany for a while and I had the impression that almost every dish contained either butter, double cream or both. The following thick soup is no exception, and I admit it is not a light dish, but as with German tradition, lightness is replaced with 'Schmackhaft' – which means it is very tasty indeed.

Serves 4

1 KG BAY BOLETES
55 G BUTTER
2 TBSP FINELY CHOPPED SPRING ONION
125 ML CHICKEN OR VEGETABLE STOCK
   (SEE PAGE 104)
1 TBSP MARJORAM OR THYME LEAVES
1 TBSP FINELY CHOPPED PARSLEY
4 TBSP DOUBLE CREAM
JUICE OF $\frac{1}{2}$ LEMON
SALT AND PEPPER TO TASTE

Clean and chop the mushrooms.

Put the butter in a pan with the spring onion and leave to sweat. Add the mushrooms and continue to sweat for 10 minutes. Add the stock and cook for 5 more minutes.

Add the herbs and cream and warm gently. Transfer to a blender or food processor and process to a coarse texture (and, of course, you can add more stock if you want the soup to be more liquid). Season to taste and add the lemon juice. Serve immediately with toasted bread.

Mushroom and Bean soup

Some of my most interesting recipes evolve when I experiment with ingredients. One sunny, late autumn day, I was picking some mature runner beans, which were almost shrivelled, but the beans inside the pods were so large and such a wonderful colour that I wanted to cook them straightaway. They would be delicious in a soup, I thought, so my companions and I collected some wild mushrooms as well. The result was very tasty, and was swiftly devoured by all of us. You can use any other type of bean, and in an emergency you could even use frozen ones.

Serves 4

500 g mixed late summer beans, podded
200 g mixed fresh mushrooms
20 g dried ceps
1 large onion, finely chopped
6 tbsp olive oil
1 hot fresh chilli, sliced
1.5 litres chicken or vegetable stock (see page 104)
salt and pepper to taste

Wash the beans and clean the fresh mushrooms as appropriate. Soak the dried mushrooms in warm water for about 20 minutes. Drain well, reserving the water. Fry the onion in the olive oil until transparent, then add the chilli and drained, dried ceps. Add the beans and cover with stock. Bring to the boil, reduce the heat and simmer for about 20 minutes or until the beans are soft. Now add the fresh mushrooms, either sliced or whole, and cook for a further 10 minutes. Add salt and pepper to taste and serve immediately with slices of toasted Pugliese bread rubbed with garlic and drizzled with extra virgin olive oil.

Hot Thai Soup of Oyster Mushrooms and Prawns

The herbs and aromas of Thailand are very intense indeed. At home I like to accompany this soup with a dish of plain boiled rice: I slightly dip a spoonful of rice into the soup to collect just enough of the wonderful liquid to flavour the rice. This may be not what Thai etiquette requires, but it gives me great satisfaction!

SERVES 4

200 G CULTIVATED YELLOW OYSTER
  MUSHROOMS
20 MEDIUM RAW PRAWNS
2 TBSP CORN OIL
800 ML WATER
4 LIME LEAVES
2 LEMONGRASS STALKS
A FEW LEAVES OF THAI BASIL
1 GARLIC CLOVE
1 TBSP CHILLI OIL
4 SMALL FRESH RED CHILLIES
SALT TO TASTE

Trim the oyster mushrooms and cut into small pieces. Shell the prawns, keeping the shells, and set the prawns aside.

Fry the prawn shells in a casserole in the corn oil until crisp, then add a little of the water. With a pestle, crush the shells to release all the juices. Add the rest of the water and the lime leaves, lemongrass, basil and garlic. Bring to the boil, reduce the heat, cover and simmer for about 10 minutes. Sieve and discard the shells and other ingredients.

Put the prawn stock into a pan and add the mushrooms, shelled prawns and chilli oil. Season with salt to taste. Bring to the boil and cook for 3–4 minutes. Serve in bowls with a whole red chilli on top of each.

Nameko and Miso Soup

Probably the best-known Japanese soup in the West, miso can also be found ready-made in supermarkets. This, according to Miho, my Japanese friend, is a nonsense because at best the subtlety of miso can be felt and tasted only if you add it at the end. Such bastardisation of ethnic food takes place in the West and East to the same degree, in the name of business, unfortunately diluting the culture. The nameko mushroom is essential to this soup, but don't worry, it is available cultivated.

SERVES 4

100 G NAMEKO MUSHROOMS
800 ML JAPANESE STOCK OR DASHI
  (SEE PAGE 115)
100 G FIRM TOFU, CUT INTO
  SMALL CUBES
60 G RED MISO (A THICK BEAN OR
  CEREAL PASTE)
A LITTLE MITSUBA (A GREEN STEM,
  RATHER LIKE FLAT-LEAF PARSLEY),
  OR ANY FRESH GREEN HERB CUT
  IN BATONS

Clean the mushrooms. Bring the stock or dashi to the boil. Add the mushrooms and tofu and cook for 1–2 minutes.

Meanwhile, in a small bowl dissolve the miso in a small amount of the hot stock. Add the dissolved miso to the soup, and serve garnished with mitsuba.

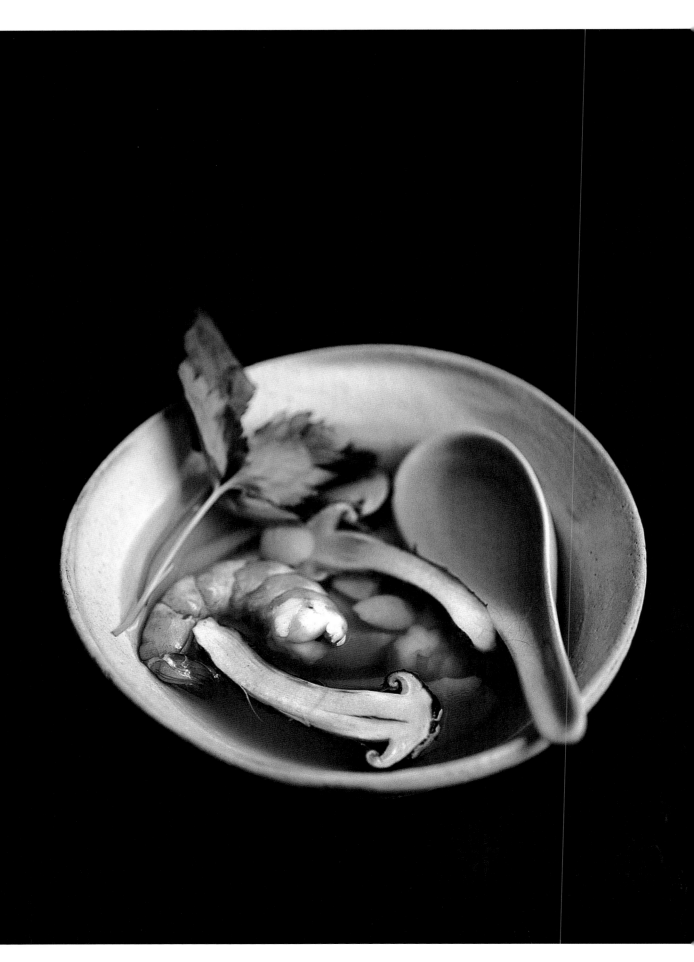

Matsutake Soup

For this recipe I had the vital help of Miho Uchida and her husband, Michiya, a Japanese couple living in London. Miho helped me get to know a great deal more about Japanese food, my knowledge previously being limited to sushi, sashimi and tempura. (I find it fascinating to discover details of other food cultures, which have been enjoyed for centuries.) They helped me even more when Michiya came back from Japan. He had been instructed to bring back some fresh matsutake, which were used in this recipe and are in the photograph. You can get all the ingredients from a Japanese food shop.

SERVES 4

4–6 MATSUTAKE MUSHROOMS
$1/2$ TSP SOY SAUCE
1 TSP SAKÉ (RICE WINE)
A FEW DROPS OF LIME JUICE (OR JAPANESE CITRON)
125 G SKINNED CHICKEN BREAST, CUT INTO SLIVERS
4 MEDIUM RAW PRAWNS, WHOLE BUT SHELLED
12 GINGKO NUTS, SHELLED
SALT
SOME FRESH MITSUBA (A GREEN STEM, RATHER LIKE FLAT-LEAF PARSLEY), OR SMALL SLIVERS OF CELERY STICK

JAPANESE STOCK (DASHI)
900 ML WATER
15 CM PIECE OF KOMBU (DRIED SEAWEED)
30 G DRIED BONITO (KATSUOBUSHI), FLAKED

Cut the mushrooms into slivers lengthways after cleaning and cutting the hard tip off the stem. Set aside.

For the stock, or dashi, heat the water in a pan over a low heat and add the kombu. When you see bubbles, add the bonito flakes. Just before the water boils, take the kombu out. Boil for 2 minutes and turn off the heat. Wait for the bonito to go to the base of the pan and discard by straining. This is a basic Japanese stock.

Add the soy sauce, saké, lime juice and a pinch of salt to the stock. Add the chicken, mushrooms and prawns and cook for 5 minutes.

Serve the soup in earthenware bowls. Add 3 gingko nuts to each bowl, and garnish with mitsuba or celery.

GAME CONSOMMÉ WITH MORELS

When morels are in season in springtime, there is still some feathered game – pheasant, grouse, partridge and pigeon – available. You can also use dried morels if it is not possible to find fresh ones, for example if you want to make this dish during the autumn game season.

SERVES 4

200 G FRESH MORELS, OR 55 G DRIED
1 SMALL PHEASANT, CLEANED
1 BOUQUET GARNI (BAY, PARSLEY, THYME)
1 CELERY STICK, FINELY CHOPPED
1 SHALLOT, FINELY SLICED
1 CARROT, FINELY CHOPPED
CHICKEN STOCK (SEE PAGE 104) OR WATER
75 ML PORT
50 ML CRÈME FRAÎCHE
1 TBSP FINELY CHOPPED CHIVES
SALT AND PEPPER TO TASTE

Clean the fresh morels carefully, or soak the dried morels in warm water for 20 minutes.

Put the pheasant into a pan with the bouquet garni, celery, shallot, carrot and some salt and pepper. Cover the pheasant with stock (or water), put the lid on and simmer for 1 hour.

Add the soaked dried morels or the fresh morels, and simmer for a further 30 minutes.

Drain everything through a fine sieve, reserving the morels, and season the consommé to taste. Add the port and warm the consommé through.

Add the crème fraîche and chives, and serve immediately with a portion of morels in each bowl.

CREAM OF CEP SOUP

It may seem extravagant to use such treasures as ceps in a soup, but it is undeniably one of the most delicious soups I have ever made. You can use them fresh – the best are the mature ones, which have a fuller flavour – or you can use them after freezing. They actually keep so well with freezing that they can be sautéed when required, but you can also just add the slices frozen to the boiling stock. If you can't find ceps, use cultivated button mushrooms as a base and for texture, with dried ceps to enhance the flavour.

SERVES 4

500 G FRESH CEPS, OR THE SAME AMOUNT OF BUTTON MUSHROOMS, PLUS 25 G DRIED CEPS
1 MEDIUM ONION, FINELY CHOPPED
4 TBSP OLIVE OIL
1.2 LITRES BEEF STOCK (SEE PAGE 104)
4 TBSP DOUBLE CREAM
SALT AND PEPPER TO TASTE

CROÛTONS
2 SLICES WHITE BREAD
25 G BUTTER

If you are using fresh ceps, clean them and cut them into pieces. Cook the onion in the oil for 3–4 minutes, then add the ceps and sauté them for 6–7 minutes. Add the stock, bring to the boil and simmer for 20 minutes.

If you are using the cultivated and dried mushrooms, soak the dried ceps in warm water for 10 minutes. Meanwhile, fry the button mushrooms together with the onion in the oil, then add the soaked ceps with their water and the stock. Simmer for about 30 minutes.

To finish either method, take the pan off the heat and blend the contents in a processor or blender. Return the soup to the pan, add the cream and some salt and pepper and heat slowly.

To make the croûtons, simply cut the bread into little cubes and fry in the butter until they are golden and crisp. Scatter the croûtons over the top of each helping.

CHAPTER TWO

LIGHT DISHES

From canapés to snacks, from antipasti to breakfasts or starters, all are united in this chapter. On the whole they are easy-to-prepare dishes, which can be enjoyed as a light meal by themselves, or as part of a meal. A couple of recipes served together would make a good lunch or supper, or you could offer a selection as a buffet, say, or as antipasti in the Italian style. The selection of light dishes also includes salads, which are increasingly in demand for their ease of preparation and health aspects. The essence of most salads is rawness – and indeed some fungi can be eaten and enjoyed raw – but you will find an interesting selection here, both raw and cooked.

By increasing the quantities of many of these dishes, they can also be eaten as a main course – especially useful for vegetarians. And of course you can increase or decrease the quantity of any of the ingredients to suit your palate. I am not offended by such a thought, and indeed, let me know about any major improvements!

THE BIG MUSHROOM SALAD

Anything can go into this salad, meaning any and all of the mushrooms you managed to collect when out picking. If you haven't enough, then you can always add some cultivated ones. The difference between this and a normal salad is that the 'vinaigrette' is cooked and the mushrooms are slightly pickled by boiling with salt and vinegar. (Some, like the honey fungus, have to be cooked before eating anyway.) The salad can also be served cold.

SERVES 4

1 KG MIXED MUSHROOMS (JUDAS' EAR, PUFFBALL, HONEY FUNGUS, AGARICS, OYSTERS, HORN OF PLENTY, ETC.), CLEANED WEIGHT
1.5 LITRES WATER
55 G SALT
500 ML WHITE WINE VINEGAR
8 TBSP OLIVE OIL
2 GARLIC CLOVES, SLICED
2 SLICES FRESH RED CHILLI
1 TBSP EACH FINELY CHOPPED PARSLEY AND CORIANDER
1 LEMON
SALT AND PEPPER TO TASTE

Clean the mushrooms as appropriate, and cut to roughly the same size.
Bring the water to the boil and add the salt and the vinegar. Add the mushrooms and cook for 10 minutes. Drain well and cool.
In a pan heat the oil, and fry the garlic and chilli to soften. Add the mushrooms, heat through, and taste for seasoning. Stir in the herbs and serve immediately, sprinkled with lemon juice.

BEEFSTEAK FUNGUS AND BEETROOT SALAD

I have experimented with beefsteak fungus for a long time, but a decent result had always eluded me. However, during the creating and testing of new recipes for this book, I came across a new way to use the 'poor man's meat' as they call it in Italy. It is actually one of the few wild mushrooms that can be eaten raw, and the combination of its acidity with the sweetness of beetroot makes, I think, for compulsive eating.

SERVES 4

200 G BEEFSTEAK FUNGUS
350 G SMALL TENDER BEETROOT, FRESHLY BOILED
EXTRA VIRGIN OLIVE OIL
2 TBSP BALSAMIC VINEGAR
2 TBSP FINELY CHOPPED CORIANDER
SALT AND PEPPER TO TASTE

TO SERVE
4 LARGE SLICES COUNTRY-STYLE BREAD, FOR BRUSCHETTA
1 GARLIC CLOVE

Clean the fungus, then cut into slices the same size as the beetroot slices will be. Skin the beetroot and slice as well.
Mix the fungus and beetroot together in a bowl with 4 tbsp of the olive oil, the balsamic vinegar, coriander and some salt and pepper to taste.
Toast the bread on both sides, then rub the garlic over each slice and brush with extra virgin olive oil.
Arrange a little of the salad on each bruschetta, or serve the salad on a plate with the bruschetta to the side.

MUSHROOM, SPINACH AND PARMA HAM SALAD

The mushroom used in this Italian recipe, Caesar's mushroom, is undoubtedly one of the prettiest and most delicate mushrooms, and it would be a sin to cook with it. Caesar's mushroom belongs to the nastiest family, the Amanitas, which includes many of the most poisonous mushrooms. But identify it well, or buy it in season from a reliable vendor, and you will enjoy a real delight.

SERVES 4

300 G CAESAR'S MUSHROOMS
250 G BABY SPINACH LEAVES
4 TBSP EXTRA VIRGIN OLIVE OIL
1 TBSP SWEET MUSTARD
2 TBSP BALSAMIC VINEGAR
SALT AND PEPPER TO TASTE
55 G PARMA HAM, SLICED 2 MM
    THICK, THEN CUT INTO STRIPS

Clean the mushrooms thoroughly, then cut them into 5mm slices. Wash the spinach well and pat dry.
Make a vinaigrette by mixing together the oil, mustard, vinegar and some salt and pepper.
Toss the spinach in the vinaigrette first, then divide between 4 plates. Garnish with the mushroom slices and strips of Parma ham. Serve accompanied by good toasted bread.

TUNA, MUSHROOMS AND BEANS

This recipe comes from the old-fashioned repertoire of many Italian restaurants over the last 30 years or so. 'Tonno e fagioli' – tuna and beans – is mostly made with tinned tuna with some canned beans included. Adding some chopped onions is usually one way of reviving the basic mixture, but I thought some mushrooms would also add flavour, especially if pickled. I would use 'ventresca di tonno', the belly, which is the most tender and best tinned tuna available. The dish is very simple to prepare.

**SERVES 4 AS A STARTER OR
2 AS A LIGHT MEAL**

1 x 180 G PICKLED MUSHROOMS
    IN OIL (SEE PAGE 102)
2 x 150 G CANS BORLOTTI BEANS
1 x 400 G CAN VENTRESCA DI TONNO
4 SPRING ONIONS, FINELY CHOPPED,
    STEM INCLUDED
3 TBSP EXTRA VIRGIN OLIVE OIL
2 TBSP BALSAMIC VINEGAR
SALT AND PEPPER TO TASTE

Drain the mushrooms from their liquid and dry slightly on a paper towel. Drain the beans and rinse them, and drain and flake the tuna.
Simply mix everything together, season with a little salt and plenty of freshly ground black pepper, and leave the flavours to penetrate for about 1 hour before eating. Serve with grissini (breadsticks).

SALAD OF CAESAR'S MUSHROOMS AND WHITE TRUFFLE

This is a marriage of wild food ingredients at the very highest level. The supreme reputation of both fungi is undisputed, and they are two of the most delicate and delicious foods in the world. I always say that this Italian dish is for gourmets and kings – and (truffle-hunting) pigs.

SERVES 4

400 G CAESAR'S MUSHROOMS, IF POSSIBLE STILL CLOSED AND YOUNG
30 G FRESH WHITE TRUFFLE
4 TBSP EXTRA VIRGIN OLIVE OIL
2 TBSP LEMON JUICE
1 TBSP VERY FINELY CHOPPED PARSLEY
40 G PARMESAN, FRESHLY SHAVED
SALT AND PEPPER TO TASTE

Clean and finely slice the mushrooms. Clean the truffle carefully.
Mix the oil with the lemon juice, parsley and some salt and pepper.
Arrange the mushroom slices on a large flat plate, sprinkle with Parmesan shavings first, then drizzle over the vinaigrette. Shave a little of the truffle over each plate. Serve with toasted bread.

SHELLFISH AND HEN OF THE WOODS SALAD

In summer you want to eat just a small amount of delicate food to combat the heat. This salad is perfect for that purpose, accompanied by some toasted bread and shared with a friend or two, perhaps in the garden, with a glass of crisp, chilled white wine. You could also use chicken of the woods or beefsteak fungus instead of the hen of the woods.

SERVES 4

500 G HEN OF THE WOODS FUNGUS
100 ML WHITE WINE VINEGAR
100 ML WATER
150 G RAW PRAWNS, NOT TOO LARGE
4–8 FRESH SCALLOPS IN SHELL
100 G COOKED CRABMEAT
6 TBSP EXTRA VIRGIN OLIVE OIL
1 TBSP EACH OF COARSELY CHOPPED CORIANDER, PARSLEY AND DILL
JUICE OF 1 LEMON
SALT AND PEPPER TO TASTE

Clean the mushrooms, separate into lobes, then cook in the vinegar and water with some salt for 2–3 minutes. Drain and cool. Shell the prawns, then cook briefly in some fresh boiling water, about 4–5 minutes. Shell the scallops (or get your fishmonger to do this for you), then cut into slices. Make sure that there are no pieces of shell in the crabmeat.
Prepare a vinaigrette with the olive oil, herbs and lemon juice, and season with salt and pepper. Marinate the scallops in the vinaigrette for 10 minutes.
Mix the fungus with the prawns and crabmeat. Add the scallops with their marinade, and mix. Adjust the seasoning, and serve the salad at room temperature.

Saint George's Mushrooms with Scrambled Egg and Wild Garlic

The 23rd April, St George's Day in Britain, marks the start of the mushroom season, and this is when this dirty white mushroom usually appears. It is deliciously delicate in flavour. Wild garlic appears in the same season (but if you can't get hold of it, use another soft herb generously).

SERVES 4

400 G ST GEORGE'S MUSHROOMS,
  CLEANED WEIGHT
55 G BUTTER
12 EGGS, BEATEN
55 G PARMESAN, FRESHLY GRATED
2 TBSP COARSELY CHOPPED WILD
  GARLIC
SALT AND PEPPER TO TASTE

If the mushrooms are large, then cut in two. Sauté them in half the butter until they start to brown at the edges. Season to taste, then set them aside, keeping them warm.

In a non-stick pan, melt the remaining butter and when hot add the beaten eggs mixed with the Parmesan. Stir with a wooden spoon to slightly solidify the mixture, but keep it soft.

Mix the wild garlic with the warm mushrooms, and arrange on a plate.

Pour the scrambled eggs on the other side of the plate. Eat with a slice of good Italian toasted bread.

Mushroom Tortilla

Eggs 'carry' many dishes, either as a part, or as a main ingredient. The entire world has specialities using eggs, because they are so nutritious and extremely easy to handle. Frittata, tortilla and omelette, all with a multitude of flavourings, have one thing in common, 'solidified' eggs. Naturally, I had to use mushrooms in this recipe, and this Spanish version contains the Spaniards' favourite, one of the russulas.

Serves 4

300 g green-cracked russula
12 eggs, beaten
1 tbsp chopped parsley
4 tbsp grated Manchego cheese
4 tbsp extra virgin olive oil
1 large onion, very finely
    chopped
salt and pepper to taste

Clean the mushrooms and quarter them if large. Mix the eggs, parsley, cheese and some salt and pepper together in a large bowl.

Heat the oil in a 25 cm non-stick frying pan and sauté the onion for 5 or so minutes, until softened. Add the mushrooms and sauté for 7–8 minutes. Add the egg mixture to the pan and with a wooden spatula stir from time to time until the egg begins to solidify. When you notice that the egg is not liquid on the top any more, leave it to build a brown crust on the base. Take a large plate and, taking care not to burn yourself, cover the pan with the plate and turn it upside down. Slide the tortilla back into the pan on its soft side and cook for a few more minutes until solid.

The tortilla may also be eaten cold, but I prefer it hot with good fresh bread.

Truffle Hunter's Breakfast

Truffle hunters are a breed of their own, having to get up very early in the morning or even when it is still dark, to avoid being seen by competitors! Their patches of ground are contested very fiercely, because the truffles command an extremely high price. If the hunters have to go far from their homes, they take with them a gas burner, a pan, a little butter, eggs and fresh bread. They can then have breakfast in the woods with some of their bounty.

The ingredients here are for one person only, as truffle hunters are loners, but you can multiply the amounts by as many as you want to feed.

Serves 1

as much truffle as you can
    afford
20 g butter
2–3 eggs
fresh crusty bread
salt and pepper to taste

Clean the truffle well before cutting or shaving.

Melt the butter in a pan, add the eggs and stir gently with a spoon to scramble. When still soft, add some salt and pepper to taste. Next add shavings of black truffle or, if you are very lucky, white truffle, and eat with the bread.

Nothing could be more delicious, especially when you are hungry after several hours' hunting. The truffle dog gets to eat the last piece of bread with which the pan is cleaned!

MORELS STUFFED WITH FOIE GRAS

This French dish is for grand occasions and is extremely opulent – just don't think about how many calories it contains! Morels are one of the few hollow mushrooms destined to be stuffed. The recipe inevitably works much better with large, fresh morels, but it is possible to use large dried ones.

I dedicate this recipe to the composer Rossini, who I'm sure would have loved this rich dish.

SERVES 4
(3 MORELS EACH AS A STARTER)

12 VERY LARGE MORELS, CLEANED
55 G BUTTER
4 TBSP CHICKEN STOCK
   (SEE PAGE 104)
2 TBSP COGNAC OR BRANDY
4 TBSP DOUBLE CREAM
1 TBSP FINELY SNIPPED CHIVES
SALT AND PEPPER TO TASTE

STUFFING
2 EGGS, BEATEN
100 G FRESH BREADCRUMBS
1 TBSP FINELY CHOPPED
   FLAT-LEAF PARSLEY
85 G PÂTÉ DE FOIE GRAS, CUT INTO
   CUBES

Cut the stem of the morels almost at the base, just leaving the hole to be stuffed. For the stuffing, mix the eggs with the breadcrumbs, parsley and some salt and pepper to obtain a smooth paste. Fill the mushroom cavities with small cubes of foie gras, then add a little of the breadcrumb mixture, remembering to leave some space as the filling expands during cooking.

Melt the butter in a frying pan and fry the stuffed morels gently, stuffed side first, then the other side, for 3–4 minutes. Add the stock and Cognac and cook for a further 5 minutes. Stir in the cream and some salt and pepper and cook for 1 minute more before finally adding the chives. Serve the morels hot with the sauce, accompanied by freshly toasted baguette slices.

RIGHT FRESH MORELS

ENOKI BUNDLES

This very nice idea – worked out with my Japanese friend, Miho – uses one of the prettiest cultivated mushrooms, the enoki. The recipe is very simple and can be made anywhere because of the general availability of the ingredients.

SERVES 4

4 x 100G PACKETS ENOKI MUSHROOMS, DIVIDED INTO 8 BUNCHES
8 THICK SLICES PARMA HAM (OR SMOKED SALMON)
4 TBSP OLIVE OIL
JUICE OF 2 LIMES
SALT AND PEPPER TO TASTE

Trim the base of the tight little mushroom bunches.
Wrap around each bunch a slice of Parma ham (or smoked salmon), and fix with a wooden cocktail stick. Sprinkle the enoki with a little salt and abundant pepper, followed by the olive oil and lime juice, and serve.

GRILLED MATSUTAKE

This is another recipe worked out with my Japanese friend Miho. When I asked her about the principles of Japanese food, she said the most important aspect was the freshness of the ingredients (although various dried items are used mainly for flavour), followed by presentation and the look of the dish, followed by taste, flavour and, but no less important, texture.

This is possibly the simplest of all the recipes, although it has a great deal of sophistication. Naturally you start by getting hold of the matsutake, the wild variety of which costs about £500 per kilo! (Even the cultivated are quite expensive.) But the rest of the ingredients are very cheap!

SERVES 4

8 OR MORE MATSUTAKE MUSHROOMS, DEPENDING ON SIZE
2 TBSP SOY SAUCE
JUICE OF 1 LEMON

Preheat a grill or barbecue. Wipe any dust off the matsutake. Clean with kitchen paper. Do not use water because this washes away aroma and flavour. Cut the hard tip off the stem. Tear each mushroom into 2–4 pieces, depending on size, starting from the stem, which will split up to the cap, leaving a sort of network of tender filaments.
Grill on each side for 1–2 minutes. Either sprinkle with a 'vinaigrette' made from the soy and lemon juice, or dip the mushrooms into a bowl containing the liquid. It's that simple.

NOTE I have tried to use other mushrooms in a similar way, but it seems that this is the only one to have this special filament structure.

ORIENTAL MUSHROOMS IN ASPIC

This recipe from Miho, my Japanese friend, is excellent. I laughed a lot when she insisted on using 'Western stock' – chicken stock cubes! Mushrooms in aspic look attractive, are practical to serve, and delicious to eat.

SERVES 4

600 G MIXED MUSHROOMS (MAITAKE, BUNA-SHIMEJI, ENOKI, SHIITAKE AND BUTTON)
1 GARLIC CLOVE, FINELY CHOPPED
1 TSP CORN OIL OR OLIVE OIL
3 TSP WHITE WINE
1/2 TSP LEMON JUICE
2 TBSP POWDERED GELATINE, DISSOLVED IN 125 ML 'WESTERN STOCK'
SALT AND PEPPER TO TASTE

TO SERVE
A HANDFUL OF SALAD LEAVES
8 CHERRY TOMATOES, HALVED
VINAIGRETTE (MADE OF 1 TBSP RICE VINEGAR, 3 TBSP SUNFLOWER OIL AND 1 TSP FRENCH MUSTARD)

Trim and wipe the mushrooms as appropriate, then slice the maitake, shiitake and button mushrooms.

Sauté the chopped garlic in the oil in a pan, then add the sliced maitake, shiitake and button mushrooms, and the trimmed buna-shimeji and enoki. Sauté over a high heat for a minute or two, then add some salt and pepper. Add the white wine and lemon juice, bring to a brisk boil, then turn off the heat. Add the dissolved gelatine and mix well.

Pour into a terrine or similar container, and leave to cool. Put in the fridge and leave to set for a couple of hours. Turn the dish upside down and turn out onto a platter. Cut into regular slices with a very sharp knife. Serve with the salad leaves and halved tomatoes sprinkled with the vinaigrette.

STUFFED SHIITAKE

This Japanese recipe also represents Chinese cooking because the shiitake mushroom, so popular now and available in every supermarket, is very commonly used in both countries (and indeed, increasingly, in the rest of the world). The recipe was suggested by my Japanese friend, Miho.

SERVES 4

12 MEDIUM-SIZED FRESH SHIITAKE
A LITTLE PLAIN FLOUR
300 G BONED CHICKEN MEAT, MINCED
150 G SHELLED RAW PRAWNS, MINCED
3 SPRING ONIONS, FINELY CHOPPED
1 TSP VERY FINELY CHOPPED ROOT GINGER
2 TBSP SAKÉ (RICE WINE)
1 TBSP SOY SAUCE
OLIVE OIL
SALT TO TASTE

SAUCE
4 TBSP SOY SAUCE
2 TBSP MIRIN (SWEETENED RICE WINE)
1 TBSP CASTER SUGAR
1 TBSP SAKÉ (RICE WINE)

Clean the shiitake well and discard the stems.

Dust the inner part of the shiitake with the flour. Mix together the chicken, prawns, spring onion, ginger, saké, soy sauce and a pinch of salt. Use a little to fill the cavity of each mushroom. Fry the stuffed mushrooms gently for 5 minutes on each side in a little olive oil, covered. Uncover and add the ingredients for the sauce. Let them heat through and evaporate a little. Serve 3 mushrooms per person, with a little sauce on each one.

EAST–WEST BRUSCHETTA

With great reluctance I accept the idea of 'fusing' ingredients from totally alien culinary cultures for the purposes of research. Very often these fusions are made for fashion or food snobbism, without complying to the rules of good taste and flavour. But here the combination of two totally different fungi, one from the East, the other from the West, makes for a light and simple, but sophisticated dish. I used the cheaper summer truffle to limit the cost, but if money is no object then you can use either Périgord or Alba truffles.

SERVES 4

2 SUMMER TRUFFLES OF ABOUT
  30 G EACH
2 x 100 G PACKETS ENOKI MUSHROOMS
4 SLICES GOOD ITALIAN BREAD FOR
  BRUSCHETTA
1 GARLIC CLOVE
JUICE OF 1 LIME
EXTRA VIRGIN OLIVE OIL
1 TSP VERY FINELY CHOPPED PARSLEY
SALT AND PEPPER TO TASTE

Clean the truffles very well and cut into thin slices, but not too thin. Cut the bases off the stalks of the enoki mushrooms

Toast the bread until it is brown and crisp on both sides and rub very gently with the garlic. Brush with oil and divide between 4 plates.

In a bowl, mix the lime juice and 2 tablespoons of the olive oil with the parsley and some salt and pepper. Mix well with the mushrooms and divide between the slices of toast. Serve as a salad or first course.

BAKED MUSHROOM BRUSCHETTA OR TOAST

Bruschetta or toast? That is the question! Whichever, this dish is a welcome snack when you feel peckish. You will need large slices of Italian country bread, toasted, or if you want to call it toast, then use sliced bread. Either way, it is delicious. You can use any mushrooms you have to hand, but a good mixture would be hedgehog fungus, giant polypore, parasols and larch boletes.

MAKES 4

300 G MUSHROOMS OF CHOICE
55 G BUTTER
4 TBSP OLIVE OIL
1 GARLIC CLOVE, FINELY CHOPPED
1 SMALL FRESH RED CHILLI, FINELY
  CHOPPED
JUICE OF $1/2$ LEMON
1 TBSP FINELY CHOPPED PARSLEY
6 TBSP DOUBLE CREAM
4 LARGE SLICES ITALIAN COUNTRY
  BREAD, TOASTED ON BOTH SIDES
100 G TALEGGIO OR MOZZARELLA
  CHEESE, CUT INTO CHUNKS
55 G FRESH BREADCRUMBS
SALT AND PEPPER TO TASTE

Preheat the oven to 230°C/Gas 8, or preheat the grill. Clean and trim the mushrooms as appropriate, and cut the larger ones into pieces if necessary. Sauté the mushrooms in the butter and oil, with the garlic and chilli, until slightly softened. Add the lemon juice and parsley and stir briefly. Add the double cream, and cook for about 10 minutes, or until the mushrooms are tender. Season to taste. Top each slice of toast with some of the mixture and dot with cheese. Sprinkle with the breadcrumbs and bake for 5 minutes in the preheated oven or put under the grill, until the cheese is bubbling. Serve immediately.

MINI BRIOCHES WITH TRUFFLE

I ate these mini brioches at a bar in Florence, where they were filled with truffle butter and a slice of fresh truffle. They make very elegant and sophisticated 'stuzzichini' (appetisers), especially when served before dinner with a glass of good champagne.

SERVES 4

12 MINI BRIOCHES
40 G SOFT BUTTER, MIXED WITH
  1 TBSP TRUFFLE OIL
1 SMALL ALBA TRUFFLE, CUT INTO
  12 THIN SLICES
SALT AND PEPPER TO TASTE

Slice the mini brioches in half, and spread one half of each with the truffle-flavoured butter. Place a truffle slice on top of the butter. Sprinkle with salt and pepper, then replace the top – and enjoy.

WILD MUSHROOM CROSTINI

This Italian dish is extremely popular because of its versatility: it can be served as a snack or antipasto, or with drinks. Crostini can be topped with chicken liver pâté, a mixture of tomato, mozzarella and basil, or grilled vegetables. This version using wild mushrooms is exceptionally good – even if you can't get hold of any wild mushrooms and have to use cultivated instead. For the photograph we used chicken of the woods, horn of plenty, brown caps or chestnut mushrooms and oyster mushrooms.

SERVES 4

400 G MIXED WILD MUSHROOMS
 (WHATEVER YOU CAN GET)
2 GARLIC CLOVES, 1 FINELY CHOPPED
1 SMALL FRESH RED CHILLI, FINELY
 CHOPPED
8 TBSP OLIVE OIL
1 TBSP COARSELY CHOPPED PARSLEY
1 TBSP MARJORAM LEAVES
 (TO REPLACE THE NEPITELLA OR
 WILD MINT USED IN TUSCANY)
4 LARGE SLICES PUGLIESE BREAD
SALT AND PEPPER TO TASTE

Clean the mushrooms thoroughly and cut them all into cubes.
Fry the finely chopped garlic and chilli in 6 tablespoons of the olive oil, and before the garlic starts to colour, add the mushrooms. Sauté or stir-fry them briefly for a few minutes only so that they retain their crisp texture. Add the parsley, marjoram and some salt and pepper.
Meanwhile, toast the slices of bread on both sides, then rub them very slightly with the whole garlic clove. Brush with the remaining olive oil and top with the mushrooms. Serve immediately.

FRIED PARASOL MUSHROOMS

Some wild mushrooms can grow so huge that one cap alone can be a meal in itself, or sometimes can even feed two or three people. The parasol is one such mushroom. The cap and the thick but tender gills underneath form a round, flat and substantial whole, just asking to be dipped in beaten egg and breadcrumbs, then shallow-fried until golden. The finished result – an Italian idea – looks like an omelette, and can easily cover your plate. Good fresh bread and a fresh green salad are all that you need for a delicious late-summer snack.

SERVES 4

4 PARASOL MUSHROOM CAPS, EACH
 ABOUT 15 CM IN DIAMETER
3 EGGS
2 TBSP VERY FINELY CHOPPED
 PARSLEY
2 TBSP FRESHLY GRATED PARMESAN
FRESH WHITE BREADCRUMBS FOR
 COATING
OLIVE OIL FOR SHALLOW-FRYING
SALT AND PEPPER TO TASTE

Clean the parasol caps, using a damp cloth to remove any dust from the top, but without washing them. Inspect the gills to check that no 'tenants' are present.
Beat the eggs and mix in the parsley, Parmesan and some salt and pepper. Dip the parasol caps in this mixture first and then into the breadcrumbs, making sure the whole of the cap is covered. Chill to allow the coating to 'set'.
Heat the oil and gently immerse the mushrooms (you'll probably have to do one at a time, if they are really large). Fry each cap over a moderate heat until golden on both sides.

Rösti with King Stropharia

The idea for this recipe came to me in India, where I saw a woman carrying a flat wicker basket on her head, full of freshly fried food. Using my highly developed culinary imagination (!), I substituted the basket with a Swiss potato rösti and covered this with sautéed fresh mushrooms. It is a wonderful 'piatto unico', a complete dish based on potatoes and fungi. Other mushrooms you could use are honey fungus, buna-shimeji, or hen of the woods.

Serves 4

600 g king stropharia mushrooms
6 tbsp olive oil
2 garlic cloves, finely chopped
2 tbsp finely chopped spring
    onion
1 small medium-hot fresh red
    chilli, finely chopped
2 tbsp chopped coriander leaves
salt and pepper to taste

Rösti baskets
1 kg waxy potatoes, peeled and
    cut into matchsticks
55 g fresh root ginger, cut into
    matchsticks
vegetable oil for frying
2 tbsp lemon juice

First of all, clean the mushrooms, and cut in two if large.

For the rösti, mix the potato and ginger sticks evenly, and divide the mixture into 4. Heat some of the oil in a 20 cm pan, and add one pile of the rösti mixture. Pat down to make a round just slightly smaller than the diameter of the pan, and fry until the potatoes stick together and are cooked and brown on one side. Turn over by covering the pan with a plate and inverting the rösti on to it. Slide back into the pan and cook the other side. Repeat to make 4 röstis. Keep them warm.

Meanwhile, in another frying pan, fry the mushrooms in the olive oil for 5 minutes. Add the garlic, spring onion, chilli and half the coriander. Stir-fry for a few more minutes, then season to taste.

Sprinkle the lemon juice over the röstis just before topping with the mushrooms, and the remaining coriander.

Potatoes and Ceps

An excellent combination of two natural ingredients, which are almost made for each other. As with many things in life, sometimes simplicity can most nearly approach perfection. In this Italian recipe, texture, flavour and looks blend superbly. To enhance the cep flavour, I didn't even add any garlic or onion.

Serves 4

200 g fresh ceps
600 g waxy firm potatoes
85 g butter
6 tbsp olive oil
12 sage leaves
salt and pepper to taste

Clean, trim and finely slice the ceps, and peel the potatoes. Boil the potatoes in salted water until soft. Drain and leave them to cool, then slice thickly.

Fry the cep slices in half the butter and half the oil until brown, then set aside. Fry the potatoes and two-thirds of the sage leaves in the rest of the butter and oil.

Mix the ceps and potatoes together in a large dish and season to taste. Scatter the remaining sage leaves over. Serve either as a starter or a side dish with meat or fish.

MUSHROOM DUMPLINGS

During the years I lived in Austria and Germany, I had many opportunities to appreciate the Germanic take on gnocchi. Dumplings there come in all shapes and sizes, from 'Klösse' up to 'Knödel' – and smaller ones, as here, known by the diminutive, 'Klösschen'. These little mushroom dumplings could be served by themselves, or accompanied by a tomato sauce. Saffron milk caps give the dish a good crunchiness, but you could use other firm-textured mushrooms: I once used chicken of the woods, and that worked well.

SERVES 4

DUMPLINGS
175 G WILD MUSHROOMS
2 TBSP OLIVE OIL
115 G BUTTER
3 EGGS
25 G ARROWROOT
1 TBSP FINELY CHOPPED PARSLEY
ABOUT 200 G FRESH WHITE
   BREADCRUMBS
SALT AND PEPPER TO TASTE

TOMATO SAUCE (optional)
1 X 400 G CAN PEELED PLUM
   TOMATOES
55 G BUTTER
1 GARLIC CLOVE, SLICED
2 FRESH BASIL LEAVES, TORN

If you are using saffron milk caps, first clean them, then blanch them and drain well. Otherwise, just clean and trim any other mushroom as appropriate.
Fry the mushrooms in the olive oil until tender, then leave to cool.
In a clean pan, melt the butter and let it cool. In a bowl, beat it to a smooth foam with the eggs. Mix in the arrowroot, parsley, mushrooms and some salt and pepper to taste, then add as much of the breadcrumbs as you need to obtain a stiff paste that is easily shaped with your hands. Set aside to rest for 30 minutes.
Take a little of the mixture at a time and form walnut-sized dumplings with your hands. Cook in simmering slightly salted water: they are ready when they rise to the surface, usually in 2–3 minutes. Serve as they are, or with the following tomato sauce.
For the tomato sauce, strain the tomatoes to remove the seeds, then purée them in a food processor. Put the butter and garlic in a small pan and cook until the garlic just starts to turn golden. Stir in the tomato purée and the basil, add salt and pepper to taste, and simmer for 10–15 minutes. Serve the dumplings with a little tomato sauce at the side.

Clams with Mushrooms

This recipe comes from Galicia, one of the most important culinary regions of Spain. Spaniards eat seafood with gusto and are equally enthusiastic about meat, but mushrooms are not as popular as they are in France or Italy. This curious but very tasty recipe is one I ate in a restaurant and then managed to recreate from memory.

Serves 4

500 g fresh ceps or orange
  birch boletes
1 kg Venus clams
1 medium onion, finely chopped
1 red pepper, de-seeded and
  cubed
2 garlic cloves, crushed
2 tbsp finely chopped parsley
4 tbsp olive oil
150 ml dry white wine
1 pinch powdered saffron
salt and pepper to taste

Clean the mushrooms, then coarsely chop. Clean the clams in fresh water. Discard any that are broken or that gape open.
Fry the onion, pepper, garlic and parsley in the oil in a large pan for 5 minutes over a low heat. Add the chopped mushrooms and continue to cook until soft. Add the wine and continue frying for a minute to let the alcohol evaporate. Add some salt and pepper and the saffron, and mix well. Finally add the clams, cover the pan and cook over a high heat until the clams open. Discard any that remain closed.
This can be eaten as a first course with bread.

Mushroom Vol-au-Vents

In recipes like this, I use mushrooms that I have frozen from the year before. The main reason for this is that the mushrooms have to be coarsely chopped anyway for freezing. The second reason is that you can bring back to mind the wonderful flavour of summer and autumn mushrooms at any time of the year. However, you can of course use fresh or dried wild mushrooms if you prefer.

The little puff pastry containers may be bought ready-made, and are usually used in Germany and Austria filled with a ragù of veal. Serve as a starter.

**Makes 16 small
vol-au-vents**

300 g frozen ceps or saffron
  milk caps
40 g butter
1 garlic clove, finely chopped
1 tsp plain flour
1 tbsp dry sherry vinegar
2 tbsp finely chopped parsley
6 tbsp double cream
16 small puff pastry cases
  (vol-au-vents)
salt and pepper to taste

Preheat the oven to 180°C/Gas 4. Blanch the mushrooms from frozen in slightly salted water for 3–4 minutes. Drain, pat dry and chop finely.
Heat the butter in a pan, add the garlic and cook briefly, without letting the garlic brown. Add the mushrooms and stir-fry for 5 minutes. Add the flour and then the sherry vinegar, continuing to stir, then add the parsley, double cream and salt and pepper to taste.
Meanwhile, heat the pastry cases through briefly in the preheated oven. Remove, and fill each case with the warm mixture.

MUSHROOM STRUDEL

Having lived for a couple of years in Vienna, strudel was known to me only as an excellent dessert, either filled with apples, pears or sour cherries, or with a paste of poppy seeds. The idea of making it savoury, with a mushroom filling, is perhaps not completely new in general terms, but it is for me, and here it is. To be lazy, I use bought filo pastry, but if you are a skilful maker of the original strudel pastry, feel free!

SERVES 4

1 x 200 G PACKET FILO PASTRY
55 G BUTTER, MELTED
1 EGG, BEATEN

FILLING
500 G MIXED WILD AND CULTIVATED
   MUSHROOMS, CLEANED WEIGHT
1 MEDIUM ONION, FINELY CHOPPED
40 G BUTTER
LOTS OF FRESHLY GRATED NUTMEG
1 TBSP DRY SHERRY
1 TBSP PLAIN FLOUR
LEAVES FROM 1 SPRIG MARJORAM
30 G PARMESAN, FRESHLY GRATED
SALT AND PEPPER TO TASTE

Preheat the oven to 200°C/Gas 6. Take 3 sheets of filo at a time. Brush 1 sheet on both sides with melted butter, then place it on top of another sheet with a third on top. Make 4 such piles of triple-layer filo. Cover with a damp cloth while you prepare the filling.

Make sure the mushrooms are dust- and sand-free, wash if appropriate (it rarely is) and trim if need be. Cook the onion in the butter and when soft add the mushrooms with the nutmeg. Stir-fry for 3–4 minutes. Add the sherry and evaporate the alcohol by cooking over a low heat for 2–3 minutes. Add the flour, marjoram and some salt and pepper, stir well, and leave to cool. The mixture will be moist. Grease a baking tray with butter and lay on it, one at a time, the 4 piles of filo. Brush the edges with beaten egg. Put a quarter of the mushroom mix on the centre of each and before folding them up, add the Parmesan. Brush with the beaten egg, turn so that the join is on the base, brush again, and bake in the preheated oven for 15 minutes. Serve warm.

MUSHROOM 'CAVIAR'

Alaskan cuisine is rich in ingredients like squirrel and moose, but the more easily accessible wild mushrooms are also much loved. This recipe proves that wherever you are in the world, mushrooms are used in cooking to prepare interesting and wonderful dishes. The word 'caviar' describes anything that has been reduced to a spreadable consistency to be eaten on toast or with vegetables or pancakes.

SERVES 4

300 G MIXED MUSHROOMS
   (PUFFBALLS, SHAGGY INK CAPS,
   SAFFRON MILK CAPS, CHICKEN OF
   THE WOODS)
1 ONION, FINELY CHOPPED
3 TBSP OLIVE OIL
2 TBSP FINELY CHOPPED CHIVES
JUICE OF $1/2$ LEMON
1 TBSP SOURED CREAM
SALT AND PEPPER TO TASTE

Clean and trim the mushrooms as appropriate, then chop them finely.

Fry the onion in the oil to soften, then add the finely chopped mushrooms and cook until tender, about 5–10 minutes. Add the chives, lemon juice, soured cream and some salt and pepper to taste.

Serve hot or cold on toasted bread, sliced tomatoes or potatoes, or with whatever you fancy.

GRILLED MUSHROOMS

Italians are very fond of grilling wild mushrooms, especially the caps of ceps and slices of puffball. Don't throw away the unused stems – use them for a duxelles (see page 105). Large puffballs look like and taste like steak – ideal for vegetarians. Eat as a starter, or as a side dish for a grilled steak. In Tuscany, they would use nepitella, a wild mint, instead of the parsley and thyme.

SERVES 4

4 YOUNG BUT LARGE FRESH CEP CAPS
   (WITH PORES STILL CREAMY)
4 SLICES PUFFBALL,
   ABOUT 2 CM THICK
4 TBSP OLIVE OIL
1 TBSP VERY FINELY CHOPPED
   PARSLEY
1 TSP THYME LEAVES
1 LARGE GARLIC CLOVE, VERY FINELY
   CHOPPED
JUICE OF $^1/_2$ LEMON
SALT AND PEPPER TO TASTE

Clean the mushrooms well and slice. Preheat the grill – an overhead one – the barbecue, or a cast-iron griddle. Mix the oil, parsley, thyme, garlic and lemon juice, and brush this all over the mushroom caps and puffball slices. Grill for a minute or so on each side. Season with salt and pepper and serve immediately.
You can also use parasol, Caesar's mushrooms or chicken of the woods for this recipe.

MUSHROOMS AND SAUERKRAUT

The recipes I create or re-create usually come to me through someone explaining them to me, or from ideas picked up when I am eating out. A Russian friend was telling me about this typical combination of mushrooms and cabbage, and here is the result, which I like very much. Meaty mushrooms are best for this recipe, especially boletes.

SERVES 4–6

200 G FRESH CEPS
200 G ORANGE BIRCH BOLETES
BUTTER
3 TBSP OLIVE OIL
1 ONION, SLICED
2 MEDIUM SWEET-SOUR PICKLED
   CUCUMBERS, SLICED
800 G SAUERKRAUT, FROM A JAR
1 TSP CASTER SUGAR
2 TBSP TOMATO PURÉE
1 TSP JUNIPER BERRIES
$^1/_2$ TSP BLACK PEPPERCORNS
2 TBSP FRESH BREADCRUMBS
SALT AND PEPPER TO TASTE

Clean the mushrooms as appropriate, then slice. Heat 40 g of the butter in a casserole dish with the oil. Add the onion and cook until soft. Add the mushrooms and fry gently for 8–10 minutes. Leave to cool, then add the cucumber and season. Place the drained sauerkraut in a separate pan with 20 g of the butter and a little water, and cook for 40–50 minutes. Add the sugar, tomato purée, juniper berries and peppercorns and cook for another 10 minutes.
Meanwhile, heat the oven to 200°C / Gas 6. Spread a layer of sauerkraut on the bottom of a casserole dish, then put the cooked mushrooms on top. Cover with another layer of sauerkraut and dot with a little butter. Sprinkle over the breadcrumbs and dot with some more butter. Bake in the preheated oven for 15 minutes. Serve with boiled potatoes. As an option, you could also add some bacon or speck to the sauerkraut. And if you would like it richer, then add 6 tablespoons double cream before baking.

RIGHT YOU CAN USE A 'BRUSH' MADE FROM A BUNDLE OF THYME TO BRUSH MUSHROOMS WITH THE OIL MIXTURE BEFORE GRILLING

SMOKED BREAST OF DUCK WITH PRESERVED MUSHROOMS

More than a recipe, this is an assemblage of preserved fungi and meats which in Italy works very well as an antipasto. The task of an appetiser is to titillate the stomach, possibly with something vinegary – which preserved mushrooms are, even though they're kept under oil. The exercise is also to offer to the guests the very best of the autumn harvest, particularly when the harvest was abundant (for it is always wonderful to eat later in the year what you preserved and kept so religiously). You could have pickled ceps or honey fungus, or some cultivated mushrooms, or a mixture. And you can use smoked goose, smoked wild boar or simply speck instead of the duck.

SERVES 4

350 G SMOKED DUCK BREAST,
   THINLY SLICED
300 G PICKLED MUSHROOMS
   IN OIL (SEE PAGE 102)
4–8 SPRIGS PARSLEY

Spread the thinly sliced duck in the middle of a large platter. Surround it with the mushrooms, draining off most of the oil in which they have been kept. Garnish with parsley and serve as an antipasto either with grissini (breadsticks) or good toasted bread.

DUCK LIVER PÂTÉ

I proudly claim this recipe as mine, but it owes a great deal to the inspiration of Santiago Gonzales, who was chef at my restaurant for some 16 years, and a master in the preparation of foie gras. I make no apologies for including it, as it is basic, easy to make and quite delicious – especially if you use the truffle.

SERVES 4

1 X 25 G BLACK TRUFFLE (SUMMER
   OR WINTER)
85 G PORK FAT, CHOPPED
1 SMALL ONION, CHOPPED
4 GARLIC CLOVES, CHOPPED
500 G CLEANED DUCK LIVERS,
   COARSELY CHOPPED
2 BAY LEAVES
1 SPRIG ROSEMARY
75 ML EACH BRANDY AND DRY
   SHERRY
60 G BUTTER
SALT AND PEPPER TO TASTE
A LITTLE ASPIC FOR
   GARNISH (OPTIONAL)

Preheat the oven to 180°C/Gas 4. Clean the truffle carefully.
Put the pork fat in a pan and stir-fry for 3–4 minutes before adding the onion and stir-frying until it is transparent. Add the garlic, chopped livers, bay leaves and rosemary, and continue to stir-fry for another 5 minutes over a moderate heat. Add some salt and pepper and the spirits. Let the alcohol evaporate for a minute, then add the butter and set aside to cool a little.
Remove and discard the bay leaves and rosemary. Put the mixture through a blender if you want it a little smoother, but it should still have some texture. Put into a terrine dish and press the truffle into the mixture so that it is just under the surface. Put the terrine in a bain-marie (a large tray containing 2.5 cm of water) and bake in the preheated oven for 1 hour. Take out and leave to cool. Cut into slices, and if you want to decorate it for a cold buffet, you could garnish the slices with some aspic cut into little cubes.

Caponata of Mushrooms

This typical Sicilian dish is the epitome of all that is fresh in that part of the world, where it is often served with the added Arabic touch of raisins and pine kernels. This variation of mine – inevitably to accommodate mushrooms – looks at first glance to be a little artificial. The end result is, however, a side dish that complements anything, and it's also good by itself as a light dish.

SERVES 4

300 G MIXED FUNGI
2 LARGE AUBERGINES, CUT INTO
   LARGE CUBES
8 TBSP OLIVE OIL
1 FRESH HOT RED CHILLI, SLICED
8 GARLIC CLOVES, SLICED
2 TBSP WHITE WINE VINEGAR
3 TBSP FINELY CHOPPED CELERY
   LEAVES
2 TBSP FINELY CHOPPED PARSLEY
1 TSP CASTER SUGAR
SALT AND PEPPER TO TASTE

Clean the mushrooms thoroughly, and if large, cut to an appropriate size. Aubergine will absorb quite a lot of oil, so to avoid that, first dip the cubes in water, then pat dry. Fry them in the oil until brown on each side, drain well and set aside.

Fry the chilli and garlic in the same pan for 1–2 minutes, then add the mushrooms. Stir-fry for a few minutes, then add the aubergine, vinegar, celery leaves, parsley and sugar, and cook everything slowly together for 10 minutes. Add salt and pepper to taste.

Serve with toast, as a light dish, or to accompany main dishes of meat or fish.

Braised Ceps

When you want to write about the real thing, the best way is to ask a native, so I spoke to a good French friend of mine, Nello Renault, on the telephone. This recipe is the result of that conversation. I have also achieved good results with this recipe by using brown cap or chestnut mushrooms with the addition of some dried ceps, which I had soaked then chopped finely. I also added some of the soaking water to the stock for flavour.

SERVES 4

300 G FRESH FIRM CEPS
2 SHALLOTS, FINELY CHOPPED
1 ONION, FINELY CHOPPED
4 TBSP OLIVE OIL
30 G BUTTER
1 TBSP PLAIN FLOUR
150 ML WHITE BORDEAUX WINE
1 LITRE CHICKEN STOCK
   (SEE PAGE 104)
2 TBSP FINELY CHOPPED PARSLEY
SALT AND PEPPER TO TASTE

Clean the ceps well, then chop them.

Fry the shallot and onion in the olive oil and butter until softened. Add the mushrooms and fry for a further 7–8 minutes. Add some salt and pepper to the mushrooms. Add the flour and stir-fry until it changes colour. Add the wine and stock and cook for a further 10 minutes.

Sprinkle with the parsley and serve immediately.

CHAPTER THREE
PASTA, RICE
AND POLENTA

Inevitably, this chapter is almost entirely Italian, because it is very traditional to combine pasta, rice and polenta with mushrooms – and few pizzas lack a slice or two of mushrooms! I have tried to give some variety in the recipes by using different types of fungi but, to be honest, when Italians talk about mushrooms they really mean only ceps (funghi porcini), which is what they use and appreciate most. (And, in fact, to improve the taste of various recipes, we often add dried ceps to sauces.) Pasta is the 'carrier' par excellence for wild mushrooms, both fresh and dried: their succulent textures complement each other perfectly, and the savoury juices exuded by cooked mushrooms provide just the right amount of lubrication. The association may be traditional, but, a word of warning. Mushroom sauces are used almost exclusively to accompany long pasta shapes such as spaghetti and tagliatelle – rarely short pasta. Different regions in Italy favour their own versions of home-made pasta and of gnocchi, while in the north, polenta and rice make equally delicious vehicles for mushrooms. Here, rice and fungi are very often seen together in risottos, but also in rice salads and soups, and polenta with fungi is used as an accompaniment to meat, usually with tomato-based sauces. Once again, the sauces and mushrooms in my recipes are interchangeable, so feel free to experiment and create your own specialities.

Tagliolini with Black Truffle

Depending on the season, this dish can be prepared with white Alba truffle, or simply with a black truffle. To give more flavour to the dish when using summer or Périgord truffle, add a few drops of truffle oil. This is a classic starter for an elegant meal.

Serves 4

400 g freshly made tagliolini
  (see page 160)
85 g butter
55 g fresh black truffle, cleaned
  and finely sliced
a few drops of truffle oil
  (optional)
55 g Parmesan, freshly grated
salt and pepper to taste

If you make your own pasta, you only need its cooking time – some 3–4 minutes – to cook the sauce! Is this the ultimate in fast food?
While the pasta is boiling in plenty of salted water (10 g salt per litre water), melt the butter in a pan, then add the sliced truffle with a few drops of truffle oil. (If using Alba truffle, the oil is not necessary.)
Drain the pasta, reserving a few tablespoons of water, and put in the pan with the butter and truffle. Add the Parmesan and some salt and pepper. Mix well, using a little of the reserved cooking water, and serve immediately with more truffle and/or more Parmesan if you like.

Pasta with Caesar's Mushrooms

The regions of Umbria and Marche in Italy, as with other regions, have developed their own shape of pasta. Ciriole, or the smaller cirioline, are like tagliatelle with a square profile. A similar pasta from other regions is called 'spaghetti alla chitarra', because it is made by hand with a tool consisting of steel strings just like a guitar. This pasta is usually made with eggs and has a delicious flavour.

SERVES 4

400 G CIRIOLE PASTA, OR TAGLIOLINI
  OR TAGLIATELLINI
60 G PARMESAN, FRESHLY GRATED
SALT AND PEPPER TO TASTE

SAUCE
300 G FRESH AND POSSIBLY STILL
  CLOSED CAESAR'S MUSHROOMS
1 GARLIC CLOVE, HALVED
55 G BUTTER
4 TBSP OLIVE OIL
A PINCH OF FRESHLY GRATED NUTMEG
1 SPRIG ROSEMARY

Clean the mushrooms carefully, then cut into chunks.

Cook the pasta for 4–6 minutes, depending on thickness, in boiling salted water. Drain, reserving some of the cooking water.

Rub a frying pan with the garlic halves, then discard the garlic. Melt the butter in the pan, then add the oil, nutmeg, some pepper and the rosemary. Leave the rosemary to cook for a few minutes, then remove and discard. Fry the mushrooms briefly in the aromatic butter and oil mixture.

Mix the drained pasta with the mushrooms and butter, and add the Parmesan. Sauté gently to amalgamate the flavours. If necessary, add a little of the cooking water for moisture. Serve with a sprinkling of extra Parmesan and a few thin slices of raw mushroom if you have them.

SPAGHETTI WITH HONEY FUNGUS

It is always around the 15th October that, seemingly out of nowhere, the honey fungus suddenly appears in the woods. I am always very excited at the sight of a colony, still with closed caps, very tightly packed in bunches at the foot of the trees, or sometimes just shooting out of the grass. When raw they have a strange smell, but once cooked they are delicious, and also lose any toxicity.

SERVES 4

500 G MEDIUM SPAGHETTI
60 G PARMESAN, COARSELY GRATED
SALT AND PEPPER TO TASTE

SAUCE
800 G FRESH AND TIGHT HONEY
   FUNGUS MUSHROOMS
8 TBSP OLIVE OIL
2 GARLIC CLOVES, SLICED
1 FRESH RED CHILLI, SLICED
2 TBSP COARSELY CHOPPED PARSLEY

Clean the honey fungus, and remove the toughest part of its stem. Boil for 3–4 minutes in slightly salted water, then drain well.
Cook the pasta in plenty of salted water for 6–7 minutes until al dente. Meanwhile, heat the oil in a large pan and add the garlic and chilli. Before the garlic browns, add the mushrooms and the parsley. Cook for a few minutes only. Drain the pasta well, and mix it with the mushroom sauce. Add the Parmesan and enjoy!

SPAGHETTI WITH MUSHROOM AND LAMB SAUCE

The Neapolitans love thin spaghetti (known also as vermicelli) that resembles little strings ('spago' means 'string'). They normally eat it with just a tomato and basil sauce, but on special occasions they add a meat sauce. The seasonal fungi added to this slowly cooked sauce makes the dish even more succulent.

SERVES 4

500 G THIN SPAGHETTI
PARMESAN OR PECORINO CHEESE,
   FRESHLY GRATED
SALT AND PEPPER TO TASTE

SAUCE
300 G FRESH HONEY FUNGUS
   MUSHROOMS
15 G DRIED CEPS, SOAKED FOR
   20 MINUTES IN WARM WATER
8 TBSP OLIVE OIL
1 LARGE ONION, FINELY SLICED
400 G RAW BONED LAMB, NOT TOO
   FATTY, COARSELY MINCED
1 FRESH HOT CHILLI, CHOPPED
150 ML DRY RED WINE
500 G TOMATO PULP (CANNED OR FRESH)

Clean the honey fungus, and remove the toughest part of its stem. Boil for 3–4 minutes in slightly salted water, then drain well and set aside. Drain the dried ceps, reserving the water, and chop. Put the olive oil into a pan, and fry the onion in it until soft. Add the meat and brown thoroughly, then stir in the chilli and wine and leave to simmer briefly. Add the chopped dried ceps and their strained soaking water, and the tomato pulp. Cook over a slow heat for 1 1/2 hours.
When ready to serve, cook the spaghetti in boiling salted water until al dente. Add the fresh mushrooms to the sauce, season and cook for a couple of minutes. Drain the spaghetti and divide between warm dishes. Top with the sauce, and sprinkle with Parmesan.

Pappardelle with Ceps

This type of pasta – like large tagliatelle – is usually combined with meat ragùs or sauces containing wild boar, game and other meats. It is very popular in my restaurant because the large size of the pasta really satisfies the palate and gives a sense of pleasure. An even larger pappardelle pasta was known in Ancient Roman times: this 'laganum' was eaten with an anchovy-based sauce.

SERVES 4

400 G PAPPARDELLE
85 G PARMESAN, FRESHLY GRATED
2 TBSP FINELY CHOPPED PARSLEY
SALT AND PEPPER TO TASTE

SAUCE
400 G FRESH, FIRM CEPS
20 G DRIED CEPS, SOAKED IN
  WARM WATER FOR 20 MINUTES
1 MEDIUM ONION, VERY FINELY
  CHOPPED
6 TBSP OLIVE OIL
40 G BUTTER
1 GARLIC CLOVE, VERY FINELY CHOPPED
4 TBSP DRY WHITE WINE

To start the sauce, clean and finely slice the fresh ceps. Drain the dried ceps, reserving the water, then chop them.

Fry the onion in the oil and butter until soft, then add the garlic. Add the chopped ceps then the wine, and simmer until the alcohol evaporates. Add the fresh ceps and the soaking water from the dried ceps and cook gently for 10 minutes. Stir well, then reduce the sauce for a few minutes. Season to taste. Cook the pasta in plenty of salted water until al dente, usually about 8–10 minutes. Drain well, then add some of the sauce. Divide this between warm plates. Pour over more of the sauce and sprinkle with Parmesan and parsley.

Cart Driver's Spaghetti

I wanted to include this recipe, despite it being in one of my previous books, as it is an example of something rather alien to me – virtually none of the ingredients in the dish is fresh! It is said to have been made by the cart drivers transporting goods from the provinces to Rome: hungry on the long journey, they would want to make themselves something that would not go off, that was quite undemanding, and that would still be delicious.

SERVES 4

25 G DRIED CEPS
4 TBSP OLIVE OIL
1 GARLIC CLOVE, CRUSHED
55 G PANCETTA, FINELY CHOPPED
1 X 200 G CAN TUNA IN OIL, DRAINED
  AND FLAKED
600 G VERY SWEET CHERRY TOMATOES
  (POMODORINI), CHOPPED, OR 500 G
  TOMATO PULP (FRESH OR CANNED)
400 G SPAGHETTI
SALT AND PEPPER TO TASTE
FRESHLY GRATED PECORINO CHEESE
  TO SERVE

Soak the ceps in warm water for 20 minutes, then drain and chop, reserving the soaking liquid.

Heat the olive oil in a frying pan, add the garlic and fry gently until soft. Add the pancetta and allow to brown a little. Stir in the ceps and tuna and fry for a few minutes, then add the tomatoes and some salt and pepper. Simmer for 20 minutes, then stir in a few tablespoons of the cep soaking liquid just to flavour the sauce, and cook for about 5 minutes longer.

Meanwhile, cook the spaghetti in a large pan of boiling salted water until al dente. Drain and mix the spaghetti with the sauce. Season with black pepper and sprinkle with grated cheese.

SARDINIAN RAVIOLI WITH FAIRY RING CHAMPIGNONS

It is interesting that two regions as far apart as Sardinia and the Veneto have a very similar way of shaping their home-made ravioli. Although the fillings are different, they both taste wonderful. You need a little patience to make these 'culurzones', but the result is very rewarding. The great footballer Gianfranco Zola was delighted when I made this dish from his home town of Oriena in Sardinia as a surprise for him. Unfortunately, the setting was less traditional – the grounds of Chelsea Football Club.

SERVES 6–7

1 QUANTITY BASIC PASTA DOUGH
  (SEE PAGE 160)
SALT AND PEPPER TO TASTE
FRESHLY GRATED PARMESAN OR
  PECORINO CHEESE

FILLING
800 G POTATOES, BOILED AND
  MASHED
200 G FRESH (DOLCE) PECORINO
  CHEESE, GRATED
55 G AGED PECORINO CHEESE,
  GRATED
125 G PARMESAN, FRESHLY GRATED
2 1/2 TBSP EXTRA VIRGIN OLIVE OIL
2 1/2 TBSP FINELY CHOPPED MINT

SAUCE
200 G FAIRY RING CHAMPIGNONS
10 G DRIED CEPS
1 SMALL SHALLOT, VERY FINELY
  DICED
55 G BUTTER
ABOUT 4 TBSP CHICKEN OR
  VEGETABLE STOCK (SEE PAGE 104)
4 TBSP DRY WHITE WINE
1 TBSP FINELY CHOPPED PARSLEY

To make the filling, mix together the potatoes, three cheeses, oil and mint, then set aside. Roll out the pasta, either by hand or with a pasta machine, until it is very thin – about 2 mm. Cut out 10 cm rounds. Knead the trimmings together, re-roll and cut out more rounds. To shape the culurzones, take a pasta round in one hand and place a teaspoon of the filling mixture off-centre on it. Turn up the bottom of the dough over the filling, then pinch a fold of dough over the right and then the left side to give a pleated effect. Pinch the top together to seal. You should end up with a money-bag shape. To prevent the pasta from drying out, it is important to work quickly and to keep the remaining pasta rounds covered.

For the sauce, clean the mushrooms, and soak the dried ceps in lukewarm water for 30 minutes. Drain well, reserving the water, then chop finely. Fry the shallot in the butter for 5 minutes, then add the mushrooms, fresh and dried, and sauté for a few more minutes. Pour in the stock and wine and continue to cook to reduce the liquid a little, before adding the parsley.

Meanwhile, cook the culurzones in plenty of lightly salted boiling water until al dente, or 6–7 minutes if you like them really soft. Drain and combine with the sauce, stirring to coat well. Serve with more grated pecorino or Parmesan – whichever you prefer.

Raviolo with Chicken of the Woods and Cauliflower Fungus

I call this an 'extrovert' raviolo because the filling is partly visible, resting between two large square sheets of pasta. It is possible to use a variety of filling, from meat to fish or vegetable. This is a vegetarian version, an elegant dish to be offered as a first course.

The minimal bother of making your own pasta dough is justified by the result, and with the addition of a little chicken or veal, it could become a dish for everybody.

Serves 4

200 G BASIC PASTA DOUGH (SEE
   PAGE 160)
OLIVE OIL
20 G BUTTER, MELTED
55 G PARMESAN, FRESHLY GRATED
SALT AND PEPPER TO TASTE

FILLING
300 G MIXED CHICKEN OF THE WOODS
   AND CAULIFLOWER MUSHROOMS,
   CLEANED WEIGHT
15 G DRIED CEPS
8 TBSP OLIVE OIL
2 GARLIC CLOVES, FINELY CHOPPED
A LITTLE FRESH RED CHILLI, FINELY
   CHOPPED
150 ML DRY WHITE WINE
4 TBSP FINELY CHOPPED PARSLEY
4 TBSP DOUBLE CREAM

Slice the fresh wild mushrooms and soak the dried ceps in lukewarm water for 20 minutes. Squeeze any excess water from the dried ceps, reserve the water and chop the ceps very finely. Heat the oil in a pan and fry the garlic, chilli and chopped ceps briefly. Add the sliced fresh mushrooms and stir-fry for a few minutes more. Add the white wine and a little of the cep soaking water and continue to cook for 2–3 minutes. Set aside.

Roll out the pasta dough to make sheets 2 mm thick. Cut into 14 cm squares. Put the pasta squares one by one in lightly salted boiling water to which, exceptionally, you will have added a few drops of oil to avoid them sticking together, and cook for 3–4 minutes, carefully stirring with a wooden spoon a couple of times. When the pasta is ready, add cold water to the pan so you will be able to handle the pasta without burning yourself, then drain all very well. Just before serving add some salt and pepper, the parsley and cream to the mushrooms, and mix well. Put a square of pasta on the bottom of each plate and add 2–3 spoonfuls of the finished filling in the centre. Cover with another sheet of pasta. Brush melted butter on top of each raviolo and sprinkle with Parmesan. Serve immediately.

Handkerchief Pasta with Morel and Truffle Sauce

This recipe has been chosen as the right place for giving instructions to make the basic pasta dough, as this shape of pasta represents what freshly made pasta is all about – silkiness and fine texture, with developing flavours that provide enormous pleasure to the palate. Once you have made your fresh sheets of pasta, any use is possible thereafter. According to its thinness, it may be used for lasagne, rolled up and cut into ribbons for tagliatelle or tagliolini, or used to make ravioli, tortellini and any other fresh pasta shapes. This same sauce can be used to flavour ravioli, other pasta shapes, rice, meat and game.

Serves 6

BASIC PASTA DOUGH
300g plain white flour, type 00 if possible
A good pinch of salt
3 medium eggs

TO SERVE
Morel and truffle sauce (see page 105)
A little stock if necessary (see page 104)
40 g butter
60 g Parmesan, freshly grated

Put the flour and salt on a marble surface if possible, or its equivalent, and form into a volcano shape with a well in the middle. Break the eggs into the well and, using a fork, gradually mix the flour into the centre. The first stage will be very crumbly and not at all workable. Now use your hands to pull the dough together, and make it as homogeneous as possible. Work it with the palms of your hands, push with alternate hands, and use the weight of your body to press down, in a movement away from you. After 10 minutes of kneading, the dough should start to be smooth and silky. If you have time, wrap it in clingfilm and leave it to rest for about 30 minutes.

Take a rolling pin and flatten the dough in a circular motion away from you, always starting from the centre and working outwards. Once you have rolled the dough to a thickness of 1mm (as thin as you can), it is ready. Cut it into whatever shapes you want (see the introduction above), but here we need large squares of about 8cm. Leave to rest on clean kitchen towels, covered.

Prepare and warm up the sauce, adding a little stock (or water) if necessary, and the butter.

Meanwhile, bring 4 litres water and 40g salt to the boil in a large pan. When it is boiling, immerse the pasta sheets one by one and cook for 1–2 minutes.

Drain these well, put in a ceramic bowl with some of the sauce, and mix. Divide between warm plates with more of the sauce poured over, and sprinkle with the Parmesan. Wonderful!

INDIVIDUAL MUSHROOM LASAGNE

Endless types of lasagne exist, with a variety of fillings. This recipe is from the area where I grew up and is extremely simple, but with a maximum of flavour.

To make the special green pasta dough for four people, follow the basic recipe opposite, but use 300 g OO plain flour, 55 g boiled spinach (very well drained and squeezed) and 2 eggs. The green dough can then be rolled out and cut into 10 cm squares.

SERVES 4

350 G FRESH YOUNG CEPS
BASIC PASTA DOUGH
    (SEE OPPOSITE PAGE), BUT MADE
    AS ABOVE
4 TBSP OLIVE OIL
1 GARLIC CLOVE, VERY FINELY
    CHOPPED
300 ML DOUBLE CREAM
2 GRATES OF NUTMEG
2 TBSP FINELY CHOPPED PARSLEY
A KNOB OF BUTTER
300 G FONTINA CHEESE, CUT INTO
    THIN SLICES
55 G PARMESAN, FRESHLY GRATED
SALT AND PEPPER TO TASTE

Clean the ceps well, and cut into thin slices. Make the pasta dough and leave to rest. Preheat the oven to 220°C/Gas 7. Roll and cut the pasta as opposite, then cover with a cloth.

Put the oil, garlic and mushrooms into a pan and fry for 3 minutes. Add the cream, nutmeg, salt and pepper then bring to the boil. Simmer to reduce a little. Remove from the heat and mix in the parsley.

Cook the pasta squares in plenty of salted water for 3 minutes, drain and dry on a cloth. Take individual serving dishes with sides, butter them and lay a sheet or two of pasta in each one. Top with some of the mushroom mixture, and cover with a few of the cheese slices. Repeat this layering of pasta, mushroom and cheese twice, finishing with the mushroom mixture. Sprinkle Parmesan on top and cook in the preheated oven for 15 minutes.

PELMENI WITH CEPS

This recipe is usually reserved for grand occasions, because wild mushrooms – collected in the autumn – are thought of as a luxury by the Russians. At other times of the year, the filling would normally be meat. Pelmeni resemble huge ravioli or dumplings, and are made with fresh pasta. Polish pierogi are similar.

SERVES 4

1 QUANTITY BASIC PASTA DOUGH
   (SEE PAGE 160)
85 G BUTTER
55 G PARMESAN, FRESHLY GRATED
A FEW DILL SPRIGS

FILLING
200 G FRESH CEPS
20 G DRIED CEPS, SOAKED IN
   WARM WATER FOR 20 MINUTES
40 G BUTTER
2 GARLIC CLOVES, VERY FINELY
   CHOPPED
2 TBSP COARSELY CHOPPED PARSLEY
1 TBSP FINELY CHOPPED DILL
85 ML CRÈME FRAÎCHE
SALT AND PEPPER TO TASTE

For the filling, clean and finely slice the fresh ceps. Drain the dried ceps, reserving the water, and chop them. Fry the fresh ceps in the butter. After a few minutes add the garlic and fry gently for 2 more minutes. Add the chopped dried ceps to the pan, frying for 2 more minutes. Season with salt and pepper, and stir in the parsley and dill. Leave to cool, then add the crème fraîche. Mix everything together well.

Roll out the fresh pasta thinly, and cut into twelve 12–14 cm squares. Line up on a work surface, and divide the filling between the squares. Moisten the edges of the pelmeni with water, and fold over to obtain a large filled triangle. Press the edges with the tines of a fork to seal. Boil in slightly salted water for 4–5 minutes. Drain well, then put in a large flat pan with the melted butter. Heat through briefly, then sprinkle with Parmesan (the Italian influence!) and garnish with the sprigs of dill.

RIGHT FRESHLY GRATED PARMESAN

STICKY RICE WITH MUSHROOMS AND GINGKO NUTS

For this Orient-inspired recipe, which is not a risotto, you could use chicken of the woods, hen of the woods, orange birch boletes, or whatever was the result of a not very successful fungus foray. Cultivated mushrooms could be used too: buna-shimeji would be good. I like rice in my combination and this one should be the Japanese or Chinese sticky rice (which I find has a slight scent of bacon or pork). The dish sounds oriental, but you can make it to your liking by simply changing the seasoning.

SERVES 4

100 G PARMA HAM, FINELY DICED
1 SMALL ONION, VERY FINELY
  CHOPPED
A LITTLE OIL
300 G JAPANESE STICKY RICE,
  WASHED UNTIL THE WATER RUNS
  CLEAR
SALT TO TASTE

RAGÙ
800 G MIXED FRESH MUSHROOMS
20 G DRIED CEPS, SOAKED
  IN WARM WATER FOR 20 MINUTES
1 GARLIC CLOVE, FINELY CHOPPED
4 SPRING ONIONS, FINELY CHOPPED
4 TBSP OLIVE OIL
1 FRESH RED CHILLI, FINELY
  CHOPPED
1 TBSP FINELY CHOPPED FRESH
  ROOT GINGER
3 TBSP SOY SAUCE
JUICE OF $^1/_2$ LEMON
12 SHELLED GINGKO NUTS
A HANDFUL OF BASIL LEAVES,
  COARSELY CHOPPED
2 TBSP COARSELY CHOPPED
  CORIANDER

Make the ragù of mushrooms first. Clean the mushrooms thoroughly, and if they are big, quarter them. Drain and chop the ceps, reserving the soaking water. Sauté the garlic and spring onion in the olive oil until soft. Add the chilli, ginger, chopped ceps and the fresh mushrooms, along with the liquid from the ceps, soy sauce, lemon juice and gingko nuts. Bring to the boil, reduce the heat, then simmer for 10–15 minutes. Stir a few times to amalgamate every-thing, adjust the salt and just before serving, add the herbs.

Meanwhile, sauté the Parma ham and onion in a pan with a little oil. Add the washed rice with 500ml cold water and some salt. Bring to the boil and simmer for 2 minutes. Cover with a lid, then simmer very gently for 6 minutes. Remove the pan from the heat and leave to stand for 10 minutes, covered. Serve the rice with the mushroom ragù.

MOREL AND CEP RISOTTO

According to Italian tradition, a cep risotto is a must in the autumn, and in my opinion is one of the best dishes, only beaten by a risotto containing white truffles! However, when experimenting one day, I found I was short of ceps, and so used some dried morels. The result was rather impressive! (You can, of course, make it with only ceps.)

SERVES 4

300 G FRESH CEPS, CLEANED WEIGHT, SLICED
55 G DRIED MORELS, SOAKED IN WARM WATER FOR 30 MINUTES
1.5 LITRES CHICKEN OR VEGETABLE STOCK (SEE PAGE 104)
2 TBSP OLIVE OIL
20 G BUTTER
1 MEDIUM ONION, FINELY SLICED
350 G CARNAROLI, VIALONE NANO OR ARBORIO RICE
SALT AND PEPPER TO TASTE

TO FINISH
55 G BUTTER
55 G PARMESAN, FRESHLY GRATED

Prepare the mushrooms, reserving the morel soaking water for use at another time. Trim the end of the morel stalks off at the base and discard. Heat the stock to a gentle simmer.

Heat the oil and butter in a large pan, then fry the onion gently until soft. Add the morels and sauté briefly. Add the rice and stir it thoroughly so that each grain is coated with oil and slightly toasted. Now start to add the hot stock, ladle by ladle, to the pan. Each time you add a ladleful, make sure that it is fully absorbed before adding the next. Stir the mixture constantly to avoid it sticking to the base of the pan, and also to create a creaminess when the starch is exuded from the grains. After 10 minutes' cooking, add the sliced ceps. Continue to cook and stir until the rice is al dente. The result should be a quite moist, but not brothy dish: this should take about 18 minutes to achieve. To finish the dish, remove from the heat, season and stir in the butter and Parmesan. Serve immediately.

RISOTTO WITH CAESAR'S MUSHROOMS

When we were taking the photographs for this book, I had to buy a whole box of fresh Caesar's mushrooms from Italy, because unfortunately they don't grow in Britain. It was lunchtime, and the recipe I created there and then for our break was stunning!

SERVES 4

200 G FRESH CAESAR'S MUSHROOMS
1.5 LITRES CHICKEN OR VEGETABLE STOCK (SEE PAGE 104)
1 MEDIUM ONION, FINELY CHOPPED
125 G BUTTER
400 G CARNAROLI RICE
60 G PARMESAN, FRESHLY GRATED
SALT AND PEPPER TO TASTE

Clean and trim the mushrooms, then cut them into small chunks. Have the stock at a steady simmer next to where you will cook the risotto.

Fry the onion in half of the butter until soft, then add the rice and stir to coat the grains with fat. Now add a ladleful of the hot stock and stir until it is absorbed. Continue in this way, stirring continuously, until all the stock has been added and the moisture has been absorbed each time. After about 15 minutes, test a grain of rice, which should be al dente, and then add the mushrooms and stir to mix. You don't really want to 'cook' them. The texture should be moist but not soupy.

Add the remaining butter, the Parmesan, and salt and pepper to taste, and stir vigorously. Serve immediately.

RIGHT MOREL AND CEP RISOTTO

FRIED PIZZA WITH MIXED MUSHROOMS AND TOMATOES

I used to believe that what my mother cooked could not be improved upon. I think that, if she were still alive, she would agree that the addition of mushrooms to her fried pizza, which we grew up with, would be desirable.

SERVES 6

PIZZA DOUGH
300 G 00 FLOUR OR PLAIN WHITE FLOUR
15 G FRESH YEAST, OR GRANULAR DRIED YEAST RECONSTITUTED IN A LITTLE LUKEWARM WATER
A PINCH OF SALT
WATER AS REQUIRED

TOPPING
400 G MIXED WILD AND CULTIVATED MUSHROOMS (CHANTERELLES, BLEWITS, HORNS OF PLENTY, ETC.)
3 GARLIC CLOVES, FINELY CHOPPED
EXTRA VIRGIN OLIVE OIL
1 MILD FRESH RED CHILLI, SLICED
300 G TOMATO PULP (DESEEDED FRESH OR CANNED)
10 BASIL LEAVES, TORN
SALT AND PEPPER TO TASTE

For the pizza dough, mix together the flour, yeast and salt. Add enough water to make a soft dough. Leave it to rise for 1–2 hours, covered with a cloth in a warm but not draughty place.

Meanwhile, for the topping, clean the mushrooms as appropriate, and coarsely chop. Fry two-thirds of the garlic in 4 tablespoons of the oil then, just before browning, add the mushrooms and chilli. Sauté for 7–8 minutes. To make the tomato sauce, fry the remaining garlic in 2 tablespoons of the oil, then add the tomato, half the basil and some salt and pepper. Keep warm.

Take a sixth of the dough and flatten it to make a disc of about 20 cm in diameter. Do the same with the rest of the dough.

Heat enough oil in a frying pan to come 2.5 cm up the sides. When hot, gently put one pizza in at a time and fry until brown and crisp on one side. Turn with tongs and fry on the other side until crisp and brown. (Interestingly, for the health conscious, this pizza doesn't absorb the oil. Instead it becomes crisp on the outside but not oily inside.) Place the fried pizza discs on a plate and top each with some of the tomato sauce. Place the mixed mushrooms on top, garnish with the remaining basil, and eat while hot.

Polenta with a Mushroom, Tomato and Sausage Sauce

One of the classic dishes of the valleys of the Italian Alps is polenta, a maize porridge. Many people don't like its simplicity, but cooked this way you won't have any complaints at all. The tomato and sausage ragù (or even tomato and chicken) makes a good combination with fungi.

Serves 6

1.5 litres water
300 g polenta flour, or 1 packet
  5-minute commercial polenta
75 g butter
55 g fontina or Taleggio cheese,
  finely diced
100 g Parmesan, freshly grated
salt and pepper to taste

Sauce
200 g button mushrooms
30 g dried ceps, soaked
  in warm water for 20 minutes
200 g luganiga sausage
1 medium onion, finely chopped
6 tbsp olive oil
1 bay leaf
400 g tomato pulp (fresh or
  canned)

For the polenta, salt the water then bring it to the boil. Slowly add the polenta flour, stirring with a wooden spoon all the time to avoid lumps. Be careful: when all the flour is in the water it will start to bubble and may burn your skin, so use a long wooden spoon. Stir occasionally for up to 40 minutes until the polenta is cooked. If the 5-minute polenta is used, just follow the packet instructions. When cooked, add the butter, the diced cheese and half the Parmesan, and amalgamate thoroughly.

Meanwhile, for the sauce, clean the fresh mushrooms and slice finely. Drain the dried ceps, reserving the water for another use, and chop. Chop the sausagemeat (removed from its skin) into small chunks. Fry the onion in the oil until soft, then add the sausagemeat and continue to cook for 10 minutes, stirring from time to time. Add the sliced mushrooms, the soaked ceps and the bay leaf, and cook for a further 5 minutes. Add the tomato pulp and cook for 20 minutes. Adjust the seasoning. Serve the sauce with the polenta either on the side or on top in a little well. Sprinkle the remaining Parmesan over before serving.

Gnocchi with Horn of Plenty and Chicken of the Woods

Many types of dumplings exist in the world, but none equals the very simple Italian version, typical of 20 regions, which is made with flour and potatoes. Their lightness, when freshly made, is the major characteristic, but when the gnocchi are combined with an appropriate sauce they become irresistible and very nourishing. They are very good simply with butter and Parmesan, exquisite with tomato and basil, excellent with pesto, a bolognese sauce or even with a Gorgonzola sauce but – and this is the first time I have done this – they are wonderful combined with mushrooms.

Serves 6

GNOCCHI
800 G FLOURY POTATOES, PEELED
    AND QUARTERED
200 G PLAIN FLOUR
1 EGG, BEATEN
SALT AND PEPPER TO TASTE

SAUCE
300 G HORN OF PLENTY MUSHROOMS,
    CLEANED WEIGHT
200 G CHICKEN OF THE WOODS
    MUSHROOMS, CLEANED WEIGHT
    (OR USE FRESH OPEN CAP OR
    BROWN CAP MUSHROOMS)
20 G DRIED CEPS
4 TBSP OLIVE OIL
55 G BUTTER
1 MEDIUM ONION, FINELY CHOPPED
150 ML DRY WHITE WINE
3 TBSP FINELY CHOPPED PARSLEY
60 G PARMESAN, FRESHLY GRATED,
    TO FINISH

Cook the potatoes in slightly salted water. When soft, drain them thoroughly. Put them back into the empty pan and stir over a gentle heat for a few seconds to get rid of any lingering moisture. Mash them finely and mix gently with the flour on a work surface, together with the egg, to make a soft dough. Keeping your hands well floured, take part of the dough and roll it with your hands into a soft sausage, about 2 cm in diameter. Cut into chunks about 2.5 cm long. With the help of a fork and more flour, press each chunk against the tines of the fork with a downwards movement, to mark and shape the gnocchi. Leave to rest on a clean cloth.

For the sauce, clean and cut the fresh mushrooms into thin strips. Soak the dried ceps for 20 minutes in warm water. Drain well, then chop them very finely, reserving their soaking water. Heat the oil and butter together in a pan and fry the onion in the mixture until soft, then add all the mushrooms. Cook very slowly for 15 minutes to reduce them. Add some of the cep soaking water and the wine and cook for a further 5–10 minutes. Add the parsley, some salt and lots of black pepper.

Plunge the gnocchi all together into abundant, slightly salted boiling water. They will be cooked when they float to the surface. Scoop them out with a slotted spoon, and add to the sauce. Mix well, divide between warm plates, and sprinkle with Parmesan.

CHAPTER FOUR
FISH

The combination of fish and mushrooms is rather modern in approach, at least in the Italian sense, although abroad, and especially in the Far East, these two items have long been eaten in partnership. In Europe in general, the pairing of fish with mushrooms is now used much more widely, and I am still discovering, through experimentation, both for my books and my restaurants, what excellent results can be achieved. For instance, I find mushrooms the perfect complement to fresh salmon and the delicate but firm white flesh of monkfish, halibut, turbot and Dover sole is ideal for cooking with fragrant wild mushrooms, since a good balance can be attained both in texture and in flavour. Dishes with mushrooms and fish can look appetising too, with the shapes and colours of certain mushrooms providing an attractive or even dramatic element of contrast. I tend not to use mushrooms with oily fish such as sardines or mackerel, as their richness calls for ingredients that act as a foil, not for the additional flavour of mushrooms.
I always use fresh mushrooms with very fresh fish, since the textures and flavours complement each other beautifully. I hope you will enjoy reproducing my results.

UMBRIAN TROUT WITH BLACK TRUFFLE

Umbria is the main black truffle region in Italy. The local Urbani brothers have the monopoly of 80 per cent of the world truffle market. When I was in Norcia, part of Umbria, I was invited to join a truffle hunt with dogs, and to eat a local trout caught in the river Nera. The trout was served with a summer truffle, with some truffle oil added for extra flavour. But if you cook with the black winter truffle (Tuber melanosporum)*, you won't need extra flavouring.*

SERVES 4

85 G BLACK TRUFFLE
4 BROWN TROUT
PLAIN FLOUR, FOR DUSTING
1 GARLIC CLOVE
60 G BUTTER
1 TSP TRUFFLE OIL (OPTIONAL)
4 TBSP DRY WHITE WINE
SALT AND PEPPER TO TASTE

Clean the truffle well, and then cut into small cubes. Clean, scale and gut the trout, then dust with flour. Rub a large frying pan with the garlic, then discard the garlic.

Melt the butter in the pan and fry the trout until slightly brown, about 4–5 minutes on each side. Add the truffle oil (if using), the cubed truffle and the wine, and deglaze the pan, by boiling for a minute or two, stirring to release any stuck-on juices. Season to taste.

Serve the fish with freshly boiled waxy potatoes and some of the sauce poured over each.

EEL FILLETS WITH BEEFSTEAK FUNGUS

If there is a fish that can match, in flavour and texture, the beefsteak fungus, it's the eel. The fungus has an acidity which compensates for the fattiness of the eel. The fish itself is actually cooked so that it loses a great deal of its natural fat: chargrilling not only melts and burns off most of the fat, but the heat also gives the fish a desirable smokiness. The marinade is also important. I have tried this recipe using conger eel, and the result was equally good. In this case you need to marinate only for 30 minutes.

SERVES 4

400 G BEEFSTEAK FUNGUS
500 G EEL FILLETS, WITH SKIN
2 TBSP OLIVE OIL
2 TBSP DOUBLE CREAM
2 TBSP CHOPPED DILL
SALT AND PEPPER TO TASTE

MARINADE
JUICE OF 2 LEMONS
4 TBSP OLIVE OIL
1 GARLIC CLOVE, FINELY CHOPPED
ABOUT 6 MINT LEAVES

Clean the fungus thoroughly, and cut into thin slices. Cut the eel into 8 cm chunks. Some 3–4 hours before cooking, mix the marinade ingredients together, adding a little salt, and pour over the eel in a suitable dish.
Heat the oil in a pan, then add the fungus slices and sauté for 5 minutes. Add the cream, dill and salt and pepper.
Grill the eel until cooked, about 5 minutes each side, then unite with the mushrooms. Stir to amalgamate the tastes. The colour will be a bit reddish: this is because the fungus exudes a reddish moisture during cooking. Accompany with bread or with some plain polenta (see page 169).

DOVER SOLE WITH FAIRY RING CHAMPIGNONS

With so many superb food ingredients on offer in Britain, the Dover sole is to me the height of marine deliciousness. Whichever way you cook a fresh Dover sole, it is always wonderful, but combined with the delicate fairy ring champignon, it becomes a dish worthy of serving at the most demanding table. To retain every morsel of full flavour I prefer to cook the fish on the bone, then fillet it before serving.

SERVES 4

4 MEDIUM DOVER SOLE
A LITTLE PLAIN FLOUR FOR DUSTING
55 G BUTTER

SAUCE
400 G FAIRY RING CHAMPIGNONS
1 SHALLOT, VERY FINELY CHOPPED
40 G BUTTER
75 ML DRY WHITE WINE
JUICE OF 1 LEMON
2 TBSP FINELY CHOPPED PARSLEY
2 TBSP DILL LEAVES (OPTIONAL)
SALT AND PEPPER TO TASTE

Clean the mushrooms well. Clean and skin the fish (or ask the fishmonger to do this for you), then dust with flour. Fry the soles on each side in the butter until crisp. You may have to use 2 large frying pans because Dover soles are always quite sizeable. While you are preparing the sauce, keep the soles warm in a low oven.

Fry the shallot in the butter until soft. Add the mushrooms and stir-fry for a few minutes. Add the wine and lemon juice, and stir for another minute. Add the herbs – saving a little of the dill for garnish – and finally some salt and pepper. Mix well and set aside.

Fillet the sole carefully by making an incision in the middle of the spine lengthways. Then cut off and discard the edges, fins, tail and head. Carefully lift one of the upper fillets, starting from the centre. If the sole is well cooked, this should come off the bone easily. Do the same with the other. When both upper fillets are off, remove the main bone leaving the lower part of the sole intact. Repeat with all four fish. To serve, put the lower fillet on a hot plate, arrange some of the mushroom mixture lengthways along this, and put the two upper fillets on top. Decorate with a little dill, if using, and serve accompanied by plain boiled potatoes.

MONKFISH WITH BUNA-SHIMEJI

This recipe uses one of the 'exotic' mushrooms, so-called because of its Eastern origins. Because it is cultivated, it is available most of the year. It has a delicate flavour, and is very easy to cook with.

SERVES 4

600 G MONKFISH FILLET, IN 4 PIECES
300 G BUNA-SHIMEJI MUSHROOMS,
   CUT AT THE BASE
PLAIN FLOUR FOR DUSTING
6 TBSP OLIVE OIL
2 GARLIC CLOVES, FINELY SLICED
1 SMALL FRESH CHILLI, FINELY
   CHOPPED
55 G BUTTER
JUICE OF 1 LIME
2 TBSP CHOPPED CORIANDER
SALT AND PEPPER TO TASTE

In this recipe, the monkfish is plainly cooked to safeguard its delicacy, as well as that of the mushrooms. Dust the fish with flour, and shake off any excess. Heat the oil in a frying pan and fry the mushrooms for 2 minutes, then add the garlic and chilli and fry for a further 2–3 minutes, stirring from time to time. Fry the fish in the butter for a couple of minutes on each side. Season with some salt and pepper and the juice of the lime.
Finish the mushrooms by stirring in the coriander and some salt and pepper. Serve the fish and mushrooms together.

SWORDFISH OLIVES WITH HONEY FUNGUS

This is an excellent combination of fish and fungi. A little patience is required to make the 'olives', but you will certainly be rewarded for your work. If you can't find honey fungus, then use cultivated buna-shimeji instead.

SERVES 4

12 THIN SWORDFISH SLICES (55 G
   EACH, ABOUT 660 G TOTAL WEIGHT)
12 TBSP FRESH WHITE BREADCRUMBS
1 TBSP FINELY CHOPPED DILL
2 TBSP PINE KERNELS
2 GHERKINS, CUT INTO SMALL CUBES
2 EGGS, BEATEN
PLAIN FLOUR FOR DUSTING
OLIVE OIL FOR FRYING
SALT AND PEPPER TO TASTE

SAUCE
300 G HONEY FUNGUS
6 TBSP OLIVE OIL
2 GARLIC CLOVES, FINELY CHOPPED
1 SMALL FRESH RED CHILLI, FINELY
   CHOPPED
4 TBSP FRESH WHITE BREADCRUMBS
100 ML VEGETABLE STOCK (SEE PAGE 104)
2 TBSP FINELY CHOPPED PARSLEY
JUICE OF 1 LEMON

Clean the honey fungus thoroughly, then blanch in salted water for 5 minutes. Drain well.
Make the stuffing for the swordfish olives with the breadcrumbs, dill, pine kernels, cubed gherkin and eggs, seasoning well with salt and pepper.
Lay the fish slices out and place 1 tablespoon of the stuffing in the centre of each one. Roll up and secure with a wooden cocktail stick. Dust with flour and fry in hot oil until brown on all sides. Keep warm.
For the sauce, heat the olive oil in another pan, then add the garlic and chilli and fry briefly before adding the honey fungus. Cook for 5 minutes. Add the breadcrumbs, stock, parsley and lemon juice and mix well, seasoning with salt and pepper to taste. When the honey fungus is cooked, add the swordfish olives, coat them with the sauce, and serve the combination warm.

RIGHT MONKFISH WITH BUNA-SHIMEJI

RED MULLET WITH CHANTERELLES

For me, there is nothing more delicious than freshly caught red mullet fried in olive oil until crisp. For you, however, the easier option might be to find a fishmonger who has already filleted some fish for you. Here I have combined the red mullet with lovely little chanterelles.

SERVES 4

250 G CHANTERELLES
4 RED MULLET FILLETS (ABOUT 400 G
  IN WEIGHT)
6 TBSP OLIVE OIL
JUICE OF 1 LIME
1 SHALLOT, VERY FINELY CHOPPED
1 TBSP BRANDY
4 TBSP DOUBLE CREAM
1 TBSP FINELY CHOPPED PARSLEY
SALT AND PEPPER TO TASTE

Clean and trim the mushrooms. Marinate the fish fillets in 2 tablespoons of the oil with the lime juice and some salt and pepper for 2 hours.
In a pan, heat the rest of the oil and fry the shallot gently to soften. Add the mushrooms and fry gently for 5 minutes. Add the brandy and, when the alcohol has evaporated, the cream, salt, pepper and parsley.
In a non-stick pan, fry the fish fillets skin side down until the skin is crisp and the flesh is cooked. This should take about 5–8 minutes. Add any remaining marinade to the pan, and heat gently.
Serve the fish immediately on hot plates with the mushrooms at the side.
Eat with bread.

TUNA STEAK WITH WILD MUSHROOMS

The Italians love tuna and swordfish, and like to grill them in steak form. I think we have increasingly been enjoying these meaty fish in this form in Britain. The delicacy of a slice of fresh tuna, just grilled or fried in olive oil and accompanied by some mixed wild mushrooms, has to be tasted to be believed! This recipe is particularly delicious with bay boletes, honey fungus and wood or field blewits, but you can use any mushrooms, even cultivated ones.

SERVES 4

500 G MIXED WILD MUSHROOMS,
  OR FRESH SHIITAKE
4 SLICES TUNA OR SWORDFISH,
  ABOUT 150 G EACH
4 TBSP OLIVE OIL
55 G BUTTER
1 GARLIC CLOVE, FINELY CHOPPED
A PINCH OF MARJORAM LEAVES
A FEW NEEDLES OF ROSEMARY
SALT AND PEPPER TO TASTE

Clean the mushrooms well, then cut into even-sized pieces.
Season the fish with salt and pepper, then fry it in the oil for 5 minutes on each side. Remove from the pan and set aside. Add the butter, mushrooms and garlic to the pan, and stir-fry for 10 minutes. Add the herbs and salt and pepper to taste.
Return the cooked fish to the pan, and stir in 1 tablespoon of water to help amalgamate the ingredients. Warm through gently, and serve immediately.

Constanza's Salt Cod with Potato and Mushrooms

Constanza Guimares is our invaluable housekeeper. When I asked her how the Portuguese would use mushrooms, she came up with the idea of combining them with what is probably the most used and best-loved ingredient in Portugal – bacalau, the salt cod from Norway. The recipe sounded so homely and comforting that I had to have a go, and here it is, using the very large brown cultivated Portobello mushroom.

Serves 4–6

800 g salt cod, cut into chunks and soaked for 2 days in water, changing the water every few hours
300 g Portobello mushrooms
6 tbsp olive oil
1 garlic clove, finely chopped
3 tbsp finely chopped parsley
400 g potatoes, cooked, peeled and sliced
200 g mature Cheddar cheese, grated
salt and pepper to taste

WHITE SAUCE
30 g plain flour
60 g butter
400 ml very hot milk
a pinch of freshly grated nutmeg

Rinse the cod and cook in boiling water for 30 minutes until tender. Leave to cool in the cooking water, then drain well. Discard all the bones and skin and flake the flesh.

Preheat the oven to 200°C/Gas 6. Clean the mushrooms thoroughly, then slice them thickly.

Meanwhile, prepare the white sauce. Fry the flour in the butter for a few minutes, stirring, then add the hot milk and whisk energetically to avoid lumps. Add some salt and pepper and the nutmeg. Cook, stirring, for 10 minutes.

Fry the mushrooms briefly in the oil, adding the garlic and most of the parsley towards the end. Take care to save the best-looking and largest mushroom slices to decorate the top of the dish.

Now assemble everything in an earthenware container, starting with a couple of spoonfuls of white sauce in the bottom. Cover this with a layer of cod flakes, then add some of the mushrooms with some potatoes and more white sauce. Sprinkle with a generous layer of Cheddar cheese, then start again with the cod, mushrooms, potatoes and white sauce, then distribute the cheese and the last layer of cod. Decorate with the reserved mushroom slices and the remaining parsley, and grind over some black pepper. Bake in the preheated oven for 25–30 minutes, then serve hot.

LEFT Constanza's Salt Cod with Potato and Mushrooms

Poached Seafood with Mushrooms

This is a recipe that you can vary infinitely. I first introduced it to my restaurant during the winter months, using dried mushrooms, as I thought the light, summery feel of the poached fish would cheer people up! But of course you can cook it at any time of year, using fresh or dried mushrooms only, or a mixture of the two. You can vary the seafood as well, of course: you just need a selection of at least three firm-textured fish. Buy the dried shiitake mushrooms in Chinese food shops.

SERVES 4

16 DRIED SHIITAKE MUSHROOMS
   PLUS 20 G DRIED CEPS, OR 300 G
   FRESH SHIITAKE
300 G RAW GIANT PRAWNS, SHELLED
   (KEEP THE SHELLS)
300 G MONKFISH FILLET
4 SOLE FILLETS (GET YOUR
   FISHMONGER TO FILLET A 500 G
   SOLE, AND GIVE YOU THE SKIN AND
   BONES)
55 G BUTTER
SALT AND PEPPER TO TASTE

FISH STOCK
FISH SCRAPS (SEE PAGE 104)
1 LITRE WATER
1 CARROT, SLICED LENGTHWAYS
1 ONION, FINELY CHOPPED
1 BAY LEAF
A LITTLE MARJORAM

Soak the dried shiitake (if using) for at least 30 minutes, then simmer in the soaking water for 30–40 minutes or until soft. Discard the stems, which are usually tough and dirty. Soak the dried ceps (if using) for 20 minutes. Reserve the soaking water. Clean any fresh mushrooms at the last minute.

Meanwhile, make the fish stock, using the prawn shells, the skin and bones from the sole, and perhaps another fish head that you have coaxed from the fishmonger. Cover these with the water, add the other stock ingredients, then boil for 1 hour, until the stock has reduced considerably. Strain and set aside.

Prepare the fish. Cut the monkfish fillet into bite-sized chunks. Roll the sole fillets up, and secure with a wooden cocktail stick.

Use a pan that is deep rather than wide so that you will not need too much liquid to cover the fish. Melt the butter in the pan and sauté the monkfish for a minute. Add the rolled fillets of sole, the mushrooms, prawns and enough fish stock – to which you could add a little mushroom soaking liquid – to cover. Poach over a gentle heat for about 10 minutes, or until the fish is cooked. Season to taste with salt and pepper.

Serve with freshly boiled potatoes, perhaps – or, better still – with a mound of buttered noodles.

PRAWNS WITH HORN OF PLENTY MUSHROOMS AND SAFFRON RICE

Horn of plenty mushrooms have some culinary peculiarities, such as becoming completely black when cooked. Here the tender little prawns are an ideal combination with these mushrooms, making the dish both elegant to look at and extremely tasty to eat.

SERVES 4

300 G HORN OF PLENTY MUSHROOMS,
   CLEANED WEIGHT
150 G CARNAROLI RICE
4 TBSP OLIVE OIL
1 SMALL ONION, FINELY SLICED
50 ML DRY WHITE WINE
400 G SMALL RAW PRAWNS, SHELLED
20 G BUTTER
A FEW SAFFRON STRANDS OR
   2 PINCHES POWDERED SAFFRON
1 TBSP LEMON JUICE
1 TSP FINELY CHOPPED PARSLEY
SALT AND PEPPER TO TASTE

Clean the mushrooms thoroughly. Cook the rice in abundant salted water for 15 minutes, then drain.

For the prawns and mushrooms, heat the oil in a pan and fry the onion until soft. Add the mushrooms and let them braise a little. After 5 minutes add the wine and let the alcohol evaporate. Then add the prawns and cook gently for a further 5 minutes.

Melt the butter in a separate pan with the saffron, lemon juice and parsley. Add the hot drained rice and mix well. Check the rice and mushroom mix for salt and pepper and serve, either with the rice mixed in with the prawns or with the prawns and mushrooms in the centre of a small circle of rice.

FRIED SEAFOOD AND MUSHROOMS

In Italy, dishes that contain seafood and other ingredients are often cooked together to produce an interesting contrast. This recipe is a perfect combination of ingredients from sea and earth. It would be fantastic eaten with an aperitif, but also as a light first course accompanied by a green salad.

SERVES 4

100 G ST GEORGE'S MUSHROOMS
150 G FRESH CEPS
100 G RAW SHRIMPS
100 G RAW SMALL PRAWNS
100 G WHITEBAIT
100 G SQUID OR SMALL OCTOPUS
2 EGGS, BEATEN
OLIVE OIL FOR DEEP-FRYING
100 G DRIED BREADCRUMBS
PLAIN FLOUR FOR DUSTING
2 LEMONS, QUARTERED
SALT AND PEPPER TO TASTE

Clean the mushrooms and cut the larger ones in halves or quarters. Prepare all the seafood, cleaning and shelling as appropriate.

Season the beaten egg, and heat the oil in a pan to 180°–190°C, until a cube of bread dropped in it browns in 30 seconds.

Dip the mushrooms first in the egg, then roll in the breadcrumbs. Fry in the hot oil until golden, then remove, drain on kitchen paper, and keep warm. Then dip the fish in the flour and fry in the hot oil until golden.

Serve immediately with the mushrooms and lemon quarters.

MUSHROOM-STUFFED SQUID

It is not so long since the idea of cooking mushrooms and fish together arrived in Europe. Eastern cultures, however, had always paired mushrooms with fish, especially in Thai, Japanese and Chinese soups. More conventionally, the Europeans combined mushrooms with game and meat. This recipe is an interesting combination of two of my favourite foods. You could use any substantial mushroom instead of the chicken of the woods.

SERVES 4

200 G CHICKEN OF THE WOODS
600 G MEDIUM-SIZED SQUID (YOU
    NEED AT LEAST 4, OR YOU COULD
    BUY MANY MORE SMALLER ONES)
8 TBSP OLIVE OIL
1 GARLIC CLOVE, VERY FINELY
    CHOPPED
1/2 TSP VERY FINELY CHOPPED FRESH
    RED CHILLI
6 TBSP FRESH BREADCRUMBS
1 TBSP FINELY CHOPPED PARSLEY
1 TBSP FINELY CHOPPED CORIANDER
2 EGGS
150 ML DRY WHITE WINE
SALT AND PEPPER TO TASTE

Clean the mushrooms very well, then dice. Clean the squid and pull away the heads and tentacles. Chop the tentacles finely.

Put half the oil into a frying pan and fry the garlic, chilli and squid tentacles briefly. Add the mushrooms to the pan and stir-fry until soft. Let as much moisture as possible evaporate. Season to taste and leave to cool.

In a large bowl, mix together the mushrooms, breadcrumbs, parsley, coriander and eggs. Adjust the salt. Now stuff the bodies of the squid with the mixture (very fiddly if you bought small squid), and hold together with a wooden cocktail stick. Fry the stuffed squid in the remaining oil for 1 minute on each side, or until starting to brown, then add the wine. Cook quickly to let the alcohol evaporate, then serve immediately, perhaps with some spinach.

SQUID WITH SHIITAKE AND JUDAS' EARS

The peculiar Judas' Ears in this recipe perfectly complement the shiitake and squid. Auricularia, wild or cultivated, are much used in Chinese and Japanese cooking, but very little in European. Indeed, this recipe leans towards the cuisines of the Far East in its use of spices and herbs. It is an interesting way of using mushrooms and can perhaps be accompanied by a little freshly boiled sticky rice.

SERVES 4

200 G FRESH SHIITAKE MUSHROOMS
150 G FRESH JUDAS' EARS, OR
   55 G DRIED, SOAKED IN WARM
   WATER FOR 30 MINUTES
700 G FRESH SQUID, CLEANED WEIGHT
6 TBSP CORN OIL
1 TBSP PEANUT OIL
4 GARLIC CLOVES, FINELY CHOPPED
1 SMALL BUNCH SPRING ONIONS,
   FINELY CHOPPED
40 G PIECE FRESH ROOT GINGER,
   PEELED AND FINELY CHOPPED
1 FRESH HOT RED CHILLI, FINELY
   CHOPPED
1 TBSP CORNFLOUR, DILUTED IN
   2 TBSP WATER (OPTIONAL)
1 TBSP SOY SAUCE
1 TBSP RICE VINEGAR
JUICE OF 1 LIME
2 TBSP COARSELY CHOPPED
   CORIANDER
SALT TO TASTE

Clean the fresh shiitake, then trim the stalks and slice the caps. Wash and rinse the Judas' Ears, fresh or dried. Cut the squid body into rings and chop the tentacles.

In a wok or frying pan, heat the oils and stir-fry the garlic, spring onions, ginger and chilli for a short while. Add the mushrooms and stir-fry for a couple of minutes more. Add the squid, and stir-fry for 3 minutes, then add the cornflour (if using), soy sauce, rice vinegar and lime juice, and stir-fry for a further 2 minutes. Add salt to taste and sprinkle the fresh coriander on top. Should you need more moisture, then use a little stock made with a cube – as every Chinese cook does (a little MSG won't kill you)!

OYSTERS WITH ZABAGLIONE AND WHITE TRUFFLE

This is the height of sophistication. Although it's very simple to prepare, it will impress any gourmet, not least because it uses that exclusive fungus, the white truffle. You are unlikely to find this in nature by yourself, because the collection of truffles, especially the white from Alba, is limited to specially licensed 'trifolau'. With the help of their trained dogs, they rummage through the Alba hills in the middle of the night (so as not to be seen) to get the most expensive food in the world. However, you only need 10 g per person. You could use black truffle, which may reduce the cost of the dish, but it also reduces the effect.

SERVES 4

1 ALBA TRUFFLE, OF ABOUT 55 G
16 FRESH OYSTERS, JUST OPENED
   AND LEFT IN THE DEEPER PART OF
   THE SHELL
20 G BUTTER
6 EGG YOLKS
150 ML DRY WHITE WINE
JUICE OF $^{1}/_{2}$ LEMON
A FEW DROPS OF TRUFFLE OIL
SALT AND PEPPER TO TASTE

Clean the truffle very carefully and at the last moment slice it very thinly with a mandolino (a special tool to shave truffles). Arrange the oysters, 4 to a plate. Preferably in a zabaglione pan (a copper bowl) over a pan of boiling water, melt the butter, then add the egg yolks, wine, lemon juice, truffle oil and some salt and pepper, and start to whisk. (You could use a double saucepan instead.) Whisk continuously until the mixture becomes semi stiff.
Spoon this sauce over the oysters, then add a few thin slices of truffle.

CHAPTER FIVE
MEAT

Meat and mushrooms are the perfect partners.
Mushroom sauces provide succulent
accompaniments to plain grilled meat, and
mushrooms are an essential ingredient of meat
casseroles and stews. Game is available at the
same time as most wild fungi, and they both seem
to complement each other so dramatically in
flavour. When testing ideas for this book, I came
across many new combinations, some using offal, a
lot of which are traditional in many diverse parts
of the world, not just in Italy. Game, red meat
and offal are strong in taste, but this can be
matched by the aromatic qualities of even the
most pungent of mushrooms. More delicate meats
such as veal or chicken also have their fungal
counterparts in the subtlety of mushrooms like
chanterelles and parasols.
There are about 40 edible mushrooms described
in this book, of which three-quarters are wild and a
quarter cultivated. Whatever meat you like, you will
certainly find one that goes with this selection
of fungi. Good luck!

CHICKEN CASSEROLE WITH TWO TYPES OF BOLETE

Chicken may be the most popular meat in the world, but very often it lacks flavour because it has been battery-raised. For this recipe you have to find the most wonderful chicken, organic and, if possible, reared outdoors. The two boletes will provide an irresistible combination to enjoy with some good friends. Bear in mind, though, that while the orange birch bolete always blackens when cooked, the cep remains immaculately white.

SERVES 4

350 G MIXED FRESH CEPS AND
   ORANGE BIRCH BOLETES, CLEANED
   WEIGHT
600 G BONELESS CHICKEN PIECES
A LITTLE PLAIN FLOUR FOR DUSTING
6 TBSP OLIVE OIL
1 MEDIUM ONION, FINELY CHOPPED
55 G BUTTER
300 G TOMATO PULP (FRESH OR
   CANNED)
A PINCH OF FRESHLY GRATED NUTMEG
1 SPRIG THYME
2 TBSP CHOPPED PARSLEY
150 ML DRY WHITE WINE
SALT AND PEPPER TO TASTE

Clean and slice the mushrooms. Dust the pieces of chicken in flour and fry them in the oil until brown all over. Put to one side.

Add the onion and butter to the oil, along with the sliced mushrooms, and fry for a minute or two. Add the tomato pulp, nutmeg, thyme and parsley and cook for a further 2 minutes. Add the wine, salt and pepper.

Return the chicken to the pan, along with any juices, and cook together for a further 15 minutes. Serve with rice.

CHICKEN ROLLS WITH DUXELLES

This is an extremely simple recipe to cook, providing you have some mushroom purée or duxelles already made.

SERVES 4

4 LARGE BONELESS CHICKEN
   BREASTS
2 QUANTITIES WILD MUSHROOM
   DUXELLES (SEE PAGE 105)
60 G BUTTER
2 TBSP OLIVE OIL
JUICE OF 1 LEMON

Beat the chicken breasts with a meat cleaver between 2 sheets of clingfilm. Spread a quarter of the duxelles over each breast, then roll up, securing with a wooden cocktail stick.

Fry in the butter and oil until brown all over, about 3 minutes on each side. Pour the lemon juice over the chicken and serve with a little of the fat. Accompany with steamed spinach and a potato purée.

CHICKEN ESCALOPES WITH SHAGGY INK CAPS

These fungi appeared on my lawn just in time for this book! You shouldn't use or drink alcohol when cooking or eating them as they may cause a reaction, so I have used a very small amount for flavour. The problem disappears in cooking.

SERVES 4

400 G YOUNG SHAGGY INK CAP MUSHROOMS
4 BONELESS CHICKEN BREASTS, SKIN REMOVED
PLAIN FLOUR FOR DUSTING
85 G BUTTER
4 TBSP OLIVE OIL
75 ML MEDIUM SHERRY
4 TBSP DILL LEAVES
JUICE OF $^{1}/_{2}$ LEMON
SALT AND PEPPER TO TASTE

Clean and trim the mushrooms.
Cut the chicken breasts into 4 pieces each, and beat them out between pieces of clingfilm until thin. Dust the pieces with flour and fry on each side in a pan in the hot butter and oil until brown. Remove the chicken and set aside. In the same pan, fry the mushrooms for a few minutes. Add the sherry and fry for a few minutes to evaporate the alcohol. Add the chicken again, along with any juices that have collected on the plate, and cook for a little longer to let the flavours amalgamate and the chicken finish cooking. Add the dill, some lemon juice and salt and pepper to taste.

MUSHROOM AND CHICKEN CASSEROLE

How lucky my friend Ken Hom is to have visited the market at Yunam in China, where they grow and sell up to 200 different varieties of mushroom. With his kind permission I have taken from one of his books this interesting recipe, which is typical of that city. I hope he doesn't mind the addition of some dried morels.

SERVES 4

25 G DRIED SHIITAKE MUSHROOMS
25 G DRIED MORELS
600 G CHICKEN THIGHS
2 TBSP PEANUT OIL
6 SLICES FRESH ROOT GINGER
1 TBSP DRY RICE WINE
1 TBSP DARK SOY SAUCE
2 TBSP CASTER SUGAR
225 ML CHICKEN STOCK (SEE PAGE 104)
1 TSP CORNFLOUR

MARINADE
1 TBSP LIGHT SOY SAUCE
2 TBSP SAKÉ (RICE WINE)
1 TSP DARK SOY SAUCE
1 TSP SESAME OIL
$^{1}/_{2}$ TSP SALT
1 TSP CORNFLOUR

Soak the dried mushrooms in warm water for 20 minutes. Cut the tough stem from the mushrooms, halve the shiitake and leave the morels whole. Skin the chicken thighs and bone them, then cut into chunks roughly 7 x 3 cm. Marinate the chicken in the marinade ingredients for 20 minutes.
Heat the peanut oil in a wok or large pan and stir-fry the ginger for 2 minutes, then add the chicken and marinade ingredients and stir-fry for a further 2 minutes. Pour the contents of the wok into a casserole dish, then add all the other ingredients, with the exception of the cornflour. Bring to the boil over a moderate heat and simmer gently for 15 minutes, covered. Remove the lid and stir in the cornflour mixed with 1 teaspoon water, then cook for a further 2 minutes. Discard the ginger before serving with plain boiled rice.

Karp Kalan Koli Curry

This recipe is from Mr P. Ganeshan, who is a commis in the kitchens of The Park Hotel in New Delhi. Morels – known there as 'gucchi' and found in Nepal, Kashmir and Tibet – are the most popular, sought-after and expensive mushrooms in India, though some years ago I got a bargain (see page 64).

Serves 4

8 boneless chicken breasts,
    (about 800 g)
butter
2 tbsp peanut oil
30 curry leaves
16 sprigs coriander
salt

STUFFING
24 medium dried morels, soaked
    in warm water for 20 minutes
2 tbsp vegetable oil
55 g finely chopped onion
1 tbsp finely chopped garlic
2 tbsp finely chopped fresh root
    ginger
1 tbsp finely chopped fresh
    green chilli
250 g skinned and boned chicken,
    minced
1 tbsp double cream (optional)

SAUCE
200 g fresh coconut flesh, grated
seeds of 5 cardamom pods
55 g shelled cashew nuts,
    soaked and drained
75 ml peanut oil
700 g onions, finely chopped
1 tbsp fresh ginger paste
2 tbsp fresh garlic paste
1 tsp ground coriander
$1/2$ tsp red chilli powder
$1/4$ tsp ground turmeric
500 g fresh tomato purée

Preheat the oven to 200°C/Gas 6. Skin the chicken breasts and split nearly through horizontally. Open out, cover with a piece of clingfilm, and beat out to flatten and enlarge.

For the stuffing, start by draining the morels (reserving the soaking water). Finely chop half of them and cut the remainder into thin julienne strips. (These will be used for the sauce and garnish.) Heat the vegetable oil in a non-stick pan and sauté the onion, garlic, ginger and chilli to soften, then add the chopped morels and the chicken mince. Cook until the mince is well cooked, then add a little of the reserved morel liquor, season with salt, and remove from the heat. For additional moistness, add some of the cream.

Season the flattened chicken breasts with salt and spread them with the prepared mixture. Roll the breasts up tightly in buttered foil, and twist the edges until the 'packages' are firm.

For the sauce, combine the coconut, cardamom seeds and cashew nuts in a mortar and grind them to a fine paste. Put the groundnut oil into a heavy-based pan, heat it over a moderate heat until almost smoking, then add the chopped onion and sauté until the onion is light brown. Add the ginger and garlic pastes, and keep stirring until the aroma of ginger and garlic is apparent. Add the coconut paste followed by the ground spices, and stir for 2 minutes. Add the fresh tomato purée and half the reserved morel liquor. Bring the sauce to the boil and simmer gently for 20 minutes.

Meanwhile, put the stuffed chicken rolls in an ovenproof dish and bake in the preheated oven for 20 minutes.

To finish, heat the 2 tablespoons groundnut oil and fry the curry leaves for a few seconds. Reserve half for garnishing, and add the other half to the sauce. Simmer the sauce for a further 5–6 minutes, and check the seasoning and consistency. Add the warm cooked chicken rolls and stir gently to coat.

Sauté the julienned morels in 15 g butter for a minute or so, then add half to the sauce. Reserve the other half for garnishing.

Serve two pieces of chicken per portion with some sauce. Garnish with the remaining julienned morels, fried curry leaves and sprigs of coriander.

CHICKEN WITH FRIED MUSHROOMS

Chicken and veal are common in Italian cooking, and many cuts are beaten, as here, to make them thinner. This makes the cooking time so short that you could almost consider dishes of this nature as 'fast food'. The egg coating here imparts a distinctive flavour and the mushrooms make it very special.

SERVES 4

4 BONELESS CORN-FED ORGANIC
  CHICKEN BREASTS, ABOUT 115 G EACH,
  SKINNED
2 TBSP PLAIN FLOUR
1 TSP FINELY CHOPPED PARSLEY
  (OR CORIANDER OR OTHER SOFT HERB)
2 EGGS, BEATEN
OLIVE OIL FOR FRYING
SALT AND PEPPER TO TASTE

MUSHROOMS
400 G CULTIVATED BLEWITS
55 G BUTTER
1 GARLIC CLOVE, FINELY CHOPPED
2–3 TBSP CHICKEN STOCK
  (SEE PAGE 104) OR WATER
1 TBSP CHOPPED PARSLEY

Clean the mushrooms, and quarter them if large.

Melt the butter in a frying pan, then add the garlic. Fry for a few seconds. Add the mushrooms and sauté for 8–10 minutes. Add the stock or water, some salt and pepper, and the parsley.

Meanwhile, prepare the chicken breasts. Flatten them with a meat cleaver to obtain large escalopes 1cm thick. Dip them in the flour and coat all over. Add the herbs and some salt and pepper to the beaten eggs.

Dip the floured breasts in the egg mixture, then shallow-fry in a pan with a little oil. Brown on each side and serve with the mushrooms, and some potato chips if you like.

SUPREME OF DUCK WITH SAFFRON MILK CAPS

Duck is usually quite fatty, but if you use only the breast, it has all the flavour and no fat at all, provided you discard the skin. This dish is fit for a prince from Eastern Europe, where they love the mushrooms used here, but I think the lesser mortals among us will appreciate it in just the same way.

SERVES 4

200 G SAFFRON MILK CAPS
10 G DRIED MORELS, SOAKED IN
  WARM WATER FOR 20 MINUTES
4 LEAN DUCK BREASTS, SKINNED
  (ABOUT 140–175 G EACH)
3 TBSP OLIVE OIL
1 SMALL SHALLOT, FINELY CHOPPED
55 G PARMA HAM, CUT IN SMALL STRIPS
2 CORNICHONS (SMALL GHERKINS),
  FINELY CHOPPED
A KNOB OF BUTTER, ROLLED IN PLAIN
  FLOUR
2 TBSP DRY SHERRY
SALT AND PEPPER TO TASTE

Clean and trim the fresh mushrooms, then blanch in boiling water for a few minutes. Drain well and slice. Drain and trim the dried morels, reserving the water for another dish.

Fry the duck breasts in the oil for 5 minutes on each side until cooked. Remove from the pan and keep warm. Add the shallot and the ham to the pan and fry for a few minutes, then add the fresh mushrooms, the drained morels and the cornichons. Stir-fry for 5 minutes.

Return the duck to the pan with any juices that have collected on the plate. Stir in the butter and flour to thicken the sauce slightly, and cook over a moderate heat for 10 minutes. Stir in the sherry and season to taste with salt and pepper. Heat to let the sherry evaporate for a minute or so, then serve warm.

ROAST PORK WITH FOUR MUSHROOMS

I like pork! It is one of the most flavoursome meats, succulent and versatile. Here I have combined it with three cultivated and one wild mushroom. I had considered initially using three oyster mushrooms in different colours, but when we were shooting the food pictures a friend came along with a huge chicken of the woods just in peak condition! What would you have done in my place?

SERVES 6

1 LOIN OF PORK, ABOUT 1.9 KG, WITH CRACKLING, TRIMMED AND CHINED
1 TBSP SALT

BASTING MIXTURE
1 GARLIC CLOVE, FINELY CHOPPED
1/2 FRESH RED CHILLI, FINELY CHOPPED
1 TBSP ROSEMARY NEEDLES, FINELY CHOPPED
1 TBSP THYME LEAVES
2 TBSP OLIVE OIL

MUSHROOM 'STEW'
800 G MIXED MUSHROOMS (2 TYPES OF OYSTER MUSHROOMS, PINK AND YELLOW, SHIITAKE AND CHICKEN OF THE WOODS)
6 TBSP OLIVE OIL
1 GARLIC CLOVE, FINELY CHOPPED
1 MEDIUM FRESH RED CHILLI, SLICED
150 ML DRY WHITE WINE
1/2 TBSP WHITE WINE VINEGAR
2 OR 3 GRATES OF NUTMEG
2 TBSP CHERVIL LEAVES
SALT AND PEPPER TO TASTE

Preheat the oven to 220°C / Gas 7. Rub the salt into the crackling of the pork and roast in the preheated oven for 40 minutes.

While it is in the oven, mix the basting mixture ingredients together. Take the meat out of the oven and baste with the basting mixture. Return to the oven for a further 40 minutes.

Meanwhile, start the mushroom 'stew'. Clean the mushrooms well. Leave the oyster mushrooms whole if small, or cut in half if larger. Slice the shiitake and chicken of the woods. Heat the oil in a wok, add the garlic and chilli and fry briefly. Add the mushrooms and stir-fry a further 5 minutes. Add the wine and vinegar and cook gently for another couple of minutes. Just before serving add the nutmeg, some salt and pepper and lastly the chervil. Present the pork on a platter surrounded by the mushrooms, then carve on to hot plates.

Sausage, Lentils and Fungi

One of the most popular Italian dishes in autumn and winter is cotechino with lentils. Cotechino is a cooking sausage made of pure pork, including the gelatinous parts such as ear and cheek. The long cooking time makes it succulent and delicious. The combination of lentils (Castelluccio are the best) and fungi makes this dish very appetising.

Serves 4

300 g larch bolete or wood
   blewit mushrooms
2 cotechino sausages, either
   pre-cooked or raw (about
   350 g each)
8 tbsp olive oil
2 garlic cloves, finely chopped
8 cherry tomatoes, cut in half
1 carrot, finely diced
1 celery stick, finely diced
200 g Castelluccio or Puy lentils
up to 800 ml chicken stock (see
   page 104), depending on the type
   of lentils (see method)
1 sprig rosemary, finely
   chopped
salt and pepper to taste

Clean the mushrooms, and cut into halves or quarters if large. Simmer the sausages in water for 30 minutes if pre-cooked, or 2–3 hours if raw.
Put half the oil in a pan, add half the garlic and fry for 30 seconds. Add the mushrooms and cook them until soft in the moisture they will exude. Set aside. In a casserole dish, heat the remaining oil and fry the tomatoes, carrot, celery and remaining garlic until soft. Add the lentils and as much stock as necessary: Castelluccio lentils will need less stock because they are ready in 20 minutes; Puy lentils need more and a longer cooking time. Cook until the lentils are fully tender, 20–30 minutes. Add the rosemary, season to taste, then mix with the mushrooms, adding a tablespoon of water if you think it necessary.
Serve hot with slices of cotechino and perhaps some boiled potatoes.

Spring Lamb with Morels

I am passionate about eating seasonally, and the two major ingredients here could not be more seasonal. Spring lamb is wonderfully tender, and when combined with the fantastic shape, colour and flavour of the spring mushroom par excellence, the morel, you will create a dish to die for. At other times of year you can use dried morels (55 g should suffice). You can use any other cut of lamb too, but you will probably need more – up to 600 g – because of trimming.

Serves 4

400 g fresh morels
1 x 400 g boned rack of lamb
4 tbsp olive oil
1 small bunch spring onions,
   coarsely chopped
1 small sprig rosemary,
   finely chopped
salt and pepper to taste

Clean the morels, and leave them whole unless very large. Trim away any fat from the lamb, and cut it into 1 cm thick medallions.
Salt the medallions and fry them in half the oil to sear on each side. (I like them when they are still pink.) Set aside, keeping them warm. Add the rest of the oil to the pan and fry the spring onions for 5 minutes, then add the morels and rosemary and fry for a further 10–15 minutes, until the morels are cooked. (If you are using dried morels, you can add a little of their soaking water.) Return the lamb medallions to the pan, taste for seasoning, and warm through together with the morels. Serve immediately.

SHOULDER OF LAMB WITH MUSHROOMS

This is one of the most loved recipes at the Neal Street Restaurant. My chef Andrea Cavaliere has developed the lamb side, while I have taken charge of the mushroom accompaniment. We may both be Italian, but we are living and working in Britain, thus I feel that this recipe is more British in inspiration than Italian. And of course it uses some of the food bounty of Britain – its wonderful lamb and the wild mushrooms that are everywhere (if you know where and when to look!). However, in the restaurant, I must admit that we serve the lamb with the unashamedly Italian polenta.

SERVES 6

200 G HEN OF THE WOODS, CLEANED WEIGHT
15 G DRIED CEPS
4 SMALL SHOULDERS OF LAMB, BONED (GET YOUR BUTCHER TO DO THIS FOR YOU)
1 TBSP EACH OF CHOPPED PARSLEY AND ROSEMARY
1 TBSP CHOPPED GARLIC
PLAIN FLOUR FOR DUSTING
8 TBSP OLIVE OIL
1 MEDIUM ONION, FINELY CHOPPED
1 CELERY STICK, FINELY CHOPPED
1 TBSP BLACK PEPPERCORNS
500 ML CHICKEN OR VEGETABLE STOCK (SEE PAGE 104)
300 ML WHITE WINE
2 TBSP WORCESTERSHIRE SAUCE
SALT AND PEPPER TO TASTE

Clean the fresh mushrooms thoroughly, and separate into small lobes. Soak the dried ceps in warm water for 20 minutes, then drain, reserving the water, and finely chop. Remove most of the fat from the lamb shoulders, trimming them well. You want each piece to weigh about 200 g. Lay the pieces, boned side up, on the work surface.

Mix the chopped herbs and garlic together, season with salt and pepper, and divide between the pieces of lamb, spreading the mixture evenly on the meat. Fold each piece of lamb over, then roll and tie into an even shape with kitchen string. Dust with flour and fry in a casserole in the oil until brown on all sides, turning every few minutes. Add the onion, celery and peppercorns to the casserole and sauté briefly, then add the stock, wine and Worcestershire sauce. Cover with a lid and cook on top of the stove over a gentle heat for 1 hour. Turn occasionally.

After an hour, much of the liquid will have evaporated, but there should still be enough to serve as a sauce. Add the mushrooms, fresh and dried, plus a little of the soaking water if necessary, and cook for a further 30 minutes. Check the seasoning before serving. I like to serve the lamb with polenta. You can use traditional or 5-minute (see page 169), flavoured with Parmesan and butter.

BEEF WELLINGTON

To celebrate living in Britain for nearly 30 years, I have taken the two British ingredients that most impressed me and united them in this fairly classic recipe. Because of my passion for mushrooms – and the plethora of mushrooms growing in the wild in Britain – they both had to be honoured here. The dish does require some preparation, I agree, but you can do this in advance, giving you time to receive your guests, while the oven does the rest.

SERVES 6–8

800 G–1 KG BEST FILLET OF BEEF
   YOU CAN BUY
30 G BUTTER
3 TBSP OLIVE OIL
250 G PUFF PASTRY
1 QUANTITY WILD MUSHROOM
   DUXELLES (SEE PAGE 105)
2 EGG YOLKS, BEATEN
SALT AND PEPPER TO TASTE

PANCAKE
125 ML MILK
55 G PLAIN FLOUR
1 EGG, BEATEN
BUTTER FOR GREASING

SAUCE
55 G CARROT, FINELY CUBED
55 G CELERY, FINELY CUBED
1 SMALL ONION, FINELY CHOPPED
6 BLACK PEPPERCORNS, CRUSHED
3 BAY LEAVES
1/2 TSP THYME LEAVES
1 TBSP PLAIN FLOUR
100 ML STRONG RED WINE
500 ML BEEF STOCK (SEE PAGE 104)
75 ML MADEIRA
30 G BUTTER

Preheat the oven to 200°C / Gas 6.

Start by making the pancake. Put the milk, flour, egg and a pinch of salt into a blender and mix to a batter. Line a baking tray of roughly 35 cm square with baking paper, butter this well, then pour in the mixture. Bake in the preheated oven for about 10–15 minutes until set. Leave to cool.

Sprinkle the beef with salt and pepper, heat the butter and oil in a large pan and fry the beef on each side to sear.

Roll the pastry out into a rectangular shape that will completely enclose the beef. Take the rectangular pancake and spread the duxelles on it. Place the beef on the pancake and gently roll the beef in the pancake. Transfer this very gently on to the rolled-out pastry, then wrap it up completely in the pastry, making sure that the top is sealed securely. Place on a greased baking tray, brush with beaten egg yolk, and bake in the preheated oven for 25 minutes or until the pastry is golden and the meat is still pink.

Meanwhile, in the same pan as the beef was browned add the vegetables for the sauce, along with the peppercorns, bay leaves and thyme, and fry gently for a few minutes to soften. Add the flour and stir in gently, then add the wine and stir to loosen the meat juices from the base of the pan. Add the stock and bring to the boil, stirring, then continue to boil to reduce the sauce down. Discard the bay leaves and pass through a chinois sieve, or leave it as it is, although it will be a bit coarse. Add the Madeira and butter, stirring in well.

Remove the beef from the oven, cut into slices and serve on a hot plate with some spinach or French beans, pouring over some of the sauce. It may be a long procedure – but it's well worth while!

Scottish Beef with Shiitake

The combination of beef and mushrooms is well loved, and the shiitake, together with the chilli and coriander, add a touch of Eastern promise and make this a truly memorable dish. If you wanted, you could use other mushrooms, such as king oysters.

Serves 4

4 TBSP OLIVE OIL
2 TBSP BALSAMIC VINEGAR
1 TBSP ENGLISH MUSTARD
1 X 450 G FILLET OF BEEF
SALT AND PEPPER TO TASTE

MUSHROOMS
400 G FRESH CAPS OF SHIITAKE
3 TBSP OLIVE OIL
2 TBSP FINELY SLICED SPRING ONION
1 GARLIC CLOVE, CRUSHED
1 SMALL FRESH RED CHILLI, FINELY
   CHOPPED
2 TBSP DRY RED WINE
2 TBSP CORIANDER LEAVES

Mix together 2 tablespoons of the oil, the vinegar, mustard, and salt and pepper, and marinate the meat in this mixture for a few hours.

To cook the fillet, heat the remaining oil in a frying pan, add the beef and gently sear on all sides. Add some salt and pepper and cook for about 10 minutes, ensuring the beef remains pink in the middle.

While it is cooking, clean and trim the mushrooms and remove the stalks. Put the oil into a frying pan and briefly fry the spring onion, followed by the garlic and chilli. Add the mushrooms and stir-fry for a few minutes. Add the wine and some salt and pepper, then fry for a further 5 minutes. Finally add the coriander, and season.

Serve the fillet and mushrooms together, accompanied by bread, boiled rice or potato purée.

Steak, Oyster and Mushroom Pie

When I want to explore an interesting recipe from a country I don't know much about, I call a top chef from that country. Darina Allen from Eire is a friend of mine and kindly provided this recipe – a strange combination of meat, shellfish and fungi that is apparently part of the St Bridget's Day festivities.

Serves 4

225 G FIELD MUSHROOMS
60 G BUTTER
675 G BEST-QUALITY BEEF, CUBED
1 LARGE ONION, FINELY CHOPPED
2 TBSP PLAIN FLOUR
600 ML GOOD BEEF STOCK (SEE
   PAGE 104)
12 LARGE NATIVE OYSTERS
SALT AND PEPPER TO TASTE

TOPPING
250 G PUFF PASTRY
1 EGG, BEATEN

Clean the mushrooms, then slice. In a large casserole dish, melt half of the butter, season the cubes of beef, then brown on all sides. Remove the beef and reserve. Add the onion to the dish and cook for 5–6 minutes. Add the flour, stir well, then cook for a minute more before adding the stock and returning the meat to the dish. Bring to the boil, cover and simmer over a low heat for 1½–2 hours. Leave to cool. In another pan melt the remaining butter and fry the sliced mushrooms. Season and set aside.

Preheat the oven to 230°C/Gas 8. Open the oysters, reserving the juices. Add the mushrooms and oysters and their juice to the cooked meat and mix well. Leave to cool. Roll the pastry to fit the top of a pie dish. Put the meat, oyster and mushroom mixture in the dish and cover with the pastry, pressing it to the outside of the dish to seal. Brush with beaten egg and bake in the preheated oven for 10 minutes. Reduce the heat to 190°C/Gas 5 and cook for a further 15–20 minutes or until the pastry forms a puffy crust. Serve immediately.

Ossobuco with Dryad's Saddle Mushrooms

That very special Italian dish, 'ossobuco', is world-famous now, and everyone knows that the recipe's title refers to the cut of meat used. This is slices of veal shank in cross-section, with the marrow bone in the middle ('ossobuco' means a bone with a hole). Traditionally, ossobuco does not contain mushrooms, but in my opinion, their addition makes the dish even more delicious!

SERVES 4

300 G DRYAD'S SADDLE MUSHROOMS
20 G DRIED CEPS
10 G DRIED MORELS
4 x 225 G OSSOBUCO PIECES
   (CROSS-CUT VEAL SHANKS)
PLAIN FLOUR FOR DUSTING
4 TBSP OLIVE OIL
1 SMALL ONION, FINELY CHOPPED
150 ML RED WINE
1 x 400 G CAN ITALIAN PEELED
   TOMATOES, DRAINED OF HALF THE
   JUICE
SALT AND PEPPER TO TASTE

Clean the fresh mushrooms well, then slice. Soak the 2 types of dried mushrooms in warm water for 20–30 minutes, then drain. Keep the soaking water for another dish. Trim the morel stalks.

Salt the veal pieces and dust with flour. Heat the oil in a casserole dish and fry the pieces 2 at a time until brown on both sides. Remove from the dish and set aside. In the same oil, fry the chopped onion until slightly brown, then add the dried mushrooms and wine, and allow to evaporate for a minute or so. Add the fresh mushroom slices, along with the tomatoes and some salt and pepper to taste. Cover the casserole and cook over a low heat, on top of the stove, for 1½ hours, until the meat is meltingly tender. Serve with rice or gnocchi.

Veal Cutlets with Ceps

You can cook ceps with almost anything as they impart such a wonderful flavour and a touch of luxury. The combination of the delicate veal paired with ceps makes an excellent main course, preceded perhaps by something like a light broth. I would accompany this dish with cubed new potatoes sautéed with garlic and rosemary.

SERVES 4

300 G FRESH CEPS
4 VEAL CUTLETS WITH THE T-BONE,
   ABOUT 250 G EACH
PLAIN FLOUR FOR DUSTING
55 G BUTTER
8 SAGE LEAVES
4 TBSP DRY WHITE WINE
4 TBSP EXTRA VIRGIN OLIVE OIL
1 GARLIC CLOVE, CRUSHED
2 TBSP FINELY CHOPPED
   FLAT-LEAF PARSLEY
SALT AND PEPPER TO TASTE

Clean the mushrooms well, then slice them.

Dust the cutlets with flour and shake off the excess. Melt the butter in a large pan and fry the cutlets gently on each side until brown. Add the sage leaves and wine. Cook for a few more minutes, turning if necessary.

In another pan, fry the mushrooms in the oil until starting to brown, then add the garlic and parsley and stir-fry for a couple of minutes. Season to taste. Serve the cutlets with a little of the sage and wine sauce, and with the ceps and their juices.

DEVILLED KIDNEYS WITH WINTER CHANTERELLES

Whenever 'devil' is mentioned in a recipe, you can be sure of a high content of hot chilli in some form or another. This recipe is no different, although I leave it up to your own taste buds to control the degree of spice. The humble winter chanterelle seems to be perfect for this recipe because it exudes enough moisture, together with the wine, to make a lovely sauce.

SERVES 4

400 G WINTER CHANTERELLES
2 LARGE POTATOES (ABOUT 700 G IN TOTAL)
700 G CALF'S KIDNEYS, CLEANED WEIGHT
PLAIN FLOUR FOR DUSTING
8 TBSP OLIVE OIL
2 GARLIC CLOVES, SLICED
2 FRESH HOT RED CHILLIES, CHOPPED (WITH THE SEEDS!)
75 ML MEDIUM MARSALA WINE
6–8 LARGE SAGE LEAVES
JUICE OF $^1/_2$ LEMON
SALT AND PEPPER TO TASTE

Clean the mushrooms. Boil the potatoes in salted water with their skins on for 15–20 minutes, until nearly tender. Drain and leave to cool, then skin and cut into slices about 2.5 cm thick.

Cut the kidneys into slices 1cm thick, dust with flour and fry in a large pan in half the oil until crisp on both sides. Set aside.

Add the garlic and chilli to the same pan and fry briefly, then add the mushrooms. Fry for 3 minutes, then add the Marsala and sage, plus some salt and pepper. Stir-fry for 4–5 minutes, then add the kidneys and lemon juice and mix well.

Meanwhile, fry the big slices of potato in the remaining oil until crisp and brown on both sides. Serve together with the kidneys.

Sweetbread Medallions with Horn of Plenty

Not everybody likes offal in general, but sweetbreads, together with liver and kidneys, seem to be loved by most gourmets from around the world. In Italy we also appreciate other parts of the animal like spinal cord, tripe, brains, spleen and testicles, which we cook so that they become delicacies. One day, I will write an entire book about offal!

SERVES 4

350 G HORN OF PLENTY MUSHROOMS, CLEANED WEIGHT
600 G CALF'S SWEETBREADS
A LITTLE PLAIN FLOUR FOR DUSTING
2 TBSP OLIVE OIL
60 G BUTTER
2 GARLIC CLOVES, FINELY CHOPPED
1 SMALL FRESH RED CHILLI, FINELY CHOPPED
3 TBSP DRY RED WINE
2 TBSP FINELY CHOPPED PARSLEY
1 TBSP FINELY CHOPPED MINT
JUICE OF 1 LEMON
SALT AND PEPPER TO TASTE

Clean the mushrooms well. Blanch the sweetbreads in salted water for 20 minutes, drain and cool. Cut away all the muscle and nerves. Cut the sweetbreads into medallions and dust them with flour.

Heat the oil and butter in a large frying pan and fry the sweetbread medallions over a moderate heat until they are brown on each side. Remove from the pan and keep warm.

Put the garlic, chilli and mushrooms into the same frying pan and sauté briefly. Add the wine, herbs and some salt and pepper. Return the sweetbreads to the pan, add the lemon juice, and stir a little to flavour the meat. Serve either with toasted bread or with steamed rice.

VENISON CARPACCIO WITH RAW CEPS

The name 'carpaccio' today is generally used to describe raw meat or fish very thinly cut and cured instantly with lemon juice and oil, plus some additions. I introduced a carpaccio of venison, one of the healthiest red meats, to my restaurant, with enormous success.

You need fillet of venison, the most tender part. Thin slices of fillet about 5 mm thick are put between two sheets of clingfilm and then beaten gently to make them paper-thin. They are wonderful served with the raw ceps, also thinly cut from small tender specimens. The fragrance of the two, accompanied by good bread, is very appetising indeed and as a dish it is very easy to make.

SERVES 4

300 G SMALL CEPS, CLEANED WEIGHT
250 G VENISON FILLET, VERY FINELY SLICED
JUICE OF 1^1/$_2$ LEMONS
3 TBSP EXTRA VIRGIN OLIVE OIL
8 TBSP FINELY CHOPPED PARSLEY
SALT AND PEPPER TO TASTE

Clean the mushrooms well and slice them finely.

Divide the very thin slices of venison fillet between 4 plates, spreading them out to the rim.

Make a vinaigrette with the lemon juice, oil and some salt and pepper, and sprinkle some of this on to the meat. Arrange the sliced mushrooms on top. Sprinkle on the remaining vinaigrette, then sprinkle with parsley and coarsely ground pepper. Eat as a starter with bread or grissini (breadsticks).

RABBIT CASSEROLE WITH WINTER CHANTERELLES

Wild game and wild mushrooms have a wonderful affinity. While many of us can go into the country and collect edible mushrooms, it is less easy to shoot our own game. Luckily, specialist butchers can be relied upon for supplies!

SERVES 6

300 G WINTER CHANTERELLES,
  CLEANED WEIGHT
1 WHOLE RABBIT, APPROX. 800 G
A LITTLE SEASONED PLAIN FLOUR
8 TBSP OLIVE OIL
30 G BUTTER
10 MEDIUM SHALLOTS
10 GARLIC CLOVES, UNPEELED
2–3 BAY LEAVES
2–3 CLOVES
1 SPRIG ROSEMARY
1 TBSP THYME LEAVES
1 TBSP WHITE WINE VINEGAR
500 ML DRY WHITE WINE
A LITTLE CHICKEN STOCK
  (SEE PAGE 104) AS REQUIRED
SALT AND PEPPER TO TASTE

Keep the chanterelles whole, but if they are large, cut in half.
Clean and quarter the rabbit and dust the quarters with seasoned flour. Heat the olive oil and butter in a frying pan and fry the rabbit until brown all over. Set aside. Add the whole shallots and garlic cloves to the same pan and fry briefly, then transfer to a casserole. Add the rabbit, bay leaves, cloves, herbs, vinegar and wine to the casserole, and leave to cook very slowly for 40 minutes on the hob with the lid on. Add salt and pepper to taste and perhaps a little stock if required. At the very last minute add the mushrooms, and mix for a minute until cooked. Serve hot, with either boiled potatoes or rice.

BRAISED RABBIT WITH MUSTARD

The French love all game and poultry, and often cook them in a wonderful stew, or 'fricassee'. You may find local variations, mostly made with chicken. The rabbit version with mushrooms, however, makes a really delicious autumn meal.

SERVES 6

300 G BROWN CAP MUSHROOMS
1 LARGE YOUNG RABBIT, BONED, THE
  FLESH CUT INTO CHUNKS (ABOUT
  675 G BONED WEIGHT)
SEASONED PLAIN FLOUR FOR DUSTING
40 G BUTTER
100 G STREAKY BACON (OR PANCETTA)
12 SMALL ONIONS
1 GARLIC CLOVE, CRUSHED
1 BOUQUET GARNI (PARSLEY, THYME,
  BAY LEAF)
150 ML DRY WHITE WINE
200 ML CHICKEN OR BEEF STOCK
2 TBSP DIJON MUSTARD
1 TBSP FINELY CHOPPED PARSLEY
SALT AND PEPPER TO TASTE

Clean and trim the mushrooms. If large, quarter them. Dust the rabbit chunks with the seasoned flour.
Melt the butter in a large casserole until sizzling, add the rabbit and brown on each side. Add the bacon, cut into strips, the whole onions and the crushed garlic, and cook for 5 minutes. Add the bouquet garni, wine and mushrooms and, after a few minutes, the stock.
Bring to the boil, reduce heat and cook for a further 20–30 minutes or until the rabbit is tender. Stir the mustard into the sauce and taste for seasoning. Serve sprinkled with parsley, with either boiled potatoes or bread.

PHEASANT BREAST WITH CAULIFLOWER FUNGUS

I dedicate this recipe to His Royal Highness the Prince of Wales, because he once told me about his pleasure at having found this mushroom all by himself in the Balmoral woods. He was very impressed by the magnitude of the fungus, which, when weighed, was a couple of kilos. I don't know how the chefs of the royal household prepared it, but they must have done a good job for the Prince to mention it and to like it so much. I once saw a similar mushroom, dried, in a Chinese shop. You may be tempted by necessity to use it instead of the cauliflower fungus.

SERVES 4

500 G CAULIFLOWER FUNGUS
4 LARGE PHEASANT BREASTS
A LITTLE PLAIN FLOUR
8 TBSP OLIVE OIL
40 G BUTTER
1 ONION, CHOPPED
  LENGTHWAYS INTO 6
4 BAY LEAVES
1 SPRIG ROSEMARY
10 JUNIPER BERRIES
500 G BLUEBERRIES
100 ML DRY WHITE WINE
6 SUN-DRIED TOMATOES, CUBED
FRESHLY GRATED NUTMEG
SALT AND PEPPER TO TASTE

Cut the fungus into chunks the size of an apricot.

Dust the pheasant breasts with flour. Heat the oil and butter in a pan, then brown the pheasant breasts on each side in the mixture for 2–3 minutes, depending on thickness. Add the onion, bay leaves, rosemary, juniper berries and blueberries. Stir-fry for 5 minutes, then add the wine and tomatoes, and cook to evaporate the alcohol. Mix well, then add the fungus chunks, which will take a further 7–10 minutes to cook. Add salt and pepper and a dash of nutmeg to taste.

Serve with a very buttery potato purée or with roast potatoes.

EXTRAVAGANZA OF GAME AND FUNGI

The autumn mushroom season coincides with the beginning of the game season. However, although I use them here, it is seldom you will find fungi such as ceps, St George's mushrooms, chanterelles or morels, because they appear in spring-time. But to me this quartet of mushrooms represents the acme of the fungi world, and I like to combine them with the sublime flavours of the different breasts of game birds. And if you really want a feast of tastes, then add a little truffle, either shaven or in the form of oil, to the breasts. This is food nirvana!

SERVES 6

GAME
6 BREASTS EACH OF THE FOLLOWING GAME BIRDS (PHEASANT, PIGEON, QUAIL AND PARTRIDGE)
PLAIN FLOUR FOR DUSTING
85 G BUTTER
2 TBSP OLIVE OIL
2 TBSP BRANDY
1 TSP TRUFFLE OIL
2 TBSP GOOD AGED BALSAMIC VINEGAR
A LITTLE CHICKEN STOCK (SEE PAGE 104) OR WATER FROM SOAKING THE MORELS
SALT AND PEPPER TO TASTE

FUNGI
200 G ST GEORGE'S MUSHROOMS
200 G FRESH CEPS
200 G CHANTERELLES
100 G FRESH MORELS, OR 30 G DRIED, SOAKED IN WARM WATER FOR 20 MINUTES
40 G BUTTER
2 TBSP OLIVE OIL
JUICE OF 1/2 LEMON

BEETROOT SALAD (OPTIONAL)
800 G BEETROOT, FRESHLY BOILED
4 TBSP BALSAMIC VINEGAR
2 TBSP TORN CORIANDER LEAVES

First make the beetroot salad, if serving. When cool enough to handle, skin the beetroot, and cut into thin slices. Sprinkle with the vinegar, coriander and some salt and pepper, and leave to cool completely, for the flavours to merge. Prepare the mushrooms by cleaning and trimming as appropriate. Cut the St George's mushrooms into quarters. Leave the fresh ceps whole if they are small, or cut in half if larger. Halve the fresh morels. Drain the dried morels (if using), reserving their soaking water.

For the birds, first dust the breasts with flour then, starting with the largest breast, fry them in the butter and olive oil until they are lightly browned. Repeat with all the breasts, cooking the smallest and most tender – the quail – last. When all are cooked, set them aside and keep warm.

Add the brandy, truffle oil and balsamic vinegar to the pan. Boil to deglaze the pan and loosen all the cooking juices. Add some stock or water if need be. Boil until you have a liquid sauce. Adjust the seasoning. Return the breasts to the pan and keep warm.

Meanwhile, to cook the mushrooms, heat the butter and oil in another pan and add the morels, followed by the chanterelles, ceps and, lastly, the St George's mushrooms. Sauté briefly just to soften and lightly brown them. Add salt, pepper and lemon juice to finish.

To assemble, arrange the breasts on a large platter and intersperse with the fungi, so the breasts look as if they were studded with jewels. Serve the gleaming red and green beetroot salad to one side. You will then need to open some bottles of an important red wine. Forget about the cost, and just enjoy!

INDEX OF MUSHROOMS USED IN THE RECIPES

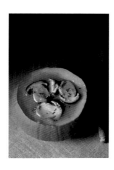

GLOSSARY

ADNATE (of gills) broadly attached to the stem

ADNEXED (of gills) narrowly attached to the stem

AGARIC large fungus family of the gilled group

ASCOMYCETES group of higher fungi whose spores are formed inside asci and are released by pressure

ASCUS (pl. asci) sac-like cell within which spores are formed

BASAL at or near the base

BASIDIA club-shaped cells on which spores are formed externally

BASIDIOMYCETES major group of higher fungi including agarics etc.,whose spores are formed externally on basidia

BOLETE mushroom with central stalk and tubes/pores

CAP the upper part of the mushroom, usually the spore-bearing part

CHLOROPHYLL green pigments found in plants that trap energy from sunlight for use in photosynthesis

CONCENTRIC (of scales) pattern of circles on the cap

CONCOLOROUS same colour as

CONVEX (of caps) rounded or domed

CROWDED (of gills) tightly packed together under the cap

CUTICLE the skin of the cap

DECURRENT (of gills) running down the stem

EPIGEAL/EPIGEOUS growing above ground

EXCENTRIC (of stems) cap central to the stem

EXOPERIDIUM outer layer of the spore case in puffballs and similar

FIBRILLOSE covered with small fibres

FREE (of gills) detached from stem

FRONDOSE (of trees) broad-leaved or deciduous

FRUIT-BODY the actual fungus growing from the mycelium

FUNGUS fruit-body formed by the meeting of hyphae, lacking chlorophyll and usually producing spores

GASTEROMYCETES group of Basidiomycetes where spores mature within the fruit-body, e.g. puffballs

GENUS a group of related species demonstrating common characteristics

GILLS blade-like strips of tissue that radiate on the underside of the cap of certain fungi, bearing little sacs in which spores are produced, e.g. in agarics. Also known as lamellae

GLEBA spore-bearing fleshy tissue within Gasteromycetes

HYMENIUM spore-bearing fertile layer of asci, basidia, etc.

HYPHA (pl. hyphae) minute individual filament from which mycelium and fruit-body are formed

HYPOGEAL/HYPOGEOUS growing underground

INROLLED with cap curling in towards the stem (as with Lactarius)

LAMELLAE gills

LATERAL (of caps) growing laterally, at the sides

MYCELIUM complex of hyphae: the vegetative portion of a fungus growing into the nutritive substrate/material

MYCOLOGIST one who studies the world of fungi

MYCOPHAGIST one who likes to eat fungi

MYCOPHILE a lover of mushrooms

MYCORRHIZA symbiotic association of the mycelium with plant and tree roots

PARASITIC drawing nutrients from living material/organisms

PERIDIUM outer skin; wall of the spore case in many Gasteromycetes

POLYPORE woody-textured fungus with tubes on underside of cap strongly attached to the flesh and built by millions of pores

PORES the mouths of the tubes in boletes and polypores

POROID consisting of pores

RETICULUM net-like mesh pattern on stalk of some boletes

RHIZOMORPH a root-like or string-like bundle of mycelial hyphae

RING remnant of a veil, present around stem of some agarics

SAPROPHYTIC living on dead matter

SCABROUS rough granular or scaly texture on stem surface

SESSILE having no stem

SINUATE (of gills) notched to the stem

SPAWN mycelium produced artificially for the purpose of cultivating mushrooms

SPORE the single reproductive unit of a fungus

STEMS the stalk or foot of a fungus, which supports the cap

SYMBIOSIS growing association with certain types of trees

TUBES sponge-like spore-producing layer, e.g. of boletes

UMBO central swelling on cap of many agarics

VEIL protective membrane enclosing entire fruit-body (universal veil), e.g. in amanitas, or joining cap cuticle to stem (partial veil), e.g. in agarics

VISCID slimy or wet

VOLVA remains of universal veil forming cup-like sac around stem base, also called 'skirt', e.g. in amanitas

RECOMMENDED READING

● G.C. Ainsworth, INTRODUCTION TO THE HISTORY OF MYCOLOGY (Cambridge University Press, 1976)
● Darina Allen, THE FESTIVE FOOD OF IRELAND (Kyle Cathie, 1992)
● David Arora, MUSHROOMS DEMYSTIFIED (Ten Speed Press, 1979)
● F.H. Brightman, THE OXFORD BOOK OF FLOWERLESS PLANTS (Peerage Books, 1966)
● Renato Brotzu, GUIDA AI FUNGHI DELLA SARDEGNA (Editrice Archivio Fotografico Sardo, 1988)
● Bruno Cetto, I FUNGHI DAL VERO, 5 vols (Arti Grafiche Saturnia-Trento, 1970)
● S.T. Chang & W.A. Hayes, THE BIOLOGY AND CULTIVATION OF EDIBLE MUSHROOMS (Academic Press, 1978)
● S.T. Chang & P.G. Miles, EDIBLE MUSHROOMS AND THEIR CULTIVATION (CRC Press, 1989)
● Heinz Denckler, DAS PILZ BUCH (Heyne Verlag, 1982)
● Colin Dickinson & John Lucas, COLOR DICTIONARY OF MUSHROOMS (Orbis, 1982)

● Manfred Enderle & Hans E. Laux, PILZE AUF HOLZ (Kosmos, 1980)
● Louise Freedman, WILD ABOUT MUSHROOMS (Aris Books, 1988)
● Sara Ann Friedman, CELEBRATING THE WILD MUSHROOM – A PASSIONATE QUEST (Dodd, Mead & Co., 1986)
● E. Garnweidner, PILZE (GU Compass, 1993)
● Jane Grigson, THE MUSHROOM FEAST (Michael Joseph, 1975)
● Hans Hvass, MAD SVAMPE I FARVER (Politiken Forlag, 1973)
● Ying Janzhe, Mao Xiaolan, M.A. Qiming, Zong Yichen & Wen Huaan, ICONS OF MEDICINAL FUNGI FROM CHINA (Science Press, 1987)
● Katsuji Komiyama, KINOKO (Nagaoko Shoten, Tokyo, 2002)
● A. Krasheninnikoya, RUSSIAN COOKING (Mir Publishers, 1978)
● J.E. Lange & M. Lange, BLV BESTIMMUNGS-BUCH (BLV Verlagsgesellschaft, 1982)

● Hans E. Laux, ESSBARE PILZE UND IHRE GIFTIGEN DOPPELGÄNGER (Kosmos, 1985)
● Carin Lindh, GOTT MED SVAMP (Bokförlaget Semic, 1983)
● Gisela Lockwald, PILZGERICHTE NOCH FINER (IHW Verlag, 1999)
● Marcel Loquin & Bengt Cortin, CHAMPIGNONS COMESTIBLES ET VÉNÉNEUX (Fernand Nathan)
● Riccardo Mazza, I FUNGHI (Manuali Somzogno, 1994)
● Orson K. Miller, MUSHROOMS OF NORTH AMERICA (E.P. Dutton, 1978)
● Roger Phillips, MUSHROOMS AND OTHER FUNGI OF GREAT BRITAIN AND EUROPE (Pan Books, 1981)
● Emil Reimers, KOSTILCHES AUS DER PILZKUCHE (BLV VerlagsGesellschaft, 1982)
● Roland Sabatier, LE LIVRE DES CHAMPIGNONS (Gallimard Editions, 1987)
● Paul Stamets, GROWING GOURMET AND MEDICINAL MUSHROOMS (Ten Speed Press, 1993)

INDEX

AUTHOR'S ACKNOWLEDGEMENTS

Alison Cathie – for publishing, Alastair Hendy – for superb photos, Susan Fleming – for invaluable editing, Priscilla – for her patience, Kate Fry – for helping to cook, Giselle Cody – for understanding my English, Mrs Tee, Yuki Sugiura, Wild Harvest (fungi), Miho & Michiya Uchida, Hugh Owens, Jane O'Shea, Hilary Mandleberg, Mary Evans, Tim Livesey (fungi), Hans Baumann, Giuseppe, Tim Neat (fungi), Tim Wisley (fungi), Dru McPherson (fungi), Roger Phillips, Flavio Giacoletto, Enzo Zaccharini, Enza Bettelli, Sumir Sarabhai, Roman Mauro, Diana & Tim Bateman, Tartuflanghe, Domenica Bartolusso, Ros Ellis, Professor Roy Watling – for mycological supervision, Giuseppe Meuro, Constanza Guimares, Mushroom Bureau (www.mushroom-uk.com), Urbani Tartufi, Priya Paul, Natasha Kilcoyne, The French Garden, Kent Down Mushrooms, Ken Hom, Darina Allen, Andrea Cavaliere, Asami Sarabhai, David Thomas, Paul Masuda.

PICTURE CREDITS

10–18 Alastair Hendy; 20 Roger Phillips; 21 above David E. Thomas; 21 below Roger Phillips; 22 Roger Phillips; 23 Alastair Hendy; 24 Roger Phillips; 25 above left Roger Phillips; 25 below left David E. Thomas; 25 above right David Thomas; 26 Roger Phillips; 27 above Felix Labhardt/Bruce Coleman; 27 Roger Phillips; 28 Alastair Hendy; 29 left Roger Phillips; 29 right Roger Phillips; 29 below right David E. Thomas; 30 David E.Thomas; 31 Roger Phillips; 32 above David E. Thomas; 32 below Roger Phillips; 33 below Roger Phillips; 33 top David E. Thomas; 34 Roger Phillips; 35-36 Alastair Hendy; 37 Roger Phillips; 38 Roger Phillips; 39 top Alastair Hendy; 39 below David E. Thomas; 40 Roger Phillips; 41 Roger Phillips; 42 Roger Phillips; 43 Alastair Hendy; 44 Alastair Hendy; 45 Roger Phillips; 46 above Roger Phillips; 46 below David E. Thomas; 47 Alastair Hendy; 48 top David E. Thomas; 48 below Roger Phillips; 49 top and right Roger Phillips; 49 below David E. Thomas; 50 above left Roger Phillips; 50 above right Roger Phillips; 50 below David E. Thomas; 51 left Alastair Hendy; 51 above Roger Phillips; 52 Roger Phillips; 53 above Roger Phillips; 53 below David E. Thomas; 54 Roger Phillips; 55 Alastair Hendy; 56 above Alastair Hendy; 56 below Alastair Hendy; 57 Roger Phillips; 58 above Roger Phillips; 58 below David E. Thomas; 59 Alastair Hendy; 60 David E. Thomas; 61 above Alastair Hendy; 61 below Roger Phillips; 62 above Alastair Hendy; 62 below David E. Thomas; 63 top David E. Thomas; 63 below Roger Phillips; 64 Roger Phillips; 65 Alastair Hendy; 66 left Hans Reinhard/Bruce Coleman; 66 right Roger Phillips; 67 above left David E. Thomas; 67 above & below right Roger Phillips; 68 Alastair Hendy; 69 above left & right Roger Phillips; 69 below David E. Thomas; 70 Roger Phillips; 71 Roger Phillips; 72 Alastair Hendy; 73 above Alastair Hendy; 73 below Roger Phillips; 74 left Alastair Hendy; 74 right Roger Phillips; 74 below Roger Phillips; 75 Roger Phillips; 76 Alastair Hendy; 78 Roger Phillips; 79 Alastair Hendy; 80 Alastair Hendy; 82 Alastair Hendy; 83 left Roger Phillips; 83 right Alastair Hendy; 84 Alastair Hendy; 85 Dr. Paul S. Masuda; 86 Alastair Hendy; 87 Alastair Hendy; 88 Alastair Hendy; 89 Alastair Hendy; 90 Alastair Hendy; 91 above Mushroom Gourmet/www.14u.co.nz; 91 below Alastair Hendy.

All the remaining photographs were taken by Alastair Hendy.